HOW THE Special Needs Brain Learns

SECOND EDITION

David A. Sousa

CORWIN PRESS
A SAGE Publications Company
Thousand Oaks, CA 91320

For information:

Corwin Press
A Sage Publications Company
2455 Teller Road
Thousand Oaks, California 91320
www.corwinpress.com

Sage Publications Ltd
1 Oliver's Yard
55 City Road
London EC1Y 1SP
United Kingdom

Sage Publications India Pvt. Ltd.
B-42, Panchsheel Enclave
Post Box 4109
New Delhi 110 017 India

Library of Congress Cataloging-in-Publication Data

Sousa, David A.
How the special needs brain learns / David A. Sousa. — 2nd ed.
    p. cm.
Includes bibliographical references and index.
ISBN 1-4129-4986-6 or 978-1-412949-86-6 (cloth) — ISBN 1-4129-4987-4 or 978-1-412949-87-3 (pbk.)
  1. Learning disabled children—Education. 2. Learning. 3. Cognition in children. I. Title.

LC4704.5.S68 2007
370.15′23—dc22

                             2006021869

Acquisitions editor: Robert D. Clouse
Editorial assistant: Jessica Wochna
Production editor: Sanford Robinson
Typesetter: C&M Digitals (P) Ltd.
Cover designer: Tracy Miller
Production artist: Lisa Miller

Contents

List of Strategies to Consider

About the Author

 **David A. Sousa,** Ed.D., is an international educational consultant. He has made presentations at national conventions of educational organizations and has conducted workshops on brain research and science education in hundreds of school districts and at several colleges and universities across the United States, Canada, Europe, and Asia.

Dr. Sousa has a bachelor of science degree in chemistry from Massachusetts State College at Bridgewater, a master of arts in teaching degree in science from Harvard University, and a doctorate from Rutgers University. His teaching experience covers all levels. He has taught junior and senior high school science, served as a K–12 director of science, and was Supervisor of Instruction for the West Orange, New Jersey, schools. He then became superintendent of the New Providence, New Jersey, public schools. He has been an adjunct professor of education at Seton Hall University and a visiting lecturer at Rutgers University. He was president of the National Staff Development Council in 1992.

Dr. Sousa has edited science books and published numerous books and articles in leading educational journals on staff development, science education, and brain research. He has received awards from professional associations and school districts for his commitment and contributions to research, staff development, and science education. He received the Distinguished Alumni Award and an honorary doctorate in education from Bridgewater (Mass.) State College.

He has appeared on the NBC *Today* show and on National Public Radio to discuss his work with schools using brain research. He makes his home in south Florida.

**Treat people as if they were what
they ought to be and
you help them to become
what they are capable of being.**

– Johann Wolfgang von Goethe

Preface to the Second Edition

Welcome to the second edition! Since the publication of the first edition, there have been major developments in our understanding of how the human brain develops and functions. Brain imaging studies now number more than 1,500 a year. New technologies, such as transcranial magnetic stimulation, have emerged for investigating cerebral processes. Researchers in genetics have found new links to physical, psychological, and learning disorders. The discovery of mirror neurons may explain why certain learning problems arise and yield clues as to how they can be treated. All of the chapters in this second edition have undergone major revisions to include these developments and the findings of new studies. In addition, I have

- Expanded and updated the chapters on attention disorders and autism spectrum disorders because of the increased interest in these conditions
- Revised the chapters on reading disabilities and emotional and behavioral disorders to reflect new research discoveries and treatments
- Recast the final chapter to include a practical framework for identifying, accommodating, and motivating students with learning difficulties
- Included references to more than 230 new scientific studies for those who wish to read the original research
- Eliminated the chapter on sleep disorders because they do not identify a special learning need

Researchers and clinicians have made considerable progress in recent years understanding the genetic and environmental triggers that result in learning problems in children and adolescents. Nonetheless, arriving at a specific diagnosis can be tricky. Teachers and parents often cannot tell the difference between a normally rambunctious child and one who may have a developmental disorder. My hope is that the information here will provide educators and parents with some of the strategies they need to help their students and children lead happy and successful lives.

David A. Sousa

Acknowledgments

Corwin Press gratefully acknowledges the contributions of the following individuals:

Beverly E.S. Alfeld
Educational Consultant & Advocate
Special Education Advocacy Services
Crystal Lake, IL

Jean Cheng Gorman
Licensed Child/School
   Psychologist
Modesto, CA

Susan M. Dannemiller
Director of Special Education
   and Pupil Services
School District of Grafton
Grafton, WI

Melba Fletcher
Administrator of Externs
Professor of Exceptional Education
   and Foundation Courses
Nova Southeastern University
Ft. Lauderdale, FL

Jackie Dorman
Special Education Teacher
Clay Middle School
Carmel, IN

Mary Novak
Multi-Categorical Teacher
Algoma Elementary School
Algoma, WI

John La Londe
Marin SELPA Director
Marin County SELPA
San Rafael, CA

Jo Bellanti
Director of Special Education
Shelby County Schools
Bartlett, TN

Lois A. Fisch
Associate Professor
   and Director of Education
Director of the Institute for
   Excellence in Education
Utica College
Utica, New York

Helen T. Dainty
Instructor
Tennessee Tech University
Cookeville, TN

Patrice W. Hallock
Assistant Professor of Education
Utica College
Utica, New York

John R. Celletti
Adjunct Professor, University of Detroit Mercy
Behavior Specialist, Lincoln Park School District
Detroit, MI

Pamela M. Schwartz
Director, Learning Support Center
Albion College
Albion, MI

Introduction

Teachers and students get up every school-day morning hoping to succeed. That hope is not always realized because many factors exist that affect the degree of success or failure in a teaching and learning situation. Some of these factors are well beyond the control of the teacher and the school staff. What teachers *do* control, of course, are the decisions they make about what to teach and about how to present the lesson so that student learning is most likely to occur. In making these decisions, teachers draw on their knowledge base and experience to design activities, ask questions, and respond to the efforts of their students.

Educators are finding themselves searching for new strategies and techniques to meet the needs of an ethnically, culturally, and socially diverse student population. Some tried-and-true strategies do not seem to be as successful as they were in the past, and more students seem to be having difficulty acquiring just the basic skills of reading, writing, and computation. The number of public school students being diagnosed with specific learning disabilities is growing. In 2002, 8.3 percent of the total public school population was classified as having specific learning disabilities and speech or language impairments, compared to 7.7 percent 10 years earlier (USDE, 2003).

This situation is generating frustration in different parts of the educational community. As a result, educators are searching for new approaches, parents are seeking alternative schooling formats (charter schools and vouchers), and state legislators are demanding higher standards and testing. Added to this mix are the demands and sanctions of the federal No Child Left Behind Act of 2001 and the 2004 Individuals with Disabilities Education Improvement Act's focus on responsiveness to intervention. All these activities are in full swing, but it remains to be seen whether these efforts will result in more effective services to students with special needs.

Meanwhile, more students diagnosed with learning disabilities are being included in regular classrooms, and teachers continue to search for new ways to help these struggling students achieve. As more students with learning difficulties enter regular classes, general education teachers are finding that they need help adjusting to the added responsibility of meeting the varied needs of these students. Consequently, special education teachers will need to collaborate more than ever with their general education colleagues on ways to differentiate instruction in the inclusive classroom.

> *General and special education teachers will need to collaborate more than ever on ways to differentiate instruction.*

1

WHO ARE SPECIAL NEEDS STUDENTS?

For the purposes of this book, the term "special needs" refers to students who are:

- Diagnosed and classified as having specific learning problems, including speech, reading, writing, mathematics, and emotional and behavioral disorders
- Enrolled in supplemental instruction programs for basic skills, such as those receiving federal funding under Title 1 of the Elementary and Secondary Education Act
- Not classified for special education or assigned to Title I programs, but still struggling with problems affecting their learning

The term, as used here, does not refer to students with learning problems resulting primarily from hearing, visual, or physical handicaps.

CAN BRAIN RESEARCH HELP?

Teachers may face significant challenges when meeting the needs of children who have learning problems. Trying to figure out what is happening in the brains of these children can be frustrating and exhausting. Until recently, science could tell us little about the causes of learning disorders and even less about ways to address them successfully.

The nature of the difficulties facing students with learning problems varies from maintaining focus, acquiring language, learning to read and write, and solving mathematical problems to remembering important information. Thanks to the development of imaging and other technologies, neuroscientists can now look inside the live brain and gain new knowledge about its structure and functions. Some of this research is already revealing clues to help guide the decisions and practices of educators working with students who have special needs.

Because of the efforts of scientists over the years to cure brain disorders, we know more about troubled brains than we do about healthy ones. Early ventures into the brain involved extensive risks that were justified by the potential for curing or improving the patient's condition. But now, essentially risk-free imaging technologies (such as functional magnetic resonance imaging or fMRI) are giving us greater knowledge about how the normal brain works. In just one project, scientists compiled a database of brain scans of about 500 children without apparent health problems aged 7 days to 18 years. This information will help researchers study different stages of brain growth and expand our understanding of what normal brain development is (Evans, 2006).

Students with learning problems comprise such a heterogeneous group that no one strategy, technique, or intervention can address all their needs. Today, more than ever, neuroscientists, psychologists, computer experts, and educators are working together in a common crusade to improve our understanding of the learning process. Comparing the functions of brains without deficits to the functions of brains with deficits is revealing some remarkable new insights about learning and behavioral disorders. Some of the findings are challenging long-held beliefs about the cause, progress, and treatment of specific learning disorders. Educators in both general and special education should be aware of this research so that they can decide what implications the findings have for their practice.

> *Comparing the functions of brains without deficits to the functions of brains with deficits is revealing some remarkable new insights about learning and behavioral disorders.*

WHAT IS IN THIS BOOK?

This book provides research information about common learning disabilities to prospective and current teachers and administrators so that they may consider alternative instructional approaches. It will help answer such questions as:

- How different are the brains of today's students?
- What kinds of strategies are particularly effective for students with learning disabilities?
- What progress is research making in discovering the causes of different learning disorders?
- Will brain research help us make more accurate diagnoses of learning problems?
- Can schools inadvertently promote ADHD-like behavior in students?
- Can students with native language problems learn another language?
- How does the brain learn to read?
- Can young brains with developmental reading problems be "rewired" to improve reading?
- How can we address the emotional needs of students in the classroom?
- What more do we know about autism spectrum disorders?

Authors must decide on the sequence that the content of a book follows. My decision here was to start with a look at basic brain structures and functions (Chapter 1) and then move on to explaining some problems that can arise during brain development (Chapter 2). Because attention is a critical component of nearly all learning, that seemed to be the next logical topic (Chapter 3). Then I turned to examining learning difficulties in the basic skill areas of speech, reading, writing, and mathematics (Chapters 4 to 7). Thereafter follows a discussion of emotional and behavioral problems (Chapter 8) and autism spectrum disorders (Chapter 9). I conclude with an effort to tie this information together into a review of effective ways to serve students with learning disabilities (Chapter 10).

Practical applications of the research can be found in the chapter sections called **Strategies to Consider,** which suggest how educators might translate the research into school and classroom practice so that students with learning difficulties can be more successful. Obviously, some of the strategies would be appropriate for all learners. However, the suggestions have been written specifically to address the special needs of students with learning difficulties.

Some of the information and suggestions found here came from advocacy organizations, including the National Institute of Mental Health, the National Information Center for Children and Youth With Disabilities, and the Learning Disability Association of America (see the **Resources** section). I have sought out original medical research reports whenever possible, and these are included in the **References** section of the book. A few of the strategies are derived or adapted from the third edition of my previous book, *How the Brain Learns*, also published by Corwin Press.

This book is not intended to be a comprehensive text describing all the types of barriers that can affect learning. Rather, it focuses on the common difficulties and disorders that any teacher is likely to encounter in the general or special education classroom. On a broader scale, the updates on research and some of the suggested strategies may benefit all who work to educate children.

As we gain a greater understanding of the human brain, we may discover that some students designated as "learning disabled" may be merely "schooling disabled." Sometimes these students are struggling to learn in an environment that is designed inadvertently to frustrate their efforts. Just changing our instructional approach may be enough to move these students to the ranks of successful learners. My hope is that this book will encourage all school professionals to learn more about how the brain learns so that they can work together for the benefit of all students.

> *As we gain a greater understanding of the human brain, we may discover that some students designated as "learning disabled" may be merely "schooling disabled."*

A WORD OF CAUTION

Several chapters contain lists of symptoms that are used to help identify specific disorders. The symptoms are included only for informational purposes, and they should not be used as a basis for diagnosis. Any individual who exhibits persistent learning problems should be referred to qualified clinical personnel for assessment.

Chapter 1

The Brain and Learning

The human brain is an amazing structure. At birth, it is equipped with more than 100 billion nerve cells designed to collect information and learn the skills necessary to keep its owner alive. Although comparatively slow in its growth and development compared to the brains of other mammals, it can learn complex skills, master any of over 6,000 languages, store memories for a lifetime, and marvel at the glory of a radiant sunset. Early in life, the brain's cells grow and connect with each other—at the rate of thousands per second—to store information and skills. Most of the connections result in the development of neural networks that will help the individual successfully face life's challenges. But sometimes, certain connections go awry, setting the stage instead for problems.

To understand the complexity of human brain growth and development, let's review some basic information about its structure. For our purposes, we will first look at major parts of the outside of the brain (Figure 1.1): the frontal, temporal, occipital, and parietal lobes; the motor cortex; and the cerebellum.

SOME EXTERIOR PARTS OF THE BRAIN

Lobes of the Brain

Although the minor wrinkles are unique in each brain, several major wrinkles and folds are common to all brains. These folds form a set of four lobes in each hemisphere. Each lobe tends to specialize for certain functions.

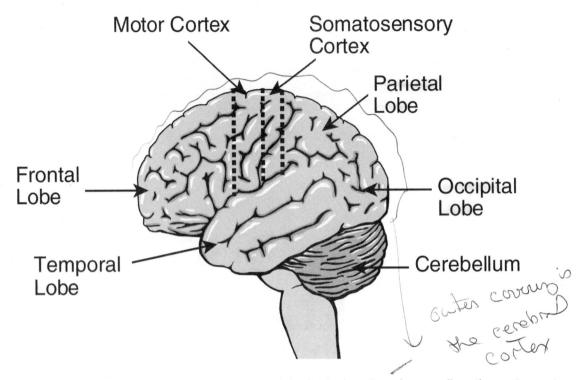

Figure 1.1 This diagram shows the four major lobes of the brain (cerebrum), as well as the motor cortex, the somatosensory cortex, and the cerebellum.

Frontal Lobe. At the front of the brain is the *frontal lobe*, containing almost 50 percent of the volume of the cerebral hemispheres. Lying just behind the forehead is a portion of the frontal lobe called the *prefrontal cortex*. The frontal lobe deals with planning and thinking. It comprises the rational and executive control center of the brain, monitoring higher-order thinking, directing problem solving, and regulating the excesses of the emotional system. Because emotions drive attention, the efficiency of this area is linked to the limbic centers.

The frontal lobe also contains our self-will area—what some might call our personality. Trauma to the frontal lobe can cause dramatic—and sometimes permanent—behavior and personality changes. (One wonders why we allow 10-year-olds to play football and soccer, where the risk of trauma to the developing frontal lobe is so high.)

Because most of the working memory is located here, it is the area where focus occurs. The frontal lobe matures slowly. MRI studies of adolescents and postadolescents reveal that the frontal lobe continues to mature into early adulthood. During this time, used neural pathways are being strengthened while unused neurons are being pruned.

> *The brain's executive system matures more slowly than the emotional system, so adolescents often resort to high-risk behavior.*

In Figure 1.2, the lighter areas on the brain images show the increasing maturation of the frontal lobe over the span of 15 years between the ages of five and 20 (Giedd et al., 1999). Thus the capability of the frontal lobe to control the excesses of the emotional system is not fully operational during adolescence, and is not likely to be fully mature until about the age of 24 (Luciana, Conklin, Hooper, & Yarger, 2005; Paus, 2005). Full maturation occurs about a year earlier in females than in males. In other words, the last part of the brain to grow up is the part capable of making rational decisions, understanding the consequences of one's actions, and putting the brakes on emotional impulses. Consequently, this slow development of the frontal lobe is one important reason that adolescents are more likely than mature adults to submit to their emotions and resort to high-risk behavior.

Temporal Lobe. Above the ears rests the *temporal lobe*, which deals with sound, music, face and object recognition, and some parts of long-term memory. It also houses the speech centers, although this is usually on the left side only.

Occipital Lobe. At the back of the brain is the *occipital lobe*, which is used almost exclusively for visual processing.

Parietal Lobe. Near the top is the *parietal lobe*, which deals mainly with spatial orientation, calculation, and certain types of recognition.

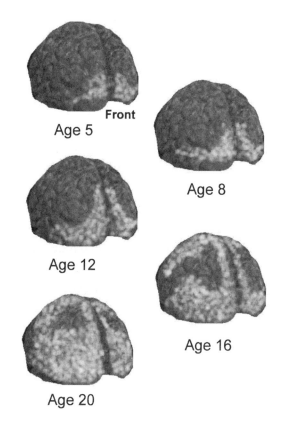

Figure 1.2 The lighter areas on these brain images show the increasing maturation of the frontal lobe over 15 years (adapted from Giedd et al., 1999).

Motor Cortex and Somatosensory Cortex

Between the parietal and frontal lobes are two bands across the top of the brain from ear to ear. The band closer to the front is the *motor cortex*. This strip controls body movement and, as we will learn later, works with the cerebellum to coordinate the learning of motor skills. Just behind the motor cortex, at the beginning of the parietal lobe, is the *somatosensory cortex,* which processes touch signals received from various parts of the body.

Cerebellum

The cerebellum (Latin for "little brain") is a two-hemisphere structure located just below the rear part of the cerebrum, right behind the brainstem. Representing about 11 percent of the brain's weight, it is a deeply folded and highly organized structure containing more neurons than all of the rest of the brain put together. The surface area of the entire cerebellum is about the same as that of one of the cerebral hemispheres.

This area coordinates movement. Because the cerebellum monitors impulses from nerve endings in the muscles, it is important in the performance and timing of complex motor tasks. It modifies and coordinates commands to swing a golf club, smooth a dancer's footsteps, and allow a hand to bring a cup to the lips without spilling its contents. The cerebellum may also store the memory of automated movements, such as touch-typing, playing a piano, and tying a shoelace. Through such automation, performance can be improved as the sequences of movements can be made with greater speed, greater accuracy, and less effort. The cerebellum also is known to be involved in the mental rehearsal of motor tasks, which also can improve performance and make it more skilled. A person whose cerebellum is damaged slows down and simplifies movement, and would have difficulty with finely tuned motion, such as catching a ball, or completing a handshake.

Recent studies indicate that the role of the cerebellum has been underestimated. Researchers now believe that it also acts as a support structure in cognitive processing by coordinating and fine-tuning our thoughts, emotions, senses (especially touch), and memories. Because the cerebellum is connected to regions of the brain that perform mental and sensory tasks, it can perform these skills automatically, without conscious attention to detail. This allows the conscious part of the brain the freedom to attend to other mental activities, thus enlarging its cognitive scope. Such enlargement of human capabilities is attributable in no small part to the cerebellum and its contribution to the automation of numerous mental activities.

SOME INTERIOR PARTS OF THE BRAIN

Brainstem

The brainstem is the oldest and deepest area of the brain. It is often referred to as the reptilian brain because it resembles the entire brain of a reptile. Of the 12 body nerves that go to the brain, 11 end in the brainstem (the olfactory nerve—for smell—goes directly to the limbic system, an evolutionary artifact). Here is where vital body functions, such as heartbeat, respiration, body temperature, and digestion, are monitored and controlled. The brainstem also houses the reticular activating system (RAS), responsible for the brain's alertness.

Limbic Area

Nestled above the brainstem and below the cerebrum lies a collection of structures commonly referred to as the limbic system and sometimes called the old mammalian brain. Many researchers now caution that viewing the limbic system as a separate functional entity is outdated because all of its components interact with many other areas of the brain.

Most of the structures in the limbic system are duplicated in each hemisphere of the brain. These structures carry out a number of different functions, including the generation of emotions and processing emotional memories. Its placement between the cerebrum and the brainstem permits the interplay of emotion and reason.

Four parts of the limbic system are important to learning and memory. They are:

The Thalamus. All incoming sensory information (except smell) goes first to the thalamus (Greek for "inner chamber"). From here it is directed to other parts of the brain for additional processing. The cerebrum and cerebellum also send signals to the thalamus, thus involving it in many cognitive activities.

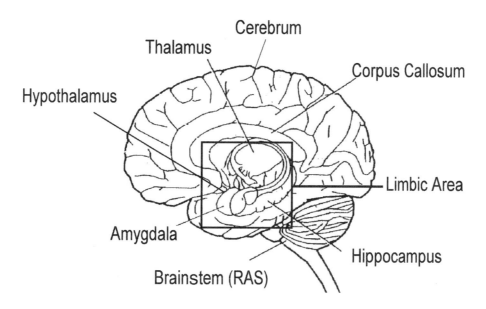

Figure 1.3 A cross section of the human brain.

The Hypothalamus. Nestled just below the thalamus is the hypothalamus. While the thalamus monitors information coming in from the outside, the hypothalamus monitors the internal systems to maintain the normal state of the body (called *homeostasis*). By controlling the release of a variety of hormones, it moderates numerous body functions, including sleep, food intake, and liquid intake. If body systems slip out of balance, it is difficult for the individual to concentrate on cognitive processing of curriculum material.

The Hippocampus. Located near the base of the limbic area is the hippocampus (the Greek word for "seahorse," because of its shape). It plays a major role in consolidating learning and in converting information from working memory via electrical signals to the long-term storage regions, a process that may take days to months. It constantly checks information relayed to working memory and compares it to stored experiences. This process is essential for the creation of meaning.

Its role was first revealed by patients whose hippocampus was damaged by lesions or removed because of disease. These patients could remember everything that happened before the surgery, but not afterward. If they were introduced to you today, you would be a stranger to them tomorrow. Because they can remember information for only a few minutes, they can read the same article repeatedly and believe on each occasion that it is the first time they have read it. Brain scans have confirmed the role of the hippocampus in permanent memory storage. Alzheimer's disease progressively destroys neurons in the hippocampus, resulting in memory loss.

Recent studies of brain-damaged patients have revealed that although the hippocampus plays an important role in the recall of facts, objects, and places, it does not seem to play much of a role in the recall of long-term personal memories (Lieberman, 2005).

The Amygdala. At the end of the hippocampus is the amygdala (Greek for "almond"). This structure plays an important role in emotions, especially fear. It regulates the individual's interactions with the environment than can affect survival, such as whether to attack, escape, mate, or eat.

Because of its proximity to the hippocampus and its activity on PET scans, researchers believe that the amygdala encodes an emotional message, if one is present, whenever a memory is tagged for long-term storage. It is not known at this time whether the emotional memories themselves are actually stored in the amygdala. One possibility is that the emotional component of a memory is stored in the amygdala while other cognitive components (names, dates, etc.) are stored elsewhere. Regardless of the storage configuration, the emotional component is recalled whenever the memory is recalled. This explains why people recalling a strong emotional memory will often experience those emotions again. The interactions between the amygdala and the hippocampus ensure that we remember for a long time those events that are important and emotional.

Teachers, of course, hope that their students will permanently remember what was taught. Thus it is worth noting that the two structures in the brain mainly responsible for long-term remembering are located in the *emotional* area of the brain.

Cerebrum

A soft jellylike mass, the cerebrum is the largest area, representing nearly 80 percent of the brain by weight. Its surface is pale gray, wrinkled, and marked by furrows called fissures. One large fissure runs from front to back and divides the cerebrum into two halves, called the *cerebral hemispheres*. For some still unexplained reason, the nerves from the left side of the body cross over to the right hemisphere, and those from the right side of the body cross to the left hemisphere. The two hemispheres are connected by a thick cable of more than 250 million nerve fibers called the *corpus callosum* (Latin for "large body"). The hemispheres use this bridge to communicate with each other and coordinate activities.

The hemispheres are covered by a thin but tough laminated *cortex* (meaning "tree bark"), rich in cells, that is about one/tenth of an inch thick and, because of its folds, has a surface area of about two square feet. That is about the size of a large dinner napkin. The cortex is composed of six layers of cells meshed in about 10,000 miles of connecting fibers per cubic inch! Here is where most of the action takes place. Thinking, memory, speech, and muscular movement are controlled by areas in the cerebrum. The cortex is often referred to as the brain's gray matter.

The neurons in the thin cortex form columns whose branches extend down through the cortical layer into a dense web below known as the white matter. Here, neurons connect with each other to form vast arrays of neural networks that carry out specific functions.

Brain Cells

The control functions and other activities of the brain are carried out by signals traveling along brain cells. The brain is composed of a trillion cells of at least two known types: nerve cells and their support cells. Nerve cells are called *neurons* and represent about one-tenth of the total number of cells—roughly 100 billion. Most of the cells are support cells, called *glial* (Greek for "glue") cells, that hold the neurons together and act as filters to keep harmful substances out of the neurons.

Neurons are the functioning core for the brain and the entire nervous system. They come in different sizes, but it takes about 30,000 brain neurons to fit on the head of a pin. Unlike other cells, the neuron (Figure 1.4) has tens of thousands of branches or *dendrites* (from the Greek word for "tree") emerging from its center. The dendrites receive electrical impulses from other neurons and transmit them along a long fiber, called the *axon* (Greek for "axis"). Each neuron has only one axon. A layer called the *myelin* (related to the

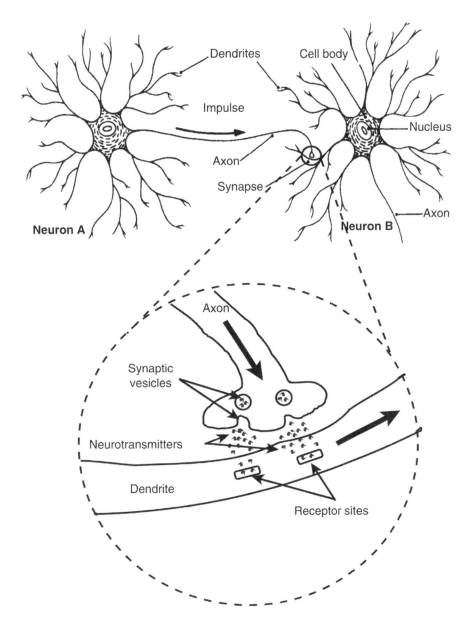

Figure 1.4 Neurons, or nerve cells, transmit impulses along an axon and across the synapse to the dendrites of the neighboring cell. The impulse is carried across the synapse to receptor sites by chemicals called neurotransmitters that lie within the synaptic vesicles.

Greek word for "marrow") *sheath* surrounds each axon. The sheath insulates the axon from the other cells and increases the speed of impulse transmission. The impulse travels along the neurons through an electro-chemical process and can move the entire length of a six-foot adult in two/tenths of a second. A neuron can transmit between 250 and 2,500 impulses per second.

Neurons have no direct contact with each other. Between each dendrite and axon is a small gap of about a millionth of an inch called a *synapse* (from the Greek meaning "to join together"). A typical neuron collects signals from others through the dendrites. The neuron sends out spikes of electrical activity (impulses) through the axon to the synapse, where the activity releases chemicals stored in sacs (called *synaptic vesicles*) at the end of the axon.

The chemicals, called *neurotransmitters*, either excite or inhibit the neighboring neuron. More than 100 neurotransmitters have been discovered so far (Gazzaniga, Ivry, & Mangun, 2002). Some of the more common neurotransmitters are acetylcholine, epinephrine, serotonin, and dopamine.

Mirror Neurons

Scientists using fMRI technology recently discovered clusters of neurons in the premotor cortex (the area in front of the motor cortex that plans movements) firing just before a person carries out a planned movement. Curiously, these neurons also fired when a person saw someone else perform the movement. For example, the firing pattern of these neurons that preceded the subject grasping a cup of coffee, was identical to the pattern when the subject saw someone else do that. Thus, similar brain areas process both the production and perception of movement. Neuroscientists believe these mirror neurons may help an individual decode the intentions and predict the behavior of others. If you see someone reach for a ball even though his hand is out of sight, your mirror neurons tell you that he is going to pick up the ball even before he does it (Fadiga, Craighero, & Olivier, 2005; Iacoboni, et al., 2005).

Studies also show that structures in the limbic area that activate during one's own pain also activate during empathy for pain. Mirror neurons allow us to re-create the experience of others within ourselves, and to understand others' emotions and empathize. Seeing the look of disgust or joy on other people's faces causes mirror neurons to trigger similar emotions in us. We start to feel their actions and sensations as though we were doing them (Singer, et al., 2004).

Mirror neurons probably explain the mimicry we see in young children when they imitate our smile and many of our other movements. We all experience this phenomenon when we attempt to stifle a yawn after seeing someone else yawning. Neuroscientists believe that mirror neurons may explain a lot about mental behaviors that have remained a mystery. For instance, there is experimental evidence that children with autism spectrum disorders may have a deficit in their mirror-neuron system. That would explain why they have difficulty inferring the intentions and mental state of others (Oberman, et al., 2005). See Chapter 9 for a discussion of these findings and their implications. Researchers also suspect that mirror neurons play a role in our ability to develop articulate speech.

LEARNING AND RETENTION

Learning occurs when the synapses make physical and chemical changes so that the influence of one neuron on another also changes. For instance, a set of neurons "learns" to fire together. Repeated firings make successive firings easier and, eventually, automatic under certain conditions. Thus, a memory is formed.

For all practical purposes, the capacity of the brain to store information is unlimited. That is, with about 100 billion neurons, each with thousands of dendrites, the number of potential neural pathways is incomprehensible. The brain will hardly run out of space to store all that an individual learns in a lifetime. Learning is the process by which we *acquire* new knowledge and skills; memory is the process by which we *retain* knowledge and skills for the future.

Investigations into the neural mechanisms required for different types of learning are revealing more about the interactions between learning new information, memory, and changes in brain structure. Just as muscles improve with exercise, the brain seems to improve with use. Although learning does not increase the number of brain cells, it does increase their size, their branches, and their ability to form more complex networks.

The brain goes through physical and chemical changes when it stores new information as the result of learning. Storing gives rise to new neural pathways and strengthens existing pathways. Hence every time we learn something, our long-term storage areas undergo anatomical changes that, together with our unique genetic makeup, constitute the expression of our individuality (Beatty, 2001).

> *Learning is the process by which we acquire knowledge; memory is the process by which we retain it.*

Learning and retention also occur in different ways. Learning involves the brain, the nervous system, and the environment, and the process by which their interplay acquires information and skills. Sometimes, we need information for just a short period of time, like the telephone number for a pizza delivery, and then the information decays after just a few seconds. Thus learning does not always involve or require long-term retention.

A good portion of the teaching done in schools centers on delivering facts and information for building concepts that explain a body of knowledge. We teach numbers, arithmetic operations, ratios, and theorems to explain mathematics. We teach about atoms, momentum, gravity, and cells to explain science. We talk about countries and famous leaders and discuss their trials and battles to explain history, and so on. Students may hold on to this information in working memory just long enough to take a test, after which the knowledge readily decays and is lost. Retention, however, requires that the learner not only give conscious attention during learning but also build conceptual frameworks that have sense and meaning for eventual consolidation into long-term storage networks.

Implications for Students With Learning Disabilities

Because students with learning disabilities can have difficulty focusing for very long, they are even more likely to perceive learning facts as a temporary effort just to please the teacher or to pass a test. It becomes increasingly important, then, for teachers of these students to emphasize *why* they need to learn certain material. Meaning (or relevancy) becomes the key to focus, learning, and retention.

Retention is the process whereby long-term memory preserves a learning in such a way that the memory can be located, identified, and retrieved accurately in the future. This is an inexact process influenced by many factors, including the degree of student focus, the length and type of rehearsal that occurred, the critical attributes that may have been identified, the student's learning style, the impact of any learning disabilities, and, of course, the inescapable influence of prior learning.

Rehearsal

The brain's decision to retain a learning seems to be based primarily on two criteria: *sense* and *meaning*. Sense refers to whether the student understands the learning: "Does this fit my perception of how the world works?" Meaning, on the other hand, refers to relevancy. Although the student may understand the learning, the more important question may be, "So what? What's this got to do with me?" Attaching sense

> *Learning is likely to be remembered if it makes sense and has meaning for the learner.*

and meaning to new learning can occur only if the learner has adequate time to process and reprocess it. This continuing reprocessing is called *rehearsal* and is a critical component in the transference of information from working memory to long-term storage.

Two major factors should be considered in evaluating rehearsal: the amount of time devoted to it, which determines whether there is both initial and secondary rehearsal, and the type of rehearsal carried out, which can be rote or elaborative.

Time for Initial and Secondary Rehearsal

Time is a critical component of rehearsal. Initial rehearsal occurs when the information first enters working memory. If the learner cannot attach sense or meaning and if there is no time for further processing, the new information is likely to be lost. Providing sufficient time to go beyond initial processing to secondary rehearsal allows the learner to review the information, to make sense of it, to elaborate on the details, and to assign value and relevance, thus increasing significantly the chance of long-term storage.

Scanning studies of the brain indicate that the frontal lobe is very much involved during the rehearsal process and, ultimately, in long-term memory formation. This makes sense because working memory is also located in the frontal lobe. Several studies using fMRI scans of humans showed that, during longer rehearsals, the amount of activity in the frontal lobe determined whether items were stored or forgotten (Buckner, Kelley, & Petersen, 1999; Goldberg, 2001; Wagner et al., 1998).

Students carry out initial and secondary rehearsal at different rates of speed and in different ways, depending on the type of information in the new learning and on their learning styles, including any learning disabilities. As the learning task changes, learners automatically shift to different patterns of rehearsal.

Rote and Elaborative Rehearsal

Rote Rehearsal. Rote rehearsal is used when learners need to remember and store information exactly as it is entered into working memory. It is a simple strategy necessary for learning information or a skill in a specific form or sequence. We employ rote rehearsal to remember a poem, the lyrics and melody of a song, multiplication tables, telephone numbers, and steps in a procedure. This rehearsal usually involves direct instruction. However, students with learning disabilities often perceive rote rehearsal as intensely boring, forcing the teacher to find creative and interesting ways to accomplish the rehearsal while keeping students on task.

> *Students with learning disabilities need more time and guidance than others to rehearse the new learning in order to determine sense and recognize meaning.*

Elaborative Rehearsal. Elaborative rehearsal is used when it is unnecessary to store information exactly as learned, and when it is important to associate new learnings with prior learnings to detect relationships. In this complex thinking process, learners review the information several times to make connections to previous learnings and assign meaning. Students use rote rehearsal to memorize a poem, but elaborative rehearsal to interpret its message. When students get very little time for, or training in, elaborative rehearsal, they resort more frequently to rote rehearsal. Consequently, they fail to make the associations or discover the relationships that only elaborative rehearsal can provide. Also, they continue to believe that the value of learning is merely the recalling of information as learned rather than the generating of new ideas, concepts, and solutions.

Students with learning disabilities need more time and guidance than others to rehearse the new learning in order to determine sense and recognize meaning. They need help with both types of rehearsal, including a rationale for each. When deciding how to use rehearsal in a lesson, teachers should consider the time available and the type of rehearsal appropriate for the specific learning objective. Keep in mind that rehearsal only contributes to, but does not guarantee, information transfer into long-term storage. However, there is almost no long-term retention *without* rehearsal.

Learning Motor Skills

Scanning studies show that a person uses the frontal lobe, motor cortex, and cerebellum while learning a new physical skill. Learning a motor skill involves following a set of procedures and can be eventually carried out largely without conscious attention. In fact, too much conscious attention directed to a motor skill while performing it can diminish the quality of its execution.

When first learning the skill, attention and awareness are obviously required. The frontal lobe is engaged because working memory is needed, and the motor cortex of the cerebrum (located across the top of the brain) interacts with the cerebellum to control muscle movement. As practice continues, the activated areas of the motor cortex become larger as nearby neurons are recruited into the new skill network. However, the memory of the skill is not established (i.e., stored) until after practice stops. It takes about four to 12 hours for this consolidation to take place in the cerebellum, and most of it occurs during deep sleep. Once the skill is mastered, brain activity shifts to the cerebellum, which organizes and coordinates the movements and the timing to perform the task. Procedural memory is the mechanism, and the brain no longer needs to use its higher-order processes as the performance of the skill becomes automatic (Penhun & Doyon, 2005; Press, Casement, Pascual-Leone, & Robertson, 2005; Walker, Stickgold, Alsop, Gaab, & Schlaug, 2005).

Continued practice of the skill changes the brain structurally, and the younger the learner is, the easier it is for these changes to occur. Most music and sports prodigies began practicing their skills very early in life. Because their brains were most sensitive to the structural changes needed to acquire the skills, they can perform them masterfully. These skills become so much a part of the individual that they are difficult to change later in life (Lacourse, Orr, Cramer, & Cohen, 2005; Schack, & Mechsner, 2006).

Learning Difficulties and Motor Skills

Children with low motor ability will have difficulty learning motor skills. But it is a mistake to assume that low motor ability also means low perceptual or intellectual ability. Research studies indicate that individuals with low motor ability often have problems interpreting visual scenes involving movement, but that this limitation does not affect their intellectual or perceptual abilities (Bonifacci, 2004). One promising technique for helping individuals with low motor ability involves the stimulation of the motor cortex (see Figure 1.1) with a strong magnetic field. The procedure, called repetitive transcranial magnetic stimulation, appears to facilitate the learning of sequential motor skills (Kim, Park, Ko, Jang, & Lee, 2004).

Individuals with developmental dyslexia often have problems learning motor skills. Researchers suspect that people with this disorder may suffer from an implicit motor learning deficit that not only affects their reading but also impairs their ability to acquire motor skills easily and accurately (Stoodley, Harrison, & Stein, 2006).

Children with attention deficits may have difficulty focusing sufficiently to acquire some specific motor skills. Often, what little focus they have is directed internally. Studies show that getting students to focus externally (i.e., on objects outside the body) enhances the acquisition and accuracy of motor skills. In these studies, the researchers suggested that the external focus of attention improves the efficiency of body movement and reduces the noise signals in the motor system that hamper the movement control and make it less reliable (Zachry, Wulf, Mercer, & Bezodis, 2005).

HOW DIFFERENT ARE THE BRAINS OF TODAY'S STUDENTS?

Teachers remark more than ever that students of today are different in the way they learn. They seem to have shorter attention spans and become bored more easily than ever before. Why is that? Is something happening in the environment of learners that alters the way they approach the learning process? Does this mean that more students will have learning problems?

The Search for Novelty

Part of our success as a species can be attributed to the brain's persistent interest in novelty, that is, changes occurring in the environment. The brain is constantly scanning its environment for stimuli. When an unexpected stimulus arises—such as a loud noise from an empty room—a rush of adrenaline closes down all unnecessary activity and focuses the brain's attention so it can spring into action. Conversely, an environment that contains mainly predictable or repeated stimuli (like some classrooms?) lowers the brain's interest in the outside world and tempts it to turn within for novel sensations.

Recent and profound changes in our culture have enhanced the brain's interest in novelty. Let's compare the environment that a child grew up in, say, 15 years ago compared to the environment that encompasses the developing brain today.

The Environment of the Past

The home environment for many children several decades ago was quite different from that of today. For example,

- The home was quieter—some might say boring compared to today.
- Parents and children did a lot of talking and reading.
- The family unit was more stable and ate together, and the dinner hour was an opportunity for parents to discuss their children's activities as well as reaffirm their love and support.
- If the home had a television, it was in a common area and controlled by adults. What children watched could be carefully monitored.

- School was an interesting place because it had television, films, field trips, and guest speakers. There were few other distractions, so school was an important influence in a child's life and the primary source of information.
- The neighborhood was also an important part of growing up. Children played together, developing their motor skills and learning the social skills needed to interact successfully with other children in the neighborhood.

The Environment of Today

In recent years, children have been growing up in a very different environment.

- Family units are not as stable as they once were. Single-parent families are more common, and children have fewer opportunities to talk with the adults who care for them. Their dietary habits are changing as home cooking is becoming a lost art.
- They are surrounded by media: cell phones, multiple televisions, movies, computers, video games, e-mail, and the Internet. Teens spend nearly 17 hours a week on the Internet and nearly 14 hours a week watching television (Guterl, 2003).
- Many 10- to 18-year-olds can now watch television and play with other technology in their own bedrooms, leading to sleep deprivation. Furthermore, with no adult present, what kind of moral compass is evolving in the impressionable preadolescent mind as a result of watching programs containing violence and sex on television and the Internet?
- They get information from many different sources besides school.
- The multimedia environment divides their attention. Even newscasts are different. In the past, only the reporter's face was on the screen. Now, the TV screen is loaded with information set in the corners and scrolling across the bottom. Children have become accustomed to these information-rich and rapidly changing messages. They can pay attention to several things at once, but they do not go into any one thing in depth.
- They spend much more time indoors with their technology, thereby missing outdoor opportunities to develop gross motor skills and socialization skills necessary to communicate and act personally with others. One unintended consequence of spending so much time indoors is the rapid rise in the number of overweight children and adolescents, now more than 15 percent of 6- to 19-year-olds.
- Young brains have responded to the technology by changing their functioning and organization to accommodate the large amount of stimulation occurring in the environment. By acclimating itself to these changes, brains respond more than ever to the unique and different—what is called *novelty*. There is a dark side to this increased novelty-seeking behavior. Some adolescents who perceive little novelty in their environment may turn to mind-altering drugs, such as ecstasy and amphetamines, for stimulation. This drug dependence can further enhance the brain's demand for novelty to the point that it becomes unbalanced and resorts to extremely risky behavior.

> *The brains of today's students are attracted more than ever to the unique and different—what is called* novelty.

- Their diet contains increasing amounts of substances that can affect brain and body functions. Caffeine is a strong brain stimulant, considered safe for most adults in small quantities. But caffeine is found in many of the foods and drinks that teens consume daily. Too much caffeine causes insomnia, anxiety, and nausea. Some teens can also develop allergies to aspartame (an artificial sugar found in children's vitamins and many "lite" foods) and other food additives. Possible symptoms of these allergic reactions include hyperactivity, difficulty concentrating, and headaches (Bateman et al., 2004; Millichap & Yee, 2003). Some children considered learning disabled may be merely displaying the symptoms of serious allergic reactions to their diet. Several dozen states now limit or prohibit the sale of foods high in caffeine and sugar in public schools, and encourage the sale of fresh fruit and other nutritious items.

When we add the changes in family lifestyles, the narcissistic values of hip-hop, as well as the temptations of alcohol and drugs, we can realize how very different the environment of today's child is from that of just 15 years ago.

Have Schools Changed to Deal With This Different Brain?

Many educators are recognizing the characteristics of the new brain, but they do not always agree on what to do about it. Granted, teaching methodologies are changing, new technologies are being used, and teachers are even introducing pop music and culture to supplement traditional classroom materials. But schools and teaching are not changing fast enough. In high schools, lecturing continues to be the main method of instruction, and the overhead projector is often the most advanced technology used. Many students remark that school is a dull, nonengaging environment that is much less interesting than what is available outside of school. They have a difficult time focusing for extended periods and are easily distracted. Because they see little novelty and relevancy in what they are learning, they keep asking the eternal question, "Why do we need to know this?" Some teachers interpret this attitude as alienation from school while other teachers see it as a sign of a learning disability. In both instances, they are likely to refer the student for counseling and diagnosis. Consequently, it is possible that more children are being referred for special education evaluation not because they have true learning difficulties but because an inflexible (though well-meaning) school environment has not adapted to their changing brains.

> *Is it possible that some children are referred for special education evaluation not because they have true learning difficulties but because a school has not adapted to their changing brains?*

Rather than ignoring the changing brain and culture, we should recognize that we must adjust schools to accommodate these changes. As we gain a more scientifically based understanding about today's novel brain and how it learns, we must rethink what we do in classrooms and schools. Maybe then more children will stay in the educational mainstream rather than be sidelined for labeling.

Some students, of course, do develop learning disabilities that need to be accurately diagnosed and addressed. The following chapters will discuss several types of learning disabilities, review recent research about them, and suggest ways of helping students who demonstrate them.

Chapter 2

When Learning Difficulties Arise

Neuron development starts in the embryo shortly after conception and proceeds at an astonishing rate. Between 50,000 and 100,000 new brain cells are generated *each second* from the fifth to the twentieth week of life. Genetic instructions govern the rate of growth and direct the migration of neurons to different levels, forming the six layers of the fetus's cerebral cortex. In the first four months of gestation, about 200 billion neurons are formed, but about half will die off during the fetus's fifth month because they fail to connect with any areas of the growing embryo. This purposeful destruction of neurons (called *apoptosis*) is genetically programmed to ensure that only those neurons that have made connections are preserved, and to prevent the brain from being overcrowded with unconnected cells. Sometimes apoptosis gets out of control, and connections that might otherwise have imparted certain intuitive skills—such as photographic memory—may be pruned as well. Defective apoptosis may also explain both the amazing abilities and deficits of autistic savants, and the impaired intelligence associated with Down syndrome. Any drugs or alcohol that the mother takes during this time can interfere with the growing brain cells, increasing the risk of fetal addiction and mental defects. Neuron growth in the fetus can also be damaged if the mother is under continual stress.

Neurons in a child's brain make many more connections than do those in an adult's brain. The 20 hours of sleep that most infants require daily preserve the energy necessary for such rapid brain development. A newborn's brain makes connections at an incredible pace as the child absorbs its environment. The richer the environment, the greater the number of interconnections that are made; consequently, learning can take place faster and with greater meaning.

As the child approaches puberty, the pace slackens, and two other processes begin: Connections the brain finds useful become permanent; those not useful are eliminated (by apoptosis) as the brain selectively strengthens and prunes connections based on experience. This process continues throughout our lives, but it appears to be most intense between the ages of 3 and 12. Thus at an early age experiences are already shaping the brain and designing the unique neural architecture that will influence how it handles future experiences in school, work, and other places.

RESEARCH EXAMINES LEARNING DISABILITIES

Possible Causes of Learning Disabilities

Neuroscientists once believed that all learning disabilities were caused by a single neurological problem. By contrast, recent research has shown that learning disabilities do not stem from a single cause but from difficulties in bringing together information from different regions of the brain. These difficulties can arise during the fetal development of the child.

> *Some children may exhibit behavior that looks like a learning disability but may simply be a delay in maturation.*

During pregnancy, the development of the brain is vulnerable to all kinds of disruptions. If the disruption occurs later in the pregnancy, errors may occur in the makeup of brain cells, their location, or the connections they make with neighboring cells. Some researchers believe that these errors may show up later as learning disorders.

Experiments with animals and imaging scans of the human brain have shown that other factors can disrupt brain development as well. Table 2.1 shows some of the factors currently under investigation and their potential impact on the development of the young brain. Problems in brain development that occur before, during, or after the birth of a child may eventually lead to learning difficulties.

Genetic Links

There is considerable evidence that genes play a role in developmental learning disabilities, especially since parents often display the same or similar learning disability as their children. In some cases, scientists have been able to link a specific gene to a specific common learning disability. But the general consensus among researchers currently is that most genes associated with common learning disabilities, such as language impairment, reading problems, and mathematics disability, are *generalist* genes, not specific ones (Plomin & Kovas, 2005). The term "generalist" means three things:

1. Genes that affect learning disabilities are largely the same genes responsible for normal variations in learning abilities.

2. Genes affecting any one aspect of a learning disability affect other aspects of that disability.

3. Genes affecting one learning disability are also likely to affect other learning disabilities.

Table 2.1	Some Factors That Affect Brain Development
Genetic Links	Because learning disabilities tend to run in families, a genetic link is likely. However, the parent's learning disability often takes a slightly different form in the child. This may indicate that inheriting a specific learning disability involves several genes. Even though a child inherits a subtle brain dysfunction that can lead to a learning disability, the dysfunction may not become evident. Some learning difficulties may stem from the family environment. Parents with an expressive language disorder, for example, may talk less to their children, or their language may be atypical. Hence the child lacks a good model for acquiring language and, consequently, may seem learning disabled.
Tobacco, Alcohol, and Other Drug Use	The mother's use of cigarettes, alcohol, or other drugs may damage the unborn child. Mothers who smoke during pregnancy often bear smaller babies who tend to be at risk for problems, including learning disorders. Alcohol can distort neural growth, which often leads to hyperactivity and intellectual impairment. Even small amounts of alcohol during pregnancy can affect the frontal lobe and lead later to problems with attention, learning, and memory. Drugs like cocaine (especially crack) seem to affect the development of the receptor cells that transmit incoming information from our senses. This receptor damage may cause children to have difficulty understanding speech sounds or letters, a common problem found in the offspring of crack-addicted mothers.
Problems During Pregnancy or Delivery	Sometimes the mother's immune system attacks the fetus, causing newly formed brain cells to settle in the wrong part of the brain. This migration may disturb the formation of neural networks needed for language and cognitive thought. During delivery, the umbilical cord may become twisted and temporarily cut off oxygen to the brain, which can damage or kill neurons and lead to learning disorders.
Toxins in the Child's Environment	Environmental toxins may disrupt brain cell growth and development in the early years. Lead and cadmium are getting particular research attention. Lead and mercury are still found in the environment, and both can cause learning difficulties and behavior problems.
Stress in the Child's Environment	Prolonged and inappropriate stress in the environment can harm the brain at any age. Corticosteroids released into the bloodstream during stress can damage the hippocampus and thus interfere with the coding of new information into memory. These chemicals also damage neurons in other brain areas, thereby increasing the risk of stroke, seizure, and infections.

Inheriting a genetic tendency for a learning problem does not necessarily mean that the trait will appear. We recognize now the powerful influence of the environment in determining whether certain genetic traits arise and affect one's behavior and learning. For example, a child born with the genetic components for expressive language problems and who lives in a household where there is little interactive conversation is

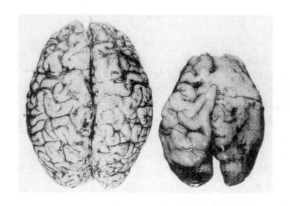

Figure 2.1 These autopsy photographs vividly demonstrate how alcohol has adversely affected the development of the newborn's brain on the right, compared to the expected normal development shown in the newborn on the left.

apt to display the symptoms of this disorder. Conversely, if the parents frequently encourage the child to participate in family discussions, then there is a smaller likelihood that the expressive language problem will emerge.

Tobacco, Alcohol, and Other Drug Use

Tobacco. It has been known for some time that mothers who smoke during pregnancy often bear children of lower than average birth weight, making these newborns more susceptible to infection, mental retardation, and cerebral palsy. More recent studies have found the nicotine in tobacco smoke affects the development of the fetal brainstem, which can lead to the death of the fetus before birth (Lavezzi, Ottaviani, & Matturri, 2005). Nicotine also affects the development of the fetal lungs and heart. After birth, these babies are more at risk for sleep apnea, labored breathing, and irregular heart rate (Hafström, Milerad, Sandberg, & Sundell, 2005).

Alcohol. Most medical professionals agree that there are no known safe times and no safe amount of alcohol to drink during pregnancy. When a pregnant woman drinks alcohol, so does her unborn baby. Alcohol passes easily and quickly through the placenta to the fetus. In the unborn baby's immature body, alcohol is broken down much more slowly than in an adult's body. As a result, the alcohol level of the baby's blood can be higher, and can remain elevated longer, than in the mother's blood. This sometimes causes the baby to suffer lifelong damage. Brain damage from alcohol runs a gamut from mild to severe. The mild forms are called Fetal Alcohol Effects, and severe damage is called Fetal Alcohol Syndrome. Fetal alcohol exposure can result in impairments in behavior, verbal learning, visual-spatial skills, attention, reaction times, and executive control functions, such as problem solving and abstract thinking (NIAAA, 2000).

Excessive drinking of alcoholic beverages during pregnancy can cause extreme and often fatal damage to the developing fetal brain. The autopsy photographs in Figure 2.1 show the dramatic difference in brain shape and size between the brain of a newborn whose mother drank alcohol excessively during pregnancy, compared to the normally developed newborn brain on the left. Apparently, the alcohol interrupts the normal growth of neurons and signals them to commit suicide, that form of cell death known as apoptosis that we discussed earlier. The cell death results in a smaller brain size (Farber & Olney, 2003).

Marijuana. Drug abuse during pregnancy can also lead to problems for the developing fetus. Studies suggest that use of marijuana during pregnancy slows fetal growth and slightly decreases the length of pregnancy. After delivery, some babies who were regularly exposed to marijuana in the womb appear to undergo withdrawal-like symptoms, including excessive crying and trembling.

There have been a limited number of studies following marijuana-exposed babies through childhood. Some did not find any increased risk of learning or behavioral problems. However, others found that children who are exposed to marijuana before birth are more likely to have subtle problems that affect their ability to pay attention and to solve visual problems. Exposed children do not appear to have a decrease in IQ. One study with more than 600 participants did find that marijuana-exposed children were much more likely to suffer depression by the age of 10 (Gray, Day, Leech, & Richardson, 2005).

Cocaine. Cocaine use during pregnancy can lead to a variety of physical problems for the baby after birth. Cocaine-exposed babies tend to have smaller heads, which generally reflect smaller brains. They may score lower than unexposed babies on tests given at birth to assess the newborn's physical condition and overall responsiveness. They may not do as well as unexposed babies on measures of motor ability, reflexes, attention, and mood control, and they appear less likely to respond to a human face or voice. As newborns, some are jittery and irritable, and they may startle and cry at the gentlest touch or sound. Generally, these behavioral disturbances are temporary and resolve over the first few months of life.

Studies now suggest that most children who are exposed to cocaine before birth have normal intelligence, although their IQ levels may have been lowered somewhat by the exposure. Furthermore, researchers have found that some of the attention

> *Some of the attention and learning difficulties that cocaine-exposed children demonstrate in early childhood can be improved in an nurturing and enriched environment.*

and learning difficulties that cocaine-exposed children demonstrate in early childhood can be improved when these children are placed in a nurturing and enriched environment (Cone-Wesson, 2005; Lewis, et al., 2004; Miller-Loncar, et al., 2005; Noland, et al., 2005). This is encouraging news for parents and early childhood educators, in light of earlier predictions that many of these children would be permanently brain damaged. Language problems may persist, however. Apparently, cocaine interferes with the development of brain cells that transmit information from the senses. This receptor damage may cause children to have difficulty hearing and discriminating speech sounds, a common problem found in the offspring of crack-addicted mothers.

Follow-up studies suggest that most adolescents who were exposed to cocaine before birth seem to function normally. However, some adolescents may have subtle impairments in the ability to control emotions, focus attention, and process language that could put them at risk for behavioral and learning problems. Researchers continue to follow cocaine-exposed children through their teen years to clarify their long-term outlook.

Problems During Pregnancy or Delivery

Problems during pregnancy can result in brain damage that affects learning. Sometimes the mother's immune system attacks the fetus, causing newly formed brain cells to settle in the wrong part of the brain. This migration may disturb the formation of neural networks needed for language and cognitive thought. Blows to the stomach area can decrease the oxygen and blood supply to the fetus, causing the death of brain cells. During delivery, the umbilical cord may become twisted and temporarily cut off oxygen to the brain, which can damage or kill neurons and lead to learning disorders.

Babies born prematurely (at or before seven months of gestation) can exhibit abnormal brain growth and injury to the white matter (Rees & Inder, 2005). Strategic areas of the brain, such as those responsible for language, emotion, and behavior, remain smaller than normal even years later. The brains of premature boys are more severely affected than the brains of premature girls (Reisster et al., 2004).

Toxins in the Child's Environment

Children are particularly susceptible to environmental toxins because, pound for pound, they drink more water, eat more food, and breathe more air than adults. Thus children have substantially heavier exposure than adults to the toxins lurking in water, food, and air. Furthermore, their hand-to-mouth behavior and their preference for playing close to the ground only add to the risk of exposure.

Lead. The effect of lead on children's health is one of those most clearly understood in the environmental field. Despite the removal of lead from gasoline and paint, more than half a million children a year in the United State exhibit signs of lead poisoning, mostly poor minority children in urban settings. For children, the primary route for lead is oral ingestion via food, water, soil, and dust. Once absorbed, lead follows the distribution of calcium in the body. Children are especially sensitive to the toxic effects of lead, because compared with adults, more is absorbed through the gastrointestinal tract, a greater proportion of circulating lead reaches the brain (especially under 5 years of age), and the developing nervous system is especially vulnerable to damage. Follow-up studies of children who had high blood levels of lead show that they have lower IQ levels and more frequent behavior problems.

Mercury. Mercury, like lead, is toxic to the developing brain. Mercury occurs in the earth's crust, and natural sources, such as volcano emissions, contribute significantly to atmospheric levels. Industrial sources of mercury emissions have declined dramatically in the past two decades. However, current main sources include waste incineration, chlorine manufacturing, and the burning of coal. Methylmercury, the more toxic form, is produced by microorganisms acting on mercury in deposits in the sea and the soil. Since mercury accumulates through the food chain, the highest levels of methylmercury occur in predatory fish, which in turn are a major source of human exposure. Increased levels of mercury and mercury compounds have been shown to impair cognitive performance in children and adolescents (Grigg, 2004).

Stress in the Child's Environment

Stress causes the body to release cortisol, a corticosteroid that arouses the brain to consider what action to take. Stress can have positive effects by encouraging individuals to raise their level of performance. But stress from living in poverty or with abusive parents has negative consequences. Continued and undesired stress can cause cortisol to remain in the body for prolonged periods, thereby damaging cells. In the child's brain, persistent stress can impair the hippocampus, the structure responsible for permanent memory storage and recall. Corticosteroids also damage neurons in other brain areas, thereby increasing the risk of stroke, seizure, and infections (Restak, 2000).

Of course, not all learning difficulties are technically disabilities. For example, many children are just slower in developing certain skills. Therefore, some children may exhibit behavior that *looks like* a learning disability but may simply be a delay in maturation.

Learning disabilities are characterized by a significant difference between a child's achievement and that individual's overall intelligence. Students with learning disabilities often exhibit a wide variety of traits, including problems with spoken and written language, reading, arithmetic, reasoning ability, and organization skills. These may be accompanied with inattention, hyperactivity, impulsivity, motor disorders, perceptual impairment, and a low tolerance for frustration. Because each of these traits can run the gamut from mild to severe, it is necessary to assess each student's disabilities carefully to determine the best approach for effective teaching.

Gender Differences

More than twice as many boys as girls are diagnosed with learning difficulties (Baron-Cohen, 2003), and four times as many boys are diagnosed with dyslexia and autism (Shaywitz, 2003; Simpson, 2005). What accounts for these gender differences? No one knows for sure, but research is shedding light on a few possible explanations. Some neuroscientists believe that male fetuses are more likely than female fetuses to invoke a foreign-body response by the mother's immune system. The response may induce a hostile environment in the womb that leads to fetal brain damage and eventual brain disorders.

Other researchers contend that an unknown factor (maybe testosterone) present during the last trimester of pregnancy slows the formation of the brain's cortex, especially in the left hemisphere. Because girls are not influenced by this mysterious factor, their brains mature normally and are therefore better able to handle the stresses of pregnancy and birth. This may explain why females recover better than males from fetal brain damage (Restak, 2000). The research continues.

A third and more likely possibility is that certain brain deficits affecting learning result from genetic mutations on the X chromosome. Females have two X chromosomes, so they are protected if the healthy chromosome can prevent the unwanted effects of the mutated one. Males, on the other hand, possess only one X chromosome, so they suffer the full consequences of any mutations on that chromosome.

What Forms of Instruction Are Most Effective?

An analysis of more than 30 years of research indicates that the following interventions are most effective with learning disabled students:

- The most effective form of teaching was one that combined direct instruction (e.g., teacher-directed lecture, discussion, and learning from textbooks) with teaching students the strategies of learning (e.g., memorization techniques, study skills). Using technology, such as computers and presentation media, can make these practice sessions more interesting and interactive.
- The component that had the greatest effect on student achievement was *control of task difficulty*, in which, for example, the teacher provided the necessary assistance or sequenced the tasks from easy to difficult. Working in small groups (five or less) and using structured questioning were also highly effective. Students also made fewer errors when teachers systematically modeled how to solve problems. See suggestions on forming these groups in **Strategies to Consider.**
- When groups of students with learning disabilities were exposed to strategy instruction (i.e., understanding how to learn), their achievement was greater than that of groups exposed solely to direct instruction.

Misconceptions About Learning Disabilities

Table 2.2 deals with some common misconceptions about the causes and implications of learning disabilities.

Table 2.2   Misconceptions About Learning Disabilities

MISCONCEPTION	EXPLANATION
Learning disabilities are common and therefore easy to diagnose.	Learning disabilities are often hidden and thus difficult to diagnose. Brain imaging continues to show promise in the diagnosis of some learning disabilities. Until this method becomes feasible, diagnosis of a learning disability needs to result from extensive observation and testing by a clinical team.
Children with learning disabilities are identified in kindergarten or first grade.	Learning disabilities often go unrecognized in the early years, and most are not identified until third grade. Bright children can mask their difficulties, and some kinds of learning problems may not surface until middle school, high school, or even college.
Children outgrow their learning disabilities.	Most learning disabilities last throughout life, and a few can be remediated. Many adults have devised strategies to cope successfully with their disabilities and lead productive lives.
Learning disabilities are caused by poor parenting.	No definitive association exists between the child-rearing skills of parents and the presence or absence of permanent learning disabilities in their children. However, home discipline, the degree of parental interaction, and other factors may affect a child's self-image and enthusiasm for success in school. Physical abuse *can* cause permanent changes in the brain.
Accommodations provided to students with learning disabilities, particularly during testing, gives them an unfair advantage over students without disabilities.	Accommodations do not favor these students. Rather, accommodations allow access to the information that gives students with a learning disability the means to demonstrate their knowledge, skills, and abilities. Without modifications, common forms of instruction and testing often inadvertently reflect a student's disability rather than the subject at hand. For example, a student who has a writing disability would be greatly impaired during a written essay exam, even though the student was skilled in the art and mechanics of composing an essay. The use of a word processor allows this student to be assessed on knowledge rather than on the limitations that the writing difficulties imposed.
Medication, diet, or other treatments can cure learning disabilities.	No quick fix exists to cure learning disabilities. Even medication given to ADHD children mediates the symptoms but does not cure the disorder. Because most learning disabilities are considered lifelong, the support and understanding of, and attention to the child's needs are basic to long-term treatment. However, certain interventions for children with dyslexia have been successful.
Students with learning disabilities don't try hard enough in school.	Ironically, brain scans show that many students with learning disabilities are working harder at certain tasks than other students, but the result is less successful. Students with learning disabilities often give up trying at school because of their fear of failure.
Learning disabilities affect everything the child does at school.	Some learning disabilities are very specific. Thus a student's weakness may affect performance in one classroom setting but not in another, or only at a particular grade level.
Children with learning disabilities are just "slow."	Most learning disabilities are independent of cognitive ability. Children at all intellectual levels—including the gifted—can have learning problems.

Gifted Children With Learning Disabilities

The notion that a gifted child can have learning disabilities strikes some people as bizarre, something like an oxymoron. Consequently, many children who are gifted in some ways and deficient in others go undetected and unserved by their schools. They tend to fall through the cracks because the system is not designed to deal with such widely different conditions occurring in the same student. Despite more than 30 years of research on these twice-exceptional students, it is only in recent years that educators have even begun to accept that high abilities and learning problems can exist together in the same person. But interest is increasing, and educators are looking to the research to help them identify these students and find ways to meet their needs.

> *Many children who are gifted in some ways and deficient in others go undetected and unserved by their schools.*

About two to five percent of all students are likely to be gifted and also have learning disabilities. Researchers continue to search for measurement activities that will accurately identify children with both talents and learning disabilities. As school districts pay more attention to twice-exceptional students, programs are emerging that address their needs. These include interventions in the regular classroom, partial pullout programs, and self-contained programs. For more information on identifying and serving twice-exceptional students, see Reis & Ruban (2005) and Sousa (2003).

RESPONSIVENESS TO INTERVENTION

Identifying and helping students with learning difficulties have never been an easy task. The number of students identified as having learning disabilities has increased more than 200 percent since the category was first established in 1977. Some researchers argue that many students have been misidentified or unidentified. The primary concern is that the right students are identified as early as practicable.

In the Individuals with Disabilities Education Act (IDEA) of 1997, the major guideline for assessing these students was a severe discrepancy between achievement and intellectual ability (IQ) in language, reading, writing, or mathematics. This type of assessment is very narrow. It relies on the difference between two scores to determine if a learning disability exists, thus tending to overidentify children with high IQs and average achievement and underidentify those with lower IQs and below-average achievement. Furthermore, this approach does not lead directly to recommendations for remediation, nor does it take into account the various neurological conditions that can affect the ability to speak, read, write, and calculate (Semrud-Clikeman, 2005).

In recent years, one method of determining whether students have learning difficulties is assessing if their responses to the methods, strategies, curriculum, and interventions they encounter lead to increased learning and appropriate progress. This concept forms the basis of the approach known as *responsiveness to intervention,* and it was addressed in the Individuals with Disabilities Education Improvement Act of 2004 (IDEA, 2004).

Key Elements of Responsiveness to Intervention

A key element of a responsiveness to intervention (RTI) approach is to provide early intervention when students first experience academic difficulties, with the goal of improving the achievement of all students, including those who may have learning disabilities. In addition to the preventive and remedial services this approach provides at-risk students, it shows promise for contributing data useful for accurately identifying learning disabilities. Thus a student exhibiting significantly low achievement and insufficient RTI may be viewed as being at risk for learning disability and possibly in need of special education services. The assumption behind this model, referred to as a dual discrepancy, is that when provided with quality instruction and remedial services, a student without disabilities will make satisfactory progress (Fuchs, Fuchs, & Speece, 2002).

A Problem-Solving Approach Using Data

Another key element of RTI is that it uses a systematic problem-solving process involving the following steps:

- Identifying and analyzing the problem, including collection of baseline data
- Generating possible scientific, research-based strategies or interventions
- Implementing an intervention plan
- Monitoring student progress to determine the student's response to these interventions
- Using the RTI data to review and revise plans as needed

The data used in the RTI process should include the following (NJCLD, 2005):

- High-quality, research-based instruction and behavioral supports in general education
- Scientific, research-based interventions focused specifically on individual student difficulties and delivered with appropriate intensity
- Use of a collaborative approach by school staff for development, implementation, and monitoring of the intervention process
- Data-based documentation reflecting continuous monitoring of student performance and progress during interventions
- Documentation of parent involvement throughout the process
- Documentation that the time lines described in the federal regulations are followed unless extended by mutual written agreement of the child's parents and a team of qualified professionals as described in these regulations
- Systematic assessment and documentation that the interventions used were implemented with fidelity

IDEA 2004 addresses the use of RTI in two respects. First, it allows for the use of RTI data as part of an evaluation for special education to assist in the identification and determination of eligibility of students with learning disabilities, as an alternative to use of the ability–achievement discrepancy criterion. Second, it creates the option of using up to 15 percent of funds for early intervention services for students who have not been identified as needing special education services but who need additional academic and behavioral support to succeed in a general education environment.

Multiple-Tiered Model

Although there is no universal RTI model, it is generally viewed as having three tiers, consisting of the following (NJCLD, 2005):

Tier 1. High-quality instructional and behavioral supports are provided for all students in general education.
- School personnel conduct universal screening of literacy skills, academics, and behavior
- Teachers implement a variety of research-supported teaching strategies and approaches
- Ongoing, curriculum-based assessment and continuous progress monitoring are used to guide high-quality instruction
- Students receive differentiated instruction based on data from ongoing assessments

Tier 2. Students whose performance and rate of progress lag behind those of peers in their classroom, school, or district receive more specialized prevention or remediation within general education.
- Curriculum-based measures are used to identify which students continue to need assistance, and with what specific kinds of skills
- Collaborative problem solving is used to design and implement instructional support for students that may consist of a standard protocol or more individualized strategies and interventions
- Identified students receive more intensive scientific, research-based instruction targeted to their individual needs
- Student progress is monitored frequently to determine intervention effectiveness and needed modifications
- Systematic assessment is conducted to determine the fidelity or integrity with which instruction and interventions are implemented
- Parents are informed and included in the planning and monitoring of their child's progress in the Tier 2 specialized interventions
- General education teachers receive support (e.g., training, consultation, direct services for students), as needed, from other qualified educators in implementing interventions and monitoring student progress

Tier 3. Comprehensive evaluation is conducted by a multidisciplinary team to determine eligibility for special education and related services.
- Parents are informed of their due process rights, and consent is obtained for the comprehensive evaluation needed to determine whether the student has a disability and is eligible for special education and related services
- Evaluation consists of multiple sources of assessment data, which may include data from standardized and norm-referenced measures, observations made by parents, students, and teachers, and data collected in Tiers 1 and 2

- Intensive, systematic, specialized instruction is provided, and additional RTI data are collected, as needed, in accordance with special education timelines and other mandates
- Procedural safeguards on evaluations and eligibility apply, as required by the IDEA 2004 mandates

Variations on this basic framework may occur. For example, Tier 2 might consist of two hierarchical steps, or subtiers (e.g., a teacher first collaborates with a single colleague, then works on problem solving with a multidisciplinary team, creating in effect a four-tiered model). Another possibility is that more than one type of intervention might be provided within Tier 2 (e.g., both a standard protocol and individualized planning, based on the student's apparent needs).

Potential Benefits of RTI

Proponents of RTI cite the following potential benefits:

- Earlier identification of students with learning disabilities using a problem-solving approach rather than an ability–achievement discrepancy formula, thus minimizing the "wait to fail" approach
- Reduction in the number of students referred for special education
- Reduction in the overidentification of minority students
- Data that have the maximum relevancy to instruction
- Focus on student outcomes with increased accountability
- Promotion of shared responsibility and collaboration

Other Issues

As school districts look for ways to implement RTI, several other issues will need to be addressed.

Extent of parental involvement. Although parental involvement is an important component of many successful interventions, questions will need to be resolved about the extent of that involvement. How will they be included in the planning? Should they be involved in all phases of the RTI process? How much training should the school provide parents in the implementation of interventions?

Identifying specific disabilities. RTI can identify a pool of at-risk students, but there are concerns about whether it can identify a specific learning disability. Research data from large-scale implementation will be needed in this area.

Implementation process. Decisions will need to be made about the structure and components to be used. How may tiers will there be, and what instructional options will be selected? How will students move through the process? What are the time lines for moving between tiers, and what data will be used to make those decisions? How much will it cost? What facilities and materials will be needed? How will student and teacher schedules be affected? How will the needed professional development be determined, provided, and followed up?

Despite the number of issues that need to be resolved when implementing RTI, supporters maintain that this approach holds greater promise than previous methods for identifying and serving students with learning disabilities. RTI moves away from the single ability–achievement discrepancy criterion and focuses on improving student achievement by enhancing the overall instructional process.

Alternatives to RTI

Not all researchers are convinced that RTI is the best method for identifying learning disabilities. Critics argue that RTI focuses almost exclusively on reading disability, neglects the evaluation of psychological processes, cannot discriminate between students with learning disabilities and those whose learning problems are due to other factors, and fails to cover the whole range of age levels from preschool to high school. They also voice concern over whether the RTI process can be implemented with integrity on a large-scale level in both special and general education. Several alternative models have been proposed that address these perceived weaknesses (Johnson, Mellard, & Byrd, 2005). See more about RTI and models for identifying learning disabilities in Chapter 10.

HELPING STUDENTS BECOME STRATEGIC LEARNERS

What actually makes learning difficult for students with learning disabilities has been the subject of research for many years. Examining the challenges of these students yields clues about the way they interact with their environment and possible interventions that may help them be more successful. This section presents suggestions offered by the National Information Center for Children and Youth With Disabilities.

What Is Learning?

Learning is an active process of acquiring and retaining knowledge so it can be applied in future situations. The ability to recall and apply new learning involves a complex interaction between the learner and the material being learned. Learning is likely to occur when a student has opportunities to practice the new information, receive feedback from the teacher, and apply the knowledge or skill in familiar and unfamiliar situations with less and less assistance from others.

Students bring to each new learning task a varied background of their own ideas, beliefs, opinions, attitudes, motivation, skills, and prior knowledge. They also bring the strategies and techniques they have learned in order to make learning more efficient. All these aspects contribute directly to students' ability to learn, and to remember and use what has been learned.

Teachers can facilitate a lifetime of successful learning by equipping students with a repertoire of strategies and tools for learning. These might include ways to organize oneself and new material; techniques to use while reading, writing, and studying mathematics or other subjects; and systematic steps to follow when working through a learning task or reflecting upon one's own learning.

Learning Difficulties of Students With Learning Disabilities

Sturomski (1997) stresses that students who have learning disabilities may have problems because they:

- Are often overwhelmed, disorganized, and frustrated in new learning situations
- Have difficulty following directions

- Have trouble with the visual or auditory perception of information
- Have problems performing school tasks, such as writing compositions, taking notes, doing written homework, or taking paper-and-pencil tests
- Have a history of academic problem and may believe that they cannot learn, that school tasks are just too difficult and not worth the effort, or that, if they do succeed at a task, it must have been due to luck
- Do not readily believe that there is a connection between what they do, the effort they make, and the likelihood of academic success. These negative beliefs about their ability to learn and the nature of learning itself that can lower self-esteem and have far-reaching academic consequences

Coping With the Difficulties

Acquiring the necessary knowledge, skills, and strategies for functioning independently in our society is as important to students with learning disabilities as it is to their peers without disabilities. Perhaps one of the most fundamental skills for everyone to learn is *how to learn*. Students can become effective, lifelong learners when they master certain techniques and strategies to assist learning and when they know which techniques are useful in different kinds of learning situations.

We all use various methods and strategies to help us remember new information or skills. Yet some of us are more conscious of our own learning processes than others. For instance, many students know little about the learning process, their own strengths and weaknesses in a learning situation, and what strategies and techniques they naturally tend to use when learning something new.

> **Students with learning disabilities need to know what strategies are useful in a learning situation and be able to use them effectively.**

Hence students with learning disabilities need to become strategic learners and not haphazardly use whatever strategies or techniques they have developed on their own. To be able to decide which strategies to use, for example, students need to observe how others think or act when using various strategies. Learning skills develop when students receive opportunities to discuss, reflect upon, and practice personal strategies with classroom materials and appropriate skills. Through feedback, teachers help students refine new strategies and monitor their choices. Over time, teachers can diminish active guidance as students assume more responsibility for their own strategic learning.

What Are Learning Strategies?

Learning strategies are efficient, effective, and organized steps or procedures used when learning, remembering, or performing. These tools and techniques help us to understand and to retain new material or skills, to integrate this new information with what we already know in a way that makes sense, and to recall the information or skill later. When we are trying to learn new information or perform a task, our strategies include both cognitive and behavioral aspects.

Strategies can be simple or complex. Simple learning strategies are cognitive activities usually associated with less challenging learning tasks. Some examples of simple strategies and the rationale for using them are the following:

- Taking notes: Adding the kinesthetic act of writing increases attention and the likelihood that the student will retain the new information.
- Making a chart or outline: Many students with learning difficulties need visual schemes to help them organize their thoughts.
- Asking the teacher questions: This clarifies any misconceptions that the students may have and forces the students to rehearse the information in their heads in order to compose the question.
- Asking ourselves questions: Helps students detect any gaps they have in their learning and decide what other information they need to fill those gaps.
- Using resource books or the Internet: Expands the number of resources where students can get information not found in the text.
- Rereading what we don't understand: This strategy gives students another opportunity to comprehend what they are reading.
- Asking someone to check our work: Peer feedback is a valuable and nonthreatening tool to verify the accuracy and completeness of the assignment.
- Developing a mnemonic device: Memory tricks like mnemonic devices are very helpful for remembering isolated facts. See **Strategies to Consider** at the end of this chapter.

Complex strategies help us accomplish tasks involving multiple steps or higher-order thinking, such as analysis or answering "What if. . .?" questions. Here are some examples of complex strategies and their rationale:

- Planning, writing, and revising an essay: These steps allow the students to organize their thoughts, decide on the central theme, and select the correct vocabulary to express their ideas.
- Identifying sources of information: Students need to recognize the importance of finding credible sources to support their arguments and of citing them to avoid plagiarism.
- Stating main ideas and supporting our position: The main theme should be clear to the reader, and the facts should support the writer's views.
- Distinguishing fact from opinion: Understanding the difference between facts and opinion is a critical skill in this day of high-pressure advertising, publicity, and news commentary.
- Searching for and correcting errors in our work: Students are less likely to repeat errors that they discover on their own.
- Keeping track of our progress: Timetables help students track the progress of their work, keep them on task, and increase the chances that their work will be submitted on time.
- Being aware of our thought processes: Reflecting on our thought processes (metacognition) helps us determine which approaches work best for solving specific problems.
- Evaluating the validity of sources: With so much information available on the Internet, students need to be able to judge the validity of what they find and the credibility of the sources.

Some of the suggestions in the research literature for strategy interventions designed to make learners more aware of what they are doing are found at the end of this chapter in **Strategies to Consider.**

Types of Learning Strategies

Learning strategies can be categorized as either cognitive or metacognitive.

Cognitive Strategies. These help a person process and manipulate information to perform tasks such as taking notes, asking questions, or filling out a chart. They tend to be task specific; that is, certain cognitive strategies are useful when learning or performing certain tasks.

Metacognitive Strategies. These are more executive in nature and are used when planning, monitoring, and evaluating learning or strategy performance. They are often referred to as self-regulatory strategies, helping students become aware of learning as a process and of what actions will facilitate that process. For example, taking the time to plan before writing assists students in writing a good composition. The ability to evaluate one's work, the effectiveness of learning, or even the use of a strategy is also metacognitive, demonstrating that a learner is aware of and thinking about how learning occurs. Students who use metacognitive strategies frequently tend to become self-regulated learners. They set goals for learning, coach themselves in positive ways, and use self-instruction to guide themselves through learning problems. Further, they monitor their comprehension or progress and reward themselves for success. Just as students can be taught cognitive, task-specific strategies, so can they be taught self-regulatory, metacognitive ones. In fact, the most effective interventions combine the use of cognitive and metacognitive strategies.

Research About the Effectiveness of Learning Strategies

Research into strategies of learning has been going on for more than 30 years, long before the availability of brain-scanning technologies. Since the 1970s, researchers at the University of Kansas have investigated the benefits of strategy instruction, especially for individuals with learning disabilities. Their work produced one of the most well-researched and well-articulated models for teaching students to use learning strategies. Known as the Strategies Integration Model, or SIM, this method

> *Learning and retention are more likely to occur when students can observe, engage in, discuss, reflect upon, and practice the new learning.*

outlines a series of steps so that educators can effectively teach any number of strategies or strategic approaches. See the model at the end of this chapter in **Strategies to Consider.**

Recent cognitive research supports the notion that learning and retention are more likely to occur when students can observe, engage in, discuss, reflect upon, and practice the new learning. When teachers help students to use learning strategies and to generalize their strategic knowledge to other academic and nonacademic situations, they are promoting student independence in the process of learning.

For students who have learning disabilities, learning-strategy instruction holds great educational promise for the following reasons:

- Instruction helps students learn how to learn and become more effective in the successful performance of academic, social, or job-related tasks. Students can better deal with immediate academic demands as well as cope with similar tasks in different settings under different conditions throughout life. The strategies are particularly powerful in the face of new learning situations.

- Instruction makes students aware of how strategies work, why they work, when they work, and where they can be used. To assist students, teachers will need to
  - talk about strategies explicitly,
  - name and describe each strategy,
  - model how each strategy is used by thinking aloud while performing tasks relevant to students,
  - provide students with multiple opportunities to use the strategies with a variety of materials, and
  - provide feedback and guidance while students refine and internalize the use of each strategy.

Ultimately, responsibility for strategy use needs to shift from teachers to students. This promotes independent learners with the cognitive flexibility necessary to address the many learning challenges they will encounter in their lives. Although no single technique or intervention can address all the varied needs of students with learning disabilities, teaching the strategies of learning will help these students become better equipped to face current and future learning tasks. By learning how to learn, they can become independent, lifelong learners—one of the primary goals of education.

> *Learning strategies help students become better equipped to face current and future learning tasks.*

How Important Is Self-Esteem?

Students with learning disabilities often have negative feelings about learning and about themselves. Because of past experiences, these students believe they cannot learn or that the work is simply too difficult. As a result, they may believe they cannot achieve success in learning through their own efforts (Gans, Kenny, & Ghany, 2003).Teachers should address this issue when presenting information on the strategies of learning. By modeling positive self-statements, teachers can convince students to attribute success in learning to their own efforts and to the use of appropriate learning strategies. For learning strategies to be successful, students need to have a positive self-image and recognize the connection between effort and success.

According to an analysis of 31 separate studies, school-based interventions designed to boost the self-esteem of students with learning disabilities were very effective. Researchers found that interventions using both skill development and self-enhancement succeeded in raising self-esteem. Interventions using group counseling techniques were effective with students at all grade levels. Academic interventions were particularly helpful for middle-school students. A major component of many of the successful academic interventions was an emphasis on students working together with their classmates and receiving feedback from classmates on their progress (Elbaum & Vaughn, 2001). See this chapter's **Strategies to Consider** for suggestions on how to build student self-esteem.

Cautions About Self-Esteem

Although research studies continue to show that raising self-esteem in students with learning disabilities can be effective, some cautions are in order. Many people assume that high self-esteem generally leads to positive outcomes and that low self-esteem often results in undesirable behaviors. But this is not always the case. In fact, the research on how self-esteem correlates with positive outcomes is mixed. Contrary to popular belief, bullies do not typically suffer from low self-esteem, nor do those prone to drug and alcohol abuse. Raising self-esteem does not automatically translate into improved academic achievement. In fact, attempts to boost self-esteem in struggling students may backfire if the focus is primarily on making them feel good about themselves. However, motivation and achievement do improve when self-esteem interventions center on instilling a sense of personal responsibility for academic performance (Baumeister, Campbell, Krueger, & Vohs, 2005). See Chapter 10 for suggestions on how to motivate students with learning disabilities.

STRATEGIES TO CONSIDER

Guidelines for Working With Students Who Have Special Needs

Teachers should consider these guidelines to help students with special needs succeed. The following general strategies are appropriate for all grade levels and subject areas.

- **Capitalize on the student's strengths.** This is more likely to give the student a feeling of success and lessen any feelings of inadequacy that flow from the disability.

- **Provide high structure and clear expectations.** These students do better in an organized environment and need to know what is expected of them. Take nothing for granted, and make sure the student is aware of acceptable and unacceptable types of behavior.

- **Use short sentences and simple vocabulary.** These students often have difficulty processing complex sentence structures and usually have a limited vocabulary. Behavior problems can arise when the student is unclear about what the teacher said.

- **Allow flexibility in classroom procedures.** For example, permit students with written language difficulties to use tape recorders for note taking and test taking.

- **Make use of self-correcting materials that provide immediate feedback without embarrassment.** Because many of these students have a short attention span, activities that give immediate feedback are desirable. Students can assess their own progress quickly and without knowing each other's results.

- **Use computers for drill and practice and for teaching word processing.** Computers are patient devices, and many programs provide varied opportunities to practice and usually give a running score of the student's progress. Word processing programs can often convince students to try creative writing despite any problems with written language.

- **Provide positive reinforcement of appropriate social skills.** Appropriate social behavior at school is likely to be repeated if it is positively reinforced. Look for opportunities to "catch the student being good."

- **Recognize that students with learning disabilities can greatly benefit from the gift of time to grow and mature.** These students often progress slowly, but many progress nonetheless. Patience with them can be rewarding for both teachers and students.

STRATEGIES TO CONSIDER

Strategies for Involvement and Retention

Students with attention difficulties need help to maximize their engagement and to improve their retention of learning. The following strategies are appropriate for all students, especially those who have learning problems (Fulk, 2000).

- **Get their attention.** Use humor, unexpected introductions, and various other attention grabbers to stimulate student interest in the lesson.

- **Make it relevant.** Relevancy (or meaning) is one of the major factors affecting retention. Students are not likely to retain what they perceive as irrelevant. Keep in mind that it is *their* perception of relevancy that matters, not *yours*.

- **Model, model, model.** Show students how to do it. Use models, simulations, and examples for simple as well as complex concepts. Ask them to develop original models.

- **Use teams.** The research indicates that these students are particularly successful when working in teams. The opportunity to discuss what they are learning keeps them actively engaged and helps them to practice interpersonal skills.

- **Set goals.** Success is a key factor in maintaining involvement. Set realistic goals with the students (e.g., "Let's try to solve three problems this time").

- **Find out what they already know.** Take the time to assess what students already know about the topic being taught. Building on this prior knowledge is an effective way of helping students establish relevancy.

- **Use visuals.** We live in a visually oriented culture, and students are acclimated to visual stimuli. Graphs, pictures, diagrams, and visual organizers are very effective learning and retention devices.

- **Go for the big picture.** The brain is a pattern seeker. Use graphics to put together the big picture, showing how concepts are connected. Discuss the patterns that emerge, and link them to what students have already learned.

- **Think and talk aloud.** When teachers think aloud, they model the steps in cognitive processing and reveal what information or skills can be used to approach and solve a problem. Talking aloud is an excellent memory enhancer, especially when students discuss open-ended questions, such as "What might have happened if. . .?" or "What would you have done instead?"

- **Suggest mnemonic devices.** All memory tricks are valuable. Teach mnemonic devices to help students remember factual information or steps in a procedure. Examples are acronyms (e.g., ROY G BIV for colors of the spectrum, HOMES for the Great Lakes), keywords or phrases (e.g., "Please excuse my dear Aunt Sally" for the order of solving arithmetic operations: parenthesis, exponents, multiplication, division, addition, and subtraction) and rhymes (e.g., "Divorced, beheaded, died; divorced, beheaded, survived" for the fate of King Henry VIII's six wives, in chronological order).

- **Use a variety of practice formats.** Practice is the key to retention but can be perceived as boring when the teacher uses only one practice format. Try small dry-erase boards, computer programs, or simulations to keep practice interesting and varied. And, if students can correctly solve five problems, do we need to give them 20?

- **Explain the value of note taking.** Writing is not only a good memory tool but also helps students organize their thoughts and focus on what is important. Gradually decrease the amount of information you give in an outline so that students need to provide more input.

- **Use closure strategies regularly.** Closure strategies, such as journal writing and group processing ("Tell your partner two things you learned today"), enhance retention of learning.

STRATEGIES TO CONSIDER

Teaching Students to Use Learning Strategies

Much has been learned through research regarding effective learning-strategy instruction. A well-articulated instructional approach, known as the Strategies Integration Model (SIM), that emerged from research conducted over a decade ago at the University of Kansas continues to be an effective intervention (Ellis, Deshler, Lenz, Schumaker, & Clark, 1991). Based on cognitive behavior modification, the SIM is one of the field's most comprehensive tools for providing strategy instruction. It can be used to teach virtually any strategic intervention.

Strategies Integration Model

Select the strategy, then ☞ ☞ ☞ ☞ ☞

STEP 1
Determine prior knowledge and generate interest in learning the strategy

STEP 2
Describe the strategy

STEP 3
Model the strategy

STEP 4
Practice the strategy

STEP 5
Provide feedback

STEP 6
Promote application to other tasks

Selecting the Strategy. First, the teacher selects a strategy that is clearly linked to the tasks students need to perform at the place they need to perform them. When the strategy is matched to student needs, they perceive relevancy and tend to be motivated to learn and use the strategy. After selecting the strategy or approach to teach, the six steps of the SIM guide the actual instruction.

Step 1—Determine prior knowledge and generate interest in learning the strategy. It is important to give a pretest to determine how much students already know about using the strategy. This information provides a starting point for instruction. Younger students, for example, may have no understanding of how they learn; older students may have already encountered their learning weaknesses. Motivate students by letting them know that gains in learning can occur when the strategy is used effectively. Studies show it is important to tell students directly that learning this strategy using effort and persistence will help them achieve whatever skill is being addressed.

Use a pretest that centers on the materials and tasks that students actually encounter in class. Following the pretest, the class should discuss the results by asking questions such as:

- How did we do?
- Were we able to perform the task successfully?
- What types of errors did we make? Why?
- What did we do, or think about, to help ourselves while taking the pretest?
- What difficulties did we have? How did we address those difficulties?

If students did not perform particularly well, then discuss a strategy or technique that will help them perform that task more successfully in the future.

According to the SIM model, it is important to obtain a commitment from students to learning the strategy. To accomplish this, teachers can discuss the value of the strategy and the fact that they are committed to helping the students. Teachers should point out the likelihood that success may not be immediate, but that success will come if the student perseveres and practices the strategy.

Student-teacher collaboration in use of the strategy is especially important with elementary school students. Teachers need to discuss and practice strategies with these young students frequently. The commitments can be verbal or in writing, but the idea here is to get the students involved and to make them aware that their participation in learning and in using the strategy is vital to their eventual success.

Step 2—Describe the strategy. In this step, teachers clearly define the strategy, give examples, discuss the benefits of learning the strategy, and ask students to determine various ways the strategy can be used. The teacher should also identify real-life assignments in specific classes in which students can apply the strategy, and ask students if they can think of other work for which the strategy might be useful. Students should also be told the various stages involved in learning the strategy, so they know what to expect.

After this overview, the students are ready to delve more deeply into hearing about and using the strategy. Instruction becomes more specific so that each step of the strategy is described in detail and presented in such a way that students can easily remember it. Acronyms can help students remember the various steps involved. An example is the COPS strategy, which helps students detect common writing errors (Shannon & Polloway, 1993). Displaying a poster or chart about the strategy and its steps will also help memory and retention. During this phase, the class discusses how this new approach to a specific task differs from what students are currently using. For closure, conclude with a review of what has been learned.

Step 3—Model the strategy. Modeling the strategy is an essential component of strategy instruction. In this step, teachers overtly use the strategy to help students perform a relevant classroom or authentic task, talking aloud as they work so that students can observe how a person thinks and what a person does while using the strategy. For example, you could model:

- Deciding which strategy to use to perform the task at hand
- Working through the task using that strategy
- Monitoring performance (i.e., is the strategy being applied correctly, and is it helping the learner effectively complete the work?)

- Revising one's strategic approach
- Making positive self-statements

The self-talk that the teacher provides as a model can become a powerful guide for students as responsibility for using the strategy transfers to them.

Acronyms Help Students Remember the Steps in Using a Strategy

COPS is the acronym for a strategic approach that helps students detect and correct common writing errors. Each letter stands for an aspect of writing that students need to check for accuracy.

C   Capitalization of appropriate letters
O   Overall appearance of paper
P   Punctuation used correctly
S   Spelling accuracy

Step 4—Practice the strategy. Practice leads to retention of learning. The more students and teachers collaborate to use the strategy, the more likely the strategy will become part of the students' strategic repertoire. Initial guided practice is designed to check for understanding and first applications.

Students should be encouraged to think aloud as they work through their practice tasks, explaining the problems they are having, the decisions they are making, or the physical actions they are taking. These student "think-alouds" should increasingly reveal the specific strategy being used to help them complete the task successfully. Initially, the think-alouds should be part of teacher-directed instruction. Later, the students benefit greatly from practicing in small groups, where they listen and help each other understand the task, why the strategy might be useful in completing the task, and how to apply the strategy to the task. Eventually, the practice sessions become self-mediated as students work independently to complete tasks while using the strategy.

As practice continues, the level of difficulty of the materials being used should gradually increase. In the beginning, students practice using the strategy with materials that are at or slightly below their comfort level, so they do not become frustrated by overly difficult content. The materials must be well matched to the strategy so that students can readily understand the strategy's value. As students become more proficient in using the strategy, teachers introduce materials that are more difficult.

Step 5—Provide feedback. The feedback that teachers give students on their use of the strategy is a critical component of the SIM model. It helps students learn how to use a strategy effectively and how to change what they are doing when a particular approach is unsuccessful. It is also important for students to reflect on their approach to and completion of the task and to self-correct when necessary. What aspects of the task did they complete well? What aspects were hard? Did any problems arise, and what did they do to solve the problems? What might they do differently the next time they have to complete a similar task?

Step 6—Promote application to other tasks (generalization). The value of using learning strategies increases greatly when students are able to apply the strategy in new situations. It may not become obvious to many students that the strategy they have been learning and practicing may be ideal for helping them to complete a learning task in a different classroom or learning situation. This is particularly true of students with learning disabilities. Thus merely exposing the students to strategy training is not sufficient for both strategy learning and strategy utilization to occur. Guided and consistent practice in generalizing how the strategies can transfer to various settings and tasks is vital for students with learning disabilities, as are repeated reminders that strategies of learning can be used in new situations.

Therefore teachers need to discuss with students what transfer is all about (Sousa, 2006) and how and when students might use the strategy in other settings. An important part of this discussion will be getting students to review the actual work that they have in other classes and discussing with students how the strategy might be useful in completing that work. Actually going through the steps of the strategy with specific work assignments can be very effective.

Students can generate their own examples of contexts in which to apply the strategy. For example, they could use the COPS strategy discussed in Step 2 for homework assignments, job applications, friendly letters, English papers, written problems in mathematics, and spelling practice. Additionally, teachers within a school may wish to coordinate among themselves to promote student use of strategies across settings, so that the strategies being taught in one classroom are mentioned and supported by other teachers as well. All of these approaches will promote student generalization of the strategy.

STRATEGIES TO CONSIDER

Techniques for Building Self-Esteem

The main purpose for building self-esteem in students with learning difficulties is to help them accept responsibility for their academic performance and to realize that their achievement is mainly the result of the effort they invest in a learning task. Praise must be genuine; insincere praise can do more harm than good. The following strategies can be used to help students build their self-esteem:

- Use students' names when addressing them.

- Have conversations with *every* student.

- Have student work occasionally assessed by other audiences (students, other teachers, parents).

- Avoid making assumptions about student behavior, and separate the behavior from the person.

- Point out positive aspects of your students' work.

- Shake hands with students, especially when you greet them.

- Allow students to explore different learning options (Internet, resource works, interviews, videotapes, DVDs, etc.).

- Display student work (with the student's permission).

- Give each student a responsibility in the classroom.

- Avoid criticizing a student's question.

- Provide multiple opportunities for students to be successful in your classroom, especially when giving tests. Could the students give oral presentations to tell you what they have learned?

- Help students turn failure into a positive learning experience.

- Celebrate your students' achievements, no matter how small.

- Allow students to make decisions about some aspects of class work (what kind of report to do, what color something can be, etc.).

- Try to get to know about the student's life outside of school (without prying).

- Provide opportunities for students to work in productive groups.

- Spend extra time with struggling students.

- Ask students about their other activities (e.g., sports, music, and drama groups).

- Encourage students to take *appropriate* risks.

- Allow students to suffer the consequences of their behavior, and avoid being overprotective.

STRATEGIES TO CONSIDER

Working With Students in Groups

Chapter 1 discusses the value of rehearsal. Group activities are effective means for students to rehearse by talking to each other about their learning. However, teachers are often concerned that special needs students may remain passive, drift off-task, or disrupt the group process.

Research studies report that group activities, especially if they include cooperative learning strategies, are particularly effective in getting struggling students to participate in the regular classroom setting. Group work is often a more effective alternative to the more traditional assignment of having a student read the text and answer questions at the end of the chapter—a practice that special needs students find frustrating. For example, speaking in front of a small group is less intimidating than speaking in front of the entire class. These students also find that their own experiences can be triggered when others in the group remember an event (Gillies, 2002).

The following suggest some of the many ways to implement this strategy. Remember to make appropriate adjustments for the age of the students.

- **Assign Students to Heterogeneous Groups**
  - o Divide the class into three sections—high, middle, and low—based on their mastery of the subject matter. Assign one student from each section to a group.
  - o If necessary, switch students so that each group is made up of students who can benefit from each other, but not so different that they are intimidated by other members of the group.
  - o Give the group assignment and stress the importance of working together. Students can read to each other, answer questions, discuss what they already know, or show a partner how to do something. The object is for all members of the group to accomplish the learning objective successfully.

- **Use the Retelling Strategy in Each Group**
  - o Ask the students to read a portion of their text, either silently or whispering to their partners. When finished, allow some think time and ask them to tell their partners what they learned and what they remembered about the text.
  - o If necessary, model this retelling strategy by telling aloud something you have read. Include analogies, personal anecdotes, and other imagery to embellish your retelling. Demonstrate how imagery and metaphors help in memory. This establishes a clear model for students to follow.
  - o Keep moving among the groups while they are retelling, asking questions to assess their progress and to assist where needed.
  - o After the students complete their retelling sessions, call on them to relate what they have read and learned. Look for opportunities to ask "What if. . .?" questions.
  - o Write the student responses on the board or overhead transparency so that all can see. Point out any differences in the responses and ask students to discuss them.

- **Some Options to Consider**
  - o Encourage students to gather information from other sources in addition to the text, such as the Internet, pictures, and charts.
  - o Within groups, give struggling students material to use that is written at an easier level.
  - o Follow-up activities can include going on a field trip, watching a video, observing an experiment, or listening to a guest speaker.

Using strategies in addition to reading is especially helpful to struggling learners whose difficulties with reading may become overly frustrating and turn them away from the learning experience.

Chapter 3

Attention Disorders

As brain research reveals more of how the brain learns, educators gain renewed hope in understanding problems that can arise during this complex process. Most learning requires the brain's attention (also called *focus*). Because emotions often drive attention, this activity occurs first in the brain's limbic area (Chapter 1) and requires the coordinated effort of three neural networks: *alerting*, *orienting*, and *executive control* (Gazzaniga, Ivry, & Mangun, 2002). Alerting occurs first in the brainstem (Figure 3.1) and helps the brain to suppress background stimuli and inhibit ongoing activity. In the central cortex and limbic areas, orienting mobilizes neural resources to turn toward and process the expected input while

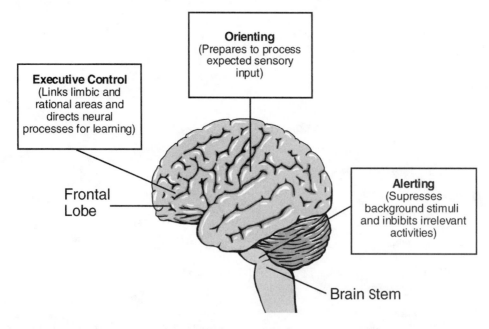

Figure 3.1 Attention for learning requires the coordinated efforts of three neural networks: alerting, orienting, and executive control.

inhibiting the transmission of all other input. Executive control links the limbic centers with the rational areas of the cerebrum, directing the various neural processes needed to decide how to respond to the specific input. Problems can arise anywhere within these three systems, and the resulting loss of attention may be accompanied by hyperactivity and impulsivity.

Let's use a simple example. Say you are taking an evening stroll, chatting with a friend, and suddenly you hear the rustling of bushes behind you. The alerting system detects the sounds, interrupts your speech, and inhibits the processing of your friend's conversation. Meanwhile, the orienting system determines the direction of the noise, turns your head to locate the source, and rapidly processes the sound information. Deciding what to do next is the job of executive control. If a frightened squirrel raises its head and runs away, your frontal lobe tells you to continue your walk and talk. However, if an angry dog shows itself, the executive, limbic, and other brain areas work together so you can make a quick retreat.

RESEARCH FINDINGS

What Is Attention-Deficit Hyperactivity Disorder (ADHD)?

Attention-deficit hyperactivity disorder (ADHD) is a syndrome that interferes with an individual's ability to focus (inattention), regulate activity level (hyperactivity), and inhibit behavior (impulsivity). It is one of the most common learning disorders in children and adolescents. It affects an estimated five percent of youths ages 9 to 17. About three times more boys than girls are diagnosed. ADHD usually becomes evident in preschool or early elementary years, frequently persisting into adolescence and adulthood. Most adults outgrow the hyperactivity part of ADHD.

Although most children have some symptoms of hyperactivity, impulsivity, and inattention, there are those in whom these behaviors persist and become the rule rather than the exception. These individuals need to be assessed by health care professionals with input from parents and teachers. The diagnosis results from a thorough review of a physical examination, a variety of psychological tests, and the observable behaviors in the child's everyday settings. These behaviors are compared to a list of symptoms contained in the fourth edition of the *Diagnostic and Statistical Manual of Mental Disorders* (DSM-IV-TR, 2000). A diagnosis of ADHD requires that six or more of the symptoms for inattention or for hyperactivity-impulsivity be present for at least six months, appear before the child is

---

Some Indicators of ADHD

(Not all indicators may be present in the same individual. Indicators should appear before the age of 7 and persist for at least 6 months in at least two of the child's environments.)

Inattention: Fails to attend to details; difficulty sustaining attention; does not seem to listen; fails to finish; has difficulty organizing tasks; avoids sustained effort; loses things; is distracted by extraneous stimuli; is forgetful.

Hyperactivity: Talks incessantly; leaves seat in classroom; may dash around or climb; difficulty playing quietly; fidgets with hands or feet; motor excess.

Impulsivity: Blurts out answers; difficulty waiting for turn; interrupts or intrudes.

seven years old, and be evident across at least two of the child's environments (e.g., at home, in school, on the playground). ADHD has been classified into three subtypes: predominantly inattentive, predominantly hyperactive-impulsive, and the combined type (APA, 2000).

Because the procedures for diagnosing ADHD involve subjective judgments, disagreements may arise over whether a child truly has the disorder. Consequently, researchers continue to look for objective measures of attention problems and hyperactivity. One such measure was developed by Martin Teicher at Harvard University. Called the Optical Tracking and Attention Test, it involves using an infrared motion sensor camera to measure a child's ability to sit still and pay attention during a 15-minute continuous performance task (Teicher, Ito, Glod, & Barber, 1996). The test has been successful in detecting inattention and hyperactivity, and has shown a high correlation with fMRI studies of children diagnosed with ADHD (Teicher, Anderson, Polcari, Glod, Maas, & Renshaw, 2000).

What Is the Difference Between ADD and ADHD?

Some children have no trouble sitting still or inhibiting their behavior, but they are inattentive and have great difficulty focusing. They tend to be withdrawn, polite, and shy. Because they lack the hyperactivity-impulsive symptoms, these children are often referred to as having Attention Deficit Disorder (ADD) without hyperactivity (i.e., predominantly inattentive). Children with several symptoms of both the inattentive and hyperactive type are diagnosed as "combined type."

ADHD and ADD are categorized as different but related disorders because there are some symptomatic differences. Table 3.1 shows some of the differences in the causes as well as the behaviors observed in students diagnosed with ADHD compared with those diagnosed with ADD. The descriptions may seem simplistic, but they do help to discriminate between two conditions that are very closely related. Although ADHD and ADD without hyperactivity are considered separate disorders, many of the strategies suggested in this chapter can apply to both groups of students.

ADHD and Intelligence

One persistent idea often found in lay publications is that children with ADHD might have unusually high IQs. But several studies focusing on this notion have shown that children with ADHD are no more likely to have an above average IQ than other children (Frazier, Demaree, & Youngstrom, 2004; Kaplan, Crawford, Dewey, & Fisher, 2000). In other words, intelligence in ADHD children can run the gamut from below average to gifted.

What Causes ADHD?

The exact causes of ADHD remain unknown. But accumulating scientific evidence indicates that this is a neurologically based medical problem, and researchers are coming closer to understanding the causes. The biological basis of the disorder appears to lie in differences in brain structure and function as well as the presence of certain genetic abnormalities.

Table 3.1 Some Differences Between ADHD and ADD		
	ADHD	**ADD Without Hyperactivity**
Cause	The size of several brain areas differ, especially in the frontal and temporal lobes Structures in limbic area and cerebellum are smaller, likely affecting neurotransmitter flow and coordinated movement	Cause may reside primarily in parietal lobe The frontal lobe processes seem intact
Primary Indicators	Persistent problems with attention, impulsivity, and hyperactivity	Low brain energy leads to difficulty with attention; seems not to listen, unorganized, forgetful in the short-term, makes careless mistakes, has problems following instructions
Decision Making	Impulsive Race from task to task	Sluggish
Attention Seeking	Shows off Egotistical Relishes in being the worst Intolerant and can become abusive Manipulative Needs instant gratification Constantly frustrated	Modest Shy Often socially withdrawn Conversation is difficult Does not need instant gratification Becomes impatient only after repeated attempts to complete task
Sense of Time	Time is poorly planned Often late	Time is poorly planned Often late
Assertiveness	Bossy Often irritating	Underassertive Overly polite and docile
Recognizing Boundaries	Intrusive Occasionally rebellious	Honors boundaries Usually polite and obedient
Popularity	Attracts new friends but has difficulty bonding Reacts strongly to criticism	Bonds but does not easily attract friends Fearful of others' displeasure
Associated Diagnoses	Oppositional Defiance Conduct Disorder (though rare)	Depression
Positive Attributes	These individuals really do well those things they know they can do	Willing to pursue areas others are afraid to try Can do well if self-employed

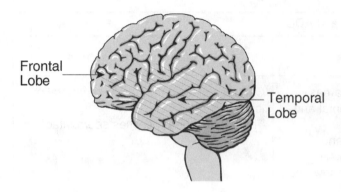

Figure 3.2   The lined area shows the parts of the frontal and temporal lobes on both sides of the brain that are smaller in children with ADHD. These areas control behavior and contain some components of the attention systems.

Comparing high-resolution MRI brain scans of children and adolescents with ADHD with scans of a non-ADHD control group, researchers found that the frontal and temporal lobes on both sides of the ADHD brains were significantly reduced in size (Figure 3.2). These cerebral areas help moderate behavior and contain some components of the attention systems (Sowell, et al., 2003). Lack of development in the frontal lobes can reduce its ability to control the excesses of emotional responses. Scans also revealed that children and adolescents with ADHD had significantly smaller total brain volumes than subjects without ADHD (Castellanos et al., 2002).

Several imaging studies have shown that ADHD brains function differently when performing the same tasks as non-ADHD brains. Although the participants with ADHD performed only slightly worse than the non-ADHD controls, they appeared to activate an entirely different network of brain areas than that seen in the non-ADHD participants (Bush et al., 1999). This may be because the impaired function of the executive control system in ADHD reduces the ability to recruit the same brain regions and strategies needed to accomplish cognitive tasks that non-ADHD individuals would use. Researchers speculate that the brain with ADHD compensates for this deficit by relying more on visual-spatial and motor processing than on verbal strategies (Fassbender & Schweitzer, 2006).

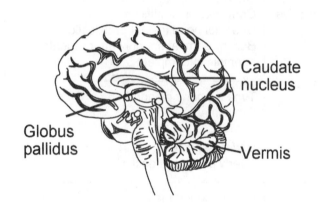

Figure 3.3   Brain scans have shown the globus pallidus, caudate nucleus, and vermis to be smaller in many ADHD adults.

Another contributing factor may be an imbalance in certain neurotransmitters that help the brain regulate focus and behavior. Deficiencies in the neurotransmitters dopamine and norepinephrine would affect arousal and alertness. Low serotonin is linked to impulsivity and erratic behavior. But what could cause the imbalance? Several neuroimaging studies have shown that two structures in the limbic area (the *cordate nucleus* and the *globus pallidus*) and one in the cerebellum (the *vermis*) are smaller in adults diagnosed with ADHD than in adults without the disorder (Figure 3.3). Further, it seems that these structural differences are strongly associated with a genetic defect.

The cordate nucleus and globus pallidus appear to be involved in the dopamine network. Dopamine is a neurotransmitter that, among other things, helps to control attention and coordinate movement. In the individual with ADHD, the smaller size of these two structures may decrease the effectiveness of dopamine, resulting in difficulty sustaining attention (Barkley, 1998; Raz, 2004). The vermis is thought to contribute to smooth motor coordination. Problems with this structure may lead to the hyperactive and impulsive behaviors seen in ADHD individuals. Another study reported that adults diagnosed with ADHD had abnormally low levels of an enzyme (DOPA decarboxylase) that produces dopamine (Swanson, Castellanos, Murias, LaHoste, & Kennedy, 1998).

High-resolution brain scans of individuals with ADHD have been very helpful in revealing more about possible anatomical origins of this complex disorder. Nonetheless, it is not likely that brain scans will be used as a standard diagnostic tool for ADHD in the foreseeable future.

Behavior Problems

The behavior problems associated with ADHD are a result of difficulties with the brain's executive control system (frontal lobe). Recall that the functions of this system include forethought, planning, inhibiting impulsive responses, and suppressing irrelevant stimuli. Deficits in these functions can result in behaviors that are perceived as indifferent, ill-mannered, and defiant. If these difficulties become part of a persistent pattern of behavior, the child receives frequent negative feedback, ultimately leading the child to anger or depression unless effective interventions occur.

Is ADHD Inherited?

Genetic predispositions for ADHD have been suspected for a long time because the disorder tends to run in families. Children with ADHD usually have at least one close relative who also has ADHD, and at least one-third of all fathers who had ADHD as a youth have children with ADHD. If one identical twin has the disorder, the other is likely to have it also. Stronger evidence of a genetic connection comes from more than 20 studies suggesting associations between ADHD and about a dozen suspected genes (Hawi et al., 2005). One suspect cause is the gene responsible for coding the neuron receptors for the key neurotransmitter dopamine (Sunohara et al., 2000). As mentioned earlier, a significant function of dopamine is to help the brain focus with intent to learn.

> **ADHD has probably been in the gene pool for thousands of years.**

The genetic markers for ADHD behavior probably have been present in the human gene pool for thousands of years, indicating that individuals with ADHD had important roles to play in the survival of early societies. In prehistoric times, for example, individuals with ADHD behavior could have been valuable as scouts to protect a hunting party from sneak attack by predators. Success in this role required people who could rapidly scan a wide area looking for danger. Impulsiveness and quick thinking were decided advantages in a hunting society. A scout who was too deeply focused on just one interesting tree or fixated on an attractive vista would likely miss the approaching predator and get eaten. ADHD traits became a mixed blessing, however, when societies relied less on hunting and more on agriculture.

Although there are genetic predispositions for ADHD, this does not imply that parenting and schooling are unimportant. On the contrary, these are likely to be susceptible—rather than dominant—genes, so the child's environment plays a major role in determining how intensely the genetic traits emerge. How the parents and school cope with a "problem" child will shape that child's development and interaction with the world (DeGrandpre & Hinshaw, 2000).

Is ADHD on the Increase?

The debate continues. Although the number of children identified with the disorder has risen, it is unclear if the rise is due to greater prevalence of the disorder, to better diagnosis and identification, or both. Certainly, heightened media interest has led to increased awareness of ADHD and the availability of effective treatments. Some scientists suggest that the changing family patterns and child-rearing problems of today may have more to do with the rise in children labeled ADHD than any biological factors. As more children are raised by total strangers, video games, and television, ADHD-like behavior may become the norm rather than the exception. One thing seems certain: Parents and teachers do not cause ADHD. However, how they react to a child with ADHD symptoms may lessen or worsen the effects of the disorder.

> *As more children are raised by total strangers, video games, and television, ADHD-like behavior may become the norm rather than the exception.*

Is It Possible to Have ADHD-Like Behavior and Not Have ADHD?

Yes. Some children diagnosed with ADHD early in life simply have the symptoms that mimic the disorder but do not have the disorder. Other factors can produce ADHD-like symptoms. Pediatric researchers are concerned about the amount of television that young children watch and the effect this viewing has on brain development. One major study showed that the more television young children watch, the more likely they are to have trouble concentrating and become restless and impulsive. The researchers noted that although ADHD has a strong genetic component, the environment also plays a key role. Hence extensive television watching may aggravate the symptoms in children who have inherited ADHD predispositions and produce ADHD-like symptoms in non-ADHD individuals (Christakis, Ebel, Rivara, & Zimmerman, 2004).

Some children have not learned the acceptable and unacceptable rules of behavior in certain environments, such as school. Their behavior, therefore, looks like ADHD, but these children may benefit more from being taught the appropriate behavior than from medication. Other children sometimes develop allergic reactions to certain foods that result in, among other things, hyperactive behavior. Again, these children will benefit from diet modification to control behavior. Additional factors could be stress reactions, other medical conditions, or intolerant schools.

Can Schools Inadvertently Enhance ADHD-Like Behavior?

As discussed in Chapter 1, most children are growing up in an environment that is very different from just a few years ago. But many schools haven't changed their instructional approaches to accommodate the resulting new brain. The possibility exists, therefore, that school and classroom operations can inadvertently create or enhance ADHD-like behavior in students when:

- Teachers under pressure to cover curriculum move too fast (even with the realization that some students need more time)

- The main mode of instruction is teacher talk (when we know that more students have visual and kinesthetic learning preferences)
- Room arrangements allow students to hide from the teacher and create mischief (the classic row-by-row formation is more conducive to isolation than collaboration)
- Discipline is arbitrary and perceived as unfair (students in secondary schools encounter six to eight teachers daily, each with a different set of rules and expectations)
- There are few or no opportunities to get up and move around (too much material to cover, so students have to sit and listen)
- The classroom is too hot or too dark (studies show students achieve more in rooms that are well-lit with plenty of natural light)
- There are few opportunities for students to interact with each other (interactive learning reduces boredom and increases retention)
- The classroom emotional climate is neutral or tense (positive emotional climate enhances learning)

Modifying the preceding situations can often change ADHD-like behavior into more positive student participation and academic success. Please do not misinterpret my comments here. I firmly believe that children who have been correctly diagnosed with ADHD should get the appropriate treatments and therapies they need, including medication. All I am suggesting is that parents, teachers, and clinicians first examine whether other possible causes of ADHD-like behavior are at work before we resort to a clinical diagnosis of a lifelong neurological disorder. See the survey at the end of this chapter in **Strategies to Consider** on how to avoid promoting ADHD-like behavior.

The Future of ADHD Research and Treatment

Research

Additional studies will need to be conducted to differentiate individuals with true ADHD from those whose symptoms mimic the disorder. Although brain-imaging studies have documented both structural and functional abnormalities in the frontal lobe and other cerebral areas, imaging methods are not yet ready to be used as diagnostic methods. The same is true of testing for the genetic variants associated with ADHD. We can expect genetic studies to yield more information on how molecular changes in the brain lead to ADHD symptoms. Both brain imaging and genetic exploration provide insights into the causes and pathology of ADHD, but more work is needed before they can be considered diagnostically useful. In the meantime, parents and clinicians will need to rely on observational evidence. Emerging knowledge about the cause and manifestations of ADHD should lead to an improved understanding of the brain mechanisms underlying the disorder, which should improve diagnostic and treatment strategies.

Treatment

Medications. Despite decades of use, concerns still linger about the long-term effects of stimulant drugs, such as methylphenidate (brand names: Concerta, Ritalin) and combinations of dextroamphetamine and amphetamine (brand name: Adderall). Can long-term use cause tics, delay growth, and kindle drug abuse?

Longitudinal studies of long-term use of stimulant drugs used to treat ADHD show that in some children tics are possible and that slight delays in growth are evident but not significant. Drug abuse actually appears less likely, for reasons not clearly understood. These results are not conclusive, so clinicians should continue to monitor children using stimulant medications for extended periods.

Nonstimulant medications seem to be effective with some patients. Atomoxetine (brand name: Strattera), for example, targets norepinephrine, the other neurotransmitter believed involved in ADHD. Modafinil (brand name: Provigil) has been prescribed for narcolepsy but has also shown to be effective in children with ADHD, although it is not clear exactly how the medication works (Biederman & Faraone, 2005).

Alternative Approaches. Scientists are also searching for treatments that do not include drugs. As brain scans reveal more about the biology of ADHD, scientists are looking at therapies that address cognitive functions, especially memory. Cognitive neuroscientists have long suspected that working and long-term memory functions are major contributors to attention and cognitive abilities. Improving memory may improve an individual's attentional and cognitive systems (Rockstroh & Scuweizer, 2001). One promising approach uses a computer software program that trains working memory. In a Swedish study, 60 percent of 20 unmedicated children with ADHD no longer met the clinical criteria for ADHD after five weeks of training. The program emphasizes the development of visual-spatial memory, which is the cognitive function that has the strongest link to inattention and ADHD (Klingberg et al., 2005).

Other studies involving behavioral therapy show that after two years, children treated with behavioral training only (i.e., parent training, school interventions, and a special summer camp program) functioned just a well as children on high-dose medication (Pelham et al., 2000). Another method that has proven effective with children who have ADHD is self-regulation, a strategy that has been successful with children with learning disabilities. In self-regulation, students use various techniques to monitor, manage, record, and assess their behavior or academic achievement. The assessment provides the feedback that allows a comparison between what the child is doing to what the child ought to be doing. Four common forms of self-regulation are self-monitoring, self-monitoring plus reinforcement, self-reinforcement, and self-management. Analyses of numerous studies showed that all four forms can be useful components as part of an intervention program for children with ADHD (Reid, Trout, & Schartz, 2005).

WHAT EDUCATORS NEED TO CONSIDER

Teachers should pinpoint areas in which each student's difficulties occur. Otherwise, valuable intervention resources may be spent where they are not effective. For example, one student with ADHD may have difficulty starting a task because the directions are not clear, while another may understand the directions but may have difficulty getting organized to begin a task. These two students need different types of interventions. Also, the sooner educational interventions begin, the better. They should be started when educational performance is affected and problems persist.

Teachers of students with ADHD should be positive, upbeat, and highly organized problem solvers. Unpredictability is a classroom constant, but teachers who use sincere praise and who are willing to put in extra effort can experience success with students who have ADHD. After all, these students want to succeed. Teachers and administrators should be constantly on the alert for school structures and classroom strategies that can unwittingly provoke any student to display ADHD-like behavior. Classrooms where students sit passively and listen mainly to teacher talk are prime breeding grounds for inattention and off-task activities.

STRATEGIES TO CONSIDER

Avoiding Instructional Strategies That Lead to School-Created ADHD-Like Behavior

Use this survey to help decide if you need to alter some of your classroom strategies.

Directions: Complete the profile below to determine whether some of your classroom or school structures can inadvertently create ADHD-like behavior in students. On a scale of 1 (lowest) to 5 (highest), circle the number that indicates the degree to which your teaching/school does the following. Connect the circles to see a profile.

1. I/We move quickly during instruction because I/we have a lot of curriculum to cover.   1   2   3   4   5

2. I/We use lecture as the main method of instruction.   1   2   3   4   5

3. I/We have classrooms arranged so it is possible for some students to be hidden from the teacher.   1   2   3   4   5

4. Each teacher determines the rules of behavior for each classroom.   1   2   3   4   5

5. I/We tend to keep students in their seats during lessons to avoid opportunities for behavior problems.   1   2   3   4   5

6. I/We usually turn down the lights when using the overhead projector or other visual aid.   1   2   3   4   5

7. I/We use the textbook as the main focus of instruction and classroom activity.   1   2   3   4   5

8. Copying information from the board is one of the main methods I/we use to give students information.   1   2   3   4   5

9. I/We tend to give more time to presenting information than to concern over students' emotional needs.   1   2   3   4   5

Scoring. If most of the circles are in the 3 to 5 range, there is a reasonable probability that some students who do not have true ADHD could be displaying ADHD-like behaviors. Changes in school operations and teacher behaviors that move those responses in the 3 to 5 range toward the 1 to 2 range are likely to decrease the incidence of ADHD-like behavior in students. Here's why:

1: Moving too quickly can lose some students who are deep processors. They want to spend more time playing with a concept before going on to the next. If the teacher doesn't allow time for processing, these students may nonetheless stay with the first idea and will be off task or become defiant about moving on. Slowing down and allowing processing time will lead to more retention of learning.

2: Fewer of today's students learn best by listening. They have been raised in a culture that emphasizes rapidly changing visual images and technology that requires their active participation. Too much teacher talk will drive some students to create visual representations of their own (doodling), and thus they will appear off task. Using a multisensory approach and keeping students actively involved is more likely to keep more students focused.

3: When some students are hidden from the teacher's sight, they can resort to off-task behavior or get into mischief, especially if there are no chances for student participation in the lesson. Classroom seating arrangements should ensure that every student can be seen by the teacher.

4: When teachers determine the rules of behavior in each classroom, chances are rules to change from one teacher to the next (elementary) or from classroom to classroom (secondary). Students then perceive the application and enforcement of discipline as arbitrary, which can result in defiance. Schools with low disciplinary problems are generally those with a few rules that all teachers enforce.

5: Brain research shows that movement opens neural pathways and retrieves memories. More students today need movement to focus. Keeping them in their seats for long periods of time may encourage some students to fidget, squirm, or get up on their own, typical signs of ADHD-like behavior.

6: Many secondary students come to school with less sleep than they need. Low lights will cause them to get drowsy and thus appear inattentive. How many sleep-deprived teachers might nod off under the same circumstances? Would that mean that the teachers have ADHD? Keep the lights on!

7: Textbooks are helpful instructional tools, but they are rarely novel. When texts are the main focus of instruction, students drift and resort to off-task behaviors. Using a variety of information sources, including the textbook, is far more interesting.

8: Many of today's students see the copying of information from a board as boring busywork. Discussing the information in groups with "What if. . .?" scenarios is far more intriguing and will less likely lead to off-task behavior.

9: More students are coming to school hoping to get their emotional needs met, mainly because this is not happening at home. Educators must recognize the importance of maintaining a purposeful, positive emotional climate in schools and classrooms. Brain research is showing us that survival ("Am I safe here?") and emotional needs ("Am I wanted here?") must be met before we can expect students to focus on the curriculum.

STRATEGIES TO CONSIDER

Strategies for Working With Students With ADHD/ADD

- Provide the student with a structured, predictable, and welcoming environment. As part of this environment,
  - Display rules and make sure students understand them
  - Post daily schedules and assignments in a clear manner
  - Call attention to any schedule changes
  - Set specific times for specific tasks
  - Design a quiet workspace that students can use on request
  - Seat problem students near positive peer models
  - Plan academic subjects for the morning hours
  - Provide regularly scheduled and frequent breaks during which students can stretch
  - Use attention-getting devices, such as secret signals, color codes, etc.
  - Do a countdown for the last several minutes of an activity
  - If a student starts getting disruptive, ask the student to read or answer a question
  - Sincerely praise students for constructive things they have done during the day
  - Shift the focus away from competition to contribution, enjoyment, and satisfaction
  - Contact parents to report good news and build a supportive relationship

- Modify the curriculum. Students with ADHD/ADD (like all students) can often benefit from the notion that less is more. If a student can demonstrate proficiency after 10 problems, then don't assign 20. Curriculum modification can also include the following:
  - Mixing activities of high and low interest
  - Avoiding more than 20 minutes of seat work or inactivity
  - Providing computerized learning materials
  - Simplifying and increasing visual presentations
  - Teaching organization and study skills
  - Using memory strategies, such as mnemonic devices
  - Using visual references for auditory instruction
  - Giving students simple decisions to make during the day to build this skill
  - Explaining your decision to students and having them explain theirs to you
  - Writing tests with easier questions dispersed throughout to keep motivation high

STRATEGIES TO CONSIDER

Getting, Focusing, and Maintaining Attention

The greatest challenges for the teacher of ADHD/ADD students are to get their attention, focus it toward a learning objective, and maintain that attention during the learning episode. The following are some suggested activities for each of these steps.

Getting Student Attention

- Start a lesson with enthusiasm, excitement, and an interesting question or problem.

- Use auditory signals, such as a bell, beeper, or timer, or play a bar of music on the piano.

- Use visual signals, such as raising your hand or flashing the room lights, to indicate the time for silence; or say, "Everybody . . . ready."

- Use color, such as colored markers on white board or on overhead transparencies or video screens. Colored paper can be used to highlight key words, steps, or patterns.

- If using an overhead projector, place an unfamiliar object on it to get attention. Frame important points with your hands or a colored box.

- Use eye contact. Students should face you when you are speaking to them, especially when you are giving instructions.

- Use humor and storytelling. Add some mystery to your story and ask students to guess the ending, either orally or in writing. Consider using props to stimulate and maintain interest.

Focusing Student Attention

- Use the overhead projector frequently when giving direct instruction. It helps focus attention, and you can write on it without turning your back to the students. You can write in color, place objects on it for interest, frame important points, and cover up irrelevant information. Be sure to remove any distracting material from the screen to avoid confusion. Use a stick or laser pointer to draw attention to the material on which you want students to focus.

- Use multisensory strategies during your presentation. Maintain your visibility and make sure you can be heard by all students. Incorporate demonstrations and hands-on activities whenever possible.

- Be aware of competing sounds in your environment, such as noisy ventilators or outside traffic, and try to limit their distraction.

- Use illustrations and encourage students to draw as much as possible. The drawings do not have to be accurate or sophisticated, just clear enough to understand a concept. Have fun with this. Even silly illustrations can help students remember a series of events, key points, steps in problem solving, or abstract information.

- Position all students so they can easily see the board or screen. Encourage them to readjust their seating whenever their view is blocked.

Maintaining Student Attention

- Present with a lively, brisk pace, keep moving to maintain your visibility, and avoid lag time. Use pictures, diagrams, manipulatives, gestures, and high-interest materials.

- Talk less. Talk is a powerful memory device, so give students opportunities to converse with each other about what they are learning. Maintain accountability by asking them to share with you what they learned from their partner.

- Ask higher-order thinking questions that are open-ended, require reasoning, and stimulate critical thinking and discussion.

- Vary the way you call on students so they cannot predict who is next. Encourage them to share answers orally with a partner or a group, or write them down in a journal.

- Use the proper structure of cooperative learning groups. ADHD students do not usually function well without the clearly defined structures and expectations that cooperative learning techniques provide.

- Allow students to use individual chalk or dry-erase boards, which are motivating and effective in checking for understanding and determining who needs extra help and practice.

- Use motivating computer programs that provide frequent feedback and self-correction for skill building and practice.

STRATEGIES TO CONSIDER

Strategies for Specific ADHD/ADD Behaviors

For Excessive Activity	For Inability to Wait	For Failure to Sustain Attention to Routine Tasks and Activities
Channel activity into acceptable avenues. For example, rather than attempting to reduce a student's activity, encourage directed movement in classrooms when this is not disruptive. Allow standing during seat work, especially at the end of a task.	Give the student substitute verbal or motor responses to make while waiting. This might include teaching the student how to continue on easier parts of the task (or a substitute task) while waiting for the teacher's help.	Decrease the length of the task. There are many ways to do this, including breaking one task into smaller parts to be completed at different times, or just assigning fewer tasks or problems.
Use activity as a reward. For example, to reward appropriate behavior, allow the student to run an errand, clean the board, or organize the teacher's desk.	When possible, permit daydreaming or planning while the student waits. For example, the student might be allowed to doodle or play with some objects while waiting. Another option is to show the student how to underline or record relevant information.	Make tasks interesting. For example, allow students to work with partners or in small groups; use an overhead projector or other device; or alternate high- and low-interest activities. Novelty can often sustain interest. Make a game out of checking students' work, and use games to help in learning rote material.
Use active responses in instruction. Teaching activities that encourage active responses (e.g., moving, talking, organizing, writing in a diary, painting, or working at the board) are helpful to ADHD students.	When inability to wait becomes impatience, encourage leadership. Do not assume that impulsive statements or behavior are aggressive in intent. Cue the student when an upcoming task will be difficult and extra control will be needed.	

For Noncompliance and Failure to Complete Tasks	For Difficulty at the Beginning of Tasks	For Completing Assignments on Time
Make sure the tasks fit within the student's learning abilities and preferred response style. Students are more likely to complete tasks when they are allowed to respond in various ways, such as with a computer, on an overhead, on tape. Make sure that disorganization is not the reason the student is failing to complete tasks.	Increase the structure of the tasks and highlight the important parts. This includes encouraging more note taking, giving directions orally as well as in writing, clearly stating the standards for acceptable work, and pointing out how tasks are structured (e.g., topic sentences, headers, table of contents, index).	Increase the student's use of lists and assignment organizers (notebook, folders). Write assignments on the board and make sure that the student has copied them.
Find ways to increase the choice and specific interest of tasks for the student. Consider allowing the student with ADHD a selection of specific tasks, topics, and activities. Determine which activities the student prefers, and use these as incentives.	Ask the student to write down the steps needed to get the task started, and have the student review the steps orally.	Establish routines for placing and retrieving commonly used objects, such as books, assignments, and clothes. Pocket folders are helpful because new work can be placed on one side and completed work on the other. Parents can be encouraged to establish places for certain things (e.g., books, homework) at home. Students can be encouraged to organize their desk or locker with labels and places for certain items.
		Teach students that, upon leaving one place for another, they will ask themselves, "Do I have everything I need?"

Source: Adapted from Fowler (2002)

STRATEGIES TO CONSIDER

Tips for Parents of Children With ADHD/ADD

Parents of children with ADHD/ADD often feel overwhelmed by the challenges associated with these disorders. The following tips, suggested by the National Information Center for Children and Youth with Disabilities (Fowler, 2002), may help parents in dealing with their children. Teachers and parents should work together to develop a consistent plan for responding to the child's needs.

- Learn about ADHD/ADD. The more you know, the more you can help yourself and your child.

- Praise your child when he or she does well. Help your child identify strengths and talents. Encourage your child's special interests and enroll your child in extracurricular activities.

- Be clear, consistent, and positive, even when disciplining the child. Set rules that tell your child what to do, not just what not to do. Be clear about what will happen if the rules are not followed. Praise good behavior and reward it.

- Create opportunities for success, no matter how large or small.

- Learn about strategies for managing your child's behavior. These include the techniques of charting, having a reward program, ignoring behaviors, natural consequences, logical consequences, and time-out. Using these strategies will lead to more positive behaviors and cut down on problem behaviors.

- Talk with your doctor about whether medication will help your child, getting second opinions if your questions go unanswered. Caution: Some people claim that ADHD/ADD can be treated primarily with megavitamins, chiropractic scalp massage, allergy treatments, and unusual diets. Be aware that these treatments have not yet stood up to scientific scrutiny. However, as new evidence emerges, an integrated approach of various treatments might be considered.

- Pay attention to your child's mental health—and your own! Be open to counseling. It can help you deal with the challenges of raising a child with ADHD/ADD. It can also help your child deal with frustration, have greater self-esteem, and learn more about social skills.

- Talk to other parents whose children have ADHD/ADD and share practical advice and emotional support. Look at the resources and organizations at the end of this book for more help.

- Meet with school officials to develop an individual educational plan (IEP) to address your child's needs. Both you and your child's teacher should get a written copy of this plan.

- Keep in touch with your child's teacher to find out how your child is doing in school. Offer support. Tell the teacher how your child is doing at home.

- Remember that as researchers continue their investigations, we may gain new knowledge that could change some of our current understandings and beliefs about the nature of ADHD and ADD, resulting in the development of alternative treatments. Keep abreast of what is happening in this field through some of the organizations listed in the **Resources** section of this book.

Chapter 4

Speech Disabilities

Human beings have developed an elaborate and complex means of spoken communication that many say is largely responsible for our place as the dominant species on this planet. Spoken language is truly a marvelous accomplishment for many reasons. At the very least, it gives form to our memories and words to express our thoughts. The human voice can pronounce about 200 vowel and 600 consonant sounds that allow it to speak any of the estimated 6,500 languages (not counting dialects) that exist today. With practice, the voice becomes so fine-tuned that it makes only about one sound error per million sounds and one word error per million words (Pinker, 1994).

Before the advent of imaging technologies, we explained how the brain produced spoken language on the basis of evidence from injured brains. In 1861, French surgeon Paul Broca noted that damage to the left frontal lobe induced language difficulties generally known as *aphasia*, wherein patients muttered sounds or lost speech completely. Broca's area is located just behind the left temple (Figure 4.1). A person with damage to Broca's area, for example, could understand language but could not speak fluently. In 1871, German neurologist Carl Wernicke described a different type of aphasia—one in which patients could not make sense of words they spoke or heard. These patients had damage in the left temporal lobe. Wernicke's area is situated above the left ear. Those with damage to Wernicke's area could speak fluently, but what they said was quite meaningless. The inferences, then, were that Broca's area stored vocabulary, grammar, and probably syntax of one's native language, while Wernicke's area was the site of native-language sense and meaning.

Recent research, using scanners, indicates that spoken-language production is a far more complex process than previously thought. When preparing to produce a spoken sentence, the brain not only uses Broca's and Wernicke's areas but also calls on several other neural networks scattered throughout the left hemisphere. Nouns are processed through one set of patterns; verbs are processed by separate neural networks. The more complex the sentence structure, the more areas that are activated, including some in the right hemisphere.

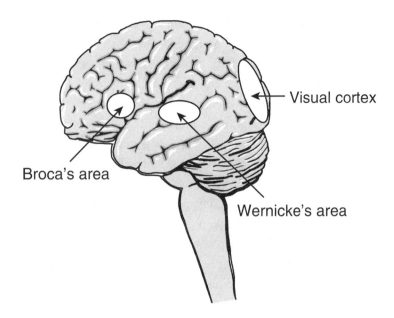

Figure 4.1 Broca's area and Wernicke's area, located in the left hemisphere in most individuals, are the two major language-processing centers of the brain. The visual cortex, across the back of both hemispheres, processes visual stimuli.

LEARNING SPOKEN LANGUAGE

Is Language Prewired in the Brain?

In the 1950s, MIT linguist Noam Chomsky theorized that young children could not possibly learn the rules of language grammar and syntax merely by imitating adults. He proposed that nature endowed humans with the ability to acquire their native language by attaching what they hear to a language template that is prewired in the brain by birth—just as baby tigers are prewired to learn how to hunt. Other linguists now suggest that language acquisition may be the result of a genetic predisposition coupled with the baby brain's incredible ability to sort through the enormous amount of information it takes in—including language—and to identify regular patterns from background noise. Although the debate over how much language is genetically prewired is far from over, researchers are gaining remarkable insights into how and when the young brain masters spoken language.

Learning Sounds Called Phonemes

The neurons in a baby's brain are capable of responding to the sounds of all the languages on this planet. At birth (some say even before) babies respond to the *prosody*—the rhythm, cadence, and pitch—of their mother's voice, not the words. Spoken language consists of minimal units of sound,

The human brain is prewired at birth to learn all the languages on this planet.

called *phonemes*, which combine to form syllables. For example, in English, the consonant sound "p" and the vowel sound "o" are both phonemes that combine to form the syllable *po-* as in *potato*.

Each language has its own set of phonemes. Surprisingly, however, the total number of basic phonemes used by all the world's languages is only about 150, although tonal variations can number in the thousands (Pinker, 1994). Although the infant's brain can perceive this entire range of phonemes, only those that are repeated get attention, and the neurons reacting to the unique sound patterns get continually stimulated and reinforced.

By the age of 10 to 12 months, the toddler's brain has begun to distinguish and remember phonemes of the native language and to ignore nonnative sounds. One study showed that at the age of 6 months, American and Japanese babies are equally good at discriminating between the "l" and "r" sounds, even though Japanese has no "l" sound. However, by age 10 months, Japanese babies have a tougher time making the distinction, while American babies have become much better at it (Cheour et al., 1998). During this and subsequent periods of growth, the ability to distinguish native sounds improves, while the ability to distinguish nonnative speech sounds diminishes. Meanwhile, pruning begins, and by one year of age, neural networks are focusing on the sounds of the language being spoken in the infant's environment (Gazzaniga, Ivry, & Mangun, 2002).

From Phonemes to Words

The next step for the brain is to detect words from the stream of sounds it is processing. This is not an easy task because people don't pause between words when speaking. Yet the brain has to recognize differences between, say, *green house* and *greenhouse*. Remarkably, babies begin to distinguish word boundaries by the age of 8 months even though they don't know what the words mean (Van Petten & Bloom, 1999). They begin to acquire new vocabulary words at the rate of about 10 a day. At the same time, memory and Wernicke's areas are becoming fully functional so the child can now attach meaning to words. Of course, learning words is one skill; putting them together to make sense is a different, more complex skill.

Learning Grammar

Chomsky believed that all languages contain some common rules that dictate how sentences are constructed and that the brain has preprogrammed circuits that respond to these rules. Modern linguists think that the brain may not be responding so much to basic language rules as to statistical regularities heard in the flow of the native tongue. It soon discerns that some words describe objects while others describe actions. Toddlers detect patterns of word order—person, action, object—so they can soon say, "Me want cookie." Other grammar features emerge, such as tense, and by the age of three years, over 90 percent of sentences uttered are grammatically correct. Errors are seldom random, but usually result from following perceived rules of grammar. If "I batted the ball" makes sense, why shouldn't "I holded the bat?" Regrettably, the toddler has yet to learn that nearly 200 of the most commonly used verbs in English are irregularly conjugated.

> *The more that children are exposed to spoken language in the early years, the more quickly they can discriminate between phonemes and recognize word boundaries.*

During the following years, practice in speaking and adult correction help the child decode some of the mysteries of grammar's irregularities, and a sophisticated language system emerges from what once was babble. No one knows how much grammar a child learns just by listening, or how much is prewired. What is certain is that the more children are exposed to spoken language in the early years, the more quickly they can discriminate between phonemes and recognize word boundaries.

Effects of Watching Television

Just letting the toddler sit in front of a television does not seem to accomplish the goal of phoneme discrimination, probably because the child's brain needs live human interaction to attach meaning to the words. Moreover, television talk is not the slow, expressive speech that parents use with their infants, which infants like and want to hear. Although toddlers may be attracted to the rapidly changing sounds and images on a television, little or no language development is in progress. Further evidence indicates that prolonged television watching can impair the growth of young brains. Susan Johnson, a pediatrician at the University of California, San Francisco, cites several studies that raise concerns over the effects of television viewing on young minds (Johnson, 1999). These studies point out that the visual system is not stimulated properly by television viewing in that there is no pupil dilation and the eyes stare at the screen and do not move from one point to the next—a skill critical for reading. The images change every 5 to 6 seconds (even faster during commercials) robbing the higher-thought areas of the brain (in the frontal lobe) of time to process the images. The wavelengths of light produced by the television tube's phosphors are very limited compared to the full spectrum of light we receive when viewing objects outdoors. Furthermore, television reduces the opportunities for the child's brain to create internal images.

Both the American Academy of Pediatrics and the National Literacy Trust in the United Kingdom recommend that parents and caregivers eliminate or strictly limit the exposure of television to toddlers under the age of two in favor of more face-to-face activities that enhance language development.

Speech and Language Patterns by Age

The human brain is programmed to learn spoken language during the child's earliest years. As language learning progresses, certain behavior patterns emerge over time, forming the building blocks of continued language growth and development. Early language development occurs in context with other skills, such as cognition (thinking, understanding, and problem solving), gross and fine motor coordination (stacking, throwing, catching, and jumping), social interaction (peer contact and group play), and taking care of one's self (washing, eating, and dressing).

The National Institute on Deafness and Other Communication Disorders (NIDCD, 2000) and the Learning Disabilities Association of America (LDA, 2006) have compiled from the research a list of speech and language behaviors that emerge for most children from birth through the age of six. Each child is different, but the list is a good indicator of speech and language progress for most children.

Birth to 5 Months

- Reacts to loud sounds
- Turns head toward a sound source

- Watches your face when you speak
- Vocalizes pleasure and displeasure sounds (laughs, giggles, or cries)
- Makes noise when talked to

Between 6 and 11 Months

- Recognizes name
- Says two to three words besides "mama" and "dada"
- Understands simple instructions
- Imitates familiar sounds
- Recognizes words as symbols for objects: cat—meows; car—points to garage

Between 12 and 17 Months

- Understands "no"
- Says two to three words to label an object (pronunciation may not be clear)
- Attends to a book or toy for about two minutes
- Follows simple directions accompanied with gestures
- Answers simple questions nonverbally
- Gives a toy when asked
- Brings an object from another room when asked
- Points to objects, pictures, and family members

Between 18 and 23 Months

- Enjoys being read to
- Uses 10 to 20 words, including names (pronunciation may not be clear)
- Follows simple directions without gestures
- Understands words like "eat" and "sleep"
- Imitates the sounds of familiar animals
- Correctly pronounces most vowels and *n, m, p,* and *h,* especially in the beginning of syllables and short words
- Asks for common foods by name
- Uses words like "more" to make wants known
- Begins to use pronouns such as "mine"
- Points to simple body parts such as nose

Between 2 and 3 Years

- Identifies body parts
- Converses with self and dolls

- Has a vocabulary of over 400 words. Asks questions, such as "What's that?"
- Uses two-word negative phrases such as "no want"
- Forms some plurals by adding an "s" to words
- Uses more pronouns, such as "you" and "I"
- Gives first name and holds up fingers to tell age
- Combines nouns and verbs, such as "daddy go"
- Knows simple time concepts, such as "tomorrow" and "last night"
- Refers to self as "me" rather than by name
- Tries to get adult attention with "watch me" phrases
- Likes to hear same story repeated
- Talks to other children as well as adults
- Answers "where" questions
- Matches three to four colors
- Understands big and little
- Names common pictures and things
- Solves problems by talking instead of hitting or crying
- Uses short sentences, such as "Me want cookie."

Between 3 and 4 Years

- Can tell a story
- Uses sentences of four to five words
- Has a vocabulary of about 1,000 words
- Uses most speech sounds but may distort more difficult sounds such as *l, r, s, sh, ch, y, v, z,* and *th*
- Strangers begin to understand much of what is said
- Uses verbs that end in "ing," such as "walking" and "talking"
- Names at least one color
- Understands "yesterday," "tonight," "summer"
- Begins to obey requests, like "Put the toy under the chair."
- Knows last name, name of street, and several nursery rhymes

Between 4 and 5 Years

- Uses past tense correctly
- Uses sentences of four to five words
- Has a vocabulary of about 1,500 words
- Defines words
- Speech is understandable but makes mistakes when pronouncing long words such as "hippopotamus"
- Uses some irregular past tense verbs such as "ran"
- Names and points to colors red, blue, yellow, and green
- Identifies triangles, circles, and squares
- Understands "in the morning," "next," and "noontime"

- Can talk of imaginary conditions, such as "I hope"
- Asks many questions, including "who" and "why"

Between 5 and 6 Years

- Uses sentences of six to eight words
- Has a vocabulary of about 2,000 words
- Defines objects by their use (you eat with a fork) and can tell what objects are made of
- Understands spatial relations like "on top," "behind," "far," and "near"
- Understands time sequences (what happened first, second)
- Knows home address
- Identifies penny, nickel, and dime
- Understands common opposites like big/little and same/different
- Counts ten objects
- Asks questions for information
- Distinguishes the left and right hands
- Uses complex sentences, for example, "Let's go to the park after we eat."
- Uses imagination to create stories

As a precaution, a child who is more than a year delayed should be examined by medical professionals for possible systemic problems, such as hearing loss. Remember that many children who have early speech and language delays eventually catch up to their developmental stage by the time they enter school.

Putting the Language Components Together

The successful use of oral language requires the brain to direct the voice box to produce sounds that follow a certain set of patterns and rules for

- Phonology—phonemes (the smallest sounds of language)
- Morphology—word formation
- Syntax—sentence formation
- Semantics—word and sentence meaning, especially idioms
- Prosody—intonation and rhythm of speech
- Pragmatics—effective use of language for different purposes, following rules of conversation, and staying on topic

Amazingly, most brains get it right. But problems can occur anywhere along the way. Some problems may just be a matter of time, i.e., the brain needs more time to discern the patterns and figure out the rules. More persistent problems may be due to physiological difficulties (e.g., hearing loss), childhood trauma (physical or psychological), genetic influences, or other factors not yet understood.

PROBLEMS IN LEARNING SPOKEN LANGUAGE

Language Problems With Children and Adolescents

Language Delay

Most toddlers begin to speak words around the age of 10 to 12 months. However, in delayed speech, children may not speak coherent words and phrases until nearly 2 years of age. The evidence suggests that a language delay to 2 years is inherited, thus representing a distinct disorder not easily remedied by environmental interventions (Dale, et al., 1998). This revelation diminishes the claim some people make that environmental influences cause most language delay. However, certain environmental factors, such as stress, *can* cause language delay in some children.

> **Language Delay**
>
> Symptoms Around Age 1½ to 2:
> - Uses only a few words during speech
> - Uses only a few phrases during speech
> - Speech is not coherent

Specific Language Impairment

A broad range of problems in learning language are grouped in the category often referred to as specific language impairment (SLI). It describes a general condition in which a child's spoken language does not develop at the expected and acceptable rate, even though the person's sensory and cognitive systems appear normal and there is no apparent environmental problem. The disorder affects about seven percent of children entering school. Parents may first become aware of SLI when their children fail to demonstrate the normal bursts of language development that occur around the age of 2 years. Many of these children will eventually achieve normal levels of language development during the subsequent two years. However, some will continue to display language difficulties at school age, having difficulty building vocabulary as well as difficulty acquiring written language.

Although most of the cognitive functions of children with SLI are normal, verbal memory deficits often occur. Montgomery (2000) tested the verbal memory of groups of children with SLI and without SLI on word recall and sentence comprehension. He found that children with SLI had less functional verbal working memory capacity and greater difficulty managing their working memory abilities than their non-SLI peers. Another study also found similar verbal working memory deficits in word recall. However, the students with SLI showed no performance difference on language processing tasks involving true/false test items (Weismer, Evans, & Hesketh, 1999). Many children identified early in life with SLI will eventually develop characteristics of dyslexia (severe reading disability).

> **Specific Language Impairment**
>
> Symptoms:
> - Complexity of speech not developing with age
> - Little or no growth in vocabulary
> - Consistently poor grammar with little or no improvement
> - Difficulty remembering recently used words

The question is whether SLI has a biological or an environmental basis, or some combination of both. Studies in recent years of children with SLI, including identical twins, support the notion of a biological basis through genetic influences and seem to point to deficits in the brain systems responsible for grammar and vocabulary processing (Bartlett et al., 2002; Choudhury & Benasich, 2003; O'Brien, Zhang, Nishimura, Tomblin, & Murray, 2003). Therefore, care must be taken in ascribing environmental factors or identifying a single intervention as a cure for SLI. Because many of the children with SLI have little or no cognitive deficit, it would seem that interventions should focus on cognitive strategies that help explain and practice the rules of grammar as well as acquire vocabulary in context.

Some children with SLI also display the symptoms of attention-deficit hyperactivity disorder (ADHD). Studies, however, suggest that these two disorders are not directly connected and originate from deficits in different cerebral systems (McInnes, Humphries, Hogg-Johnson, & Tannock, 2003; Williams, Stott, Goodyer, & Sahakian, 2000).

Expressive Language Disorder

Children with this disorder understand language but have trouble expressing themselves in speech. They often have a weak vocabulary and difficulty recalling words, using the correct tense, and constructing complex sentences. Although the cause is unknown, cerebral damage, head trauma, and malnutrition, perhaps in combination with genetic influences, have been associated with the disorder. Some children may have no problem in simple expression but have difficulties retrieving and organizing words and sentences when expressing more complicated thoughts and ideas. This is more likely to occur when they are trying to define, describe, or explain information or retell an activity or event.

Expressive Language Disorder

Symptoms:

- Below average vocabulary skills
- Difficulty producing complex sentences
- Improper use of correct tenses
- Problems in recalling words

Treatment usually involves language therapy that focuses on increasing the number of phrases a child can use. The phrases are presented as blocks, and the child practices building complex sentences from these blocks. Language therapy and similar treatments show an encouraging recovery rate, especially if interventions are started soon after diagnosis.

Receptive-Expressive Language Disorder

Symptoms:

- Impairment in language comprehension
- Impairment in language expression
- Speech containing many articulation errors
- Difficulty recalling early visual or auditory memories

Receptive Language Disorder

Those with receptive language disorder have trouble understanding certain aspects of speech. They may not respond to their names or have difficulty following directions, or point to a bell when you say "ball." Their hearing is fine, but they can't make sense out of certain sounds, words, or sentences they hear. Sometimes, they may appear inattentive. Because receiving and using speech are closely related, many people with receptive language disorder also have symptoms of expressive language disorder. The combined symptoms are referred to as Receptive-Expressive Language Disorder.

Language Problems With Adolescents

Problems with language are particularly troublesome for adolescents because language plays such a major role in secondary school subjects. The elementary years emphasize language development. The middle school grades begin to focus on specific subjects where mastery of language is assumed. But in high school, teachers expect students to have an increased vocabulary, more advanced sentence structure, and the ability to use different kinds of language for different situations.

> ### Adolescent Language Disorder
>
> Symptoms:
> - Failure to understand or follow rules of conversation, such as taking turns and staying on topic
> - Difficulty using different language for different needs of the learner or situation
> - Difficulty requesting further information to aid understanding
> - Incorrect use of grammar
> - Poor or limited vocabulary
> - Difficulty with instructions, especially those that are long or grammatically complex
> - Extreme forgetfulness
> - Difficulty understanding puns, idioms, jokes, riddles

Much effort goes into identifying and remediating language problems in young children. Yet less effort seems to be directed toward identifying adolescents with language problems. Such problems can lead to feelings of failure, low self-esteem, poor academic and social success, and a high dropout rate. Adolescents with language disorders can be those:

- Who received no interventions
- Who initially received treatment through early intervention programs but who still have some language difficulties
- Who had normal language development but experienced a disruption because of some mental, physical, emotional, or traumatic event
- Who have some other learning disability

Working with adolescents who have language difficulties requires more direct instruction aimed at treating the identified language weakness. Consistent practice is important, but the practice should not be so repetitive as to be perceived as boring. Practice using computer programs creates interest, and success in mastering these programs can enhance self-esteem.

Language and Cognitive Thought. Studies have provided strong evidence that language and cognitive thought are separated in the brain (Gazzaniga, Ivry, & Mangun, 2002). Some studies involved patients with Williams syndrome, a rare genetic disorder first described in 1961. Children

> *Because evidence exists that language and cognitive thought are separated in the brain, we should not assume that students with language problems are not intelligent.*

with this disorder have difficulty with simple spatial tasks, and many have IQ scores in the 40 to 50 range and cannot read or write above the first-grade level. Despite these inadequacies, they develop extraordinary spoken-language skills. They amass large vocabularies, speak in complex, grammatically correct sentences, and display engaging personalities. Coincidentally, many children with Williams syndrome exhibit exceptional musical talent.

Stuttering

Stuttering is a communication disorder that affects the fluency of speech. It begins during childhood and, in some cases, persists throughout life. The disorder is characterized by disruptions in the production of speech sounds. Sometimes words are repeated or preceded by interjections, and there are moments when a sound or period of silence is prolonged. Some speakers who stutter exhibit excessive physical tension in their speech or appear to be out of breath when talking.

The exact cause of stuttering is not known. Developmental stuttering typically starts between the ages of 30 to 48 months. Recent studies suggest that genetic factors play a significant role in the disorder. Many individuals who stutter inherit traits that impair their ability to string together the various muscle movements that are necessary to produce sentences fluently. Not everyone who is genetically predisposed to stuttering will develop the disorder. Environmental events can trigger stuttering. The acquisition of grammar skills appears to be another trigger for developmental stuttering. Between the ages of two and five years, children acquire many of the simpler rules of language. A child who is predisposed to stuttering may have no difficulty speaking fluently when the sentences are only two or three words long. However, the speech system may run into fluency problems when the child tries to produce longer, more complex sentences. After stuttering has begun, stress, teasing, embarrassment, and other factors often act to aggravate speech fluency.

There is no known cure for stuttering, but many treatment approaches have proven successful. Young children who have been stuttering for only a short time have a high rate of natural recovery. However, it is not possible to determine which children will recover and which will continue stuttering. Most treatment programs for those who persistently stutter are designed to teach the speaker specific skills or behaviors that lead to improved oral communication. For example, speech-language pathologists teach speakers who stutter to control and monitor their rate of speech, to initiate words in a slightly slower and less physically tense manner, and to regulate and monitor their breathing. Over time, speakers learn to produce smooth speech at progressively faster rates, in progressively longer sentences, and in progressively more challenging situations.

Treatment techniques using choral speech have shown to be effective. Researchers believe that this approach engages the mirror neuron system (see Chapter 1) to imitate fluent speech and inhibit stuttering (Kalinowski & Saltuklaroglu, 2003).

Implications at Home

Given the evidence that the brain's ability to acquire spoken language is at its peak in the early years, parents should create a rich environment that includes lots of communication activities, such as talking, singing, and reading. However, the acquisition of speech and language can be affected by a number of factors, including muscular disorders, hearing problems, or developmental delays. These factors should be investigated if a child demonstrates significant delay or difficulty in speech.

Language Deficits and Learning a Second Language

Should students with language difficulties be expected to learn a second language? For students without language difficulties, learning another language can be a rewarding experience that can enrich their lives forever. But for students with language problems, it can be a stressful, perhaps painful, experience. Continued research on how the brain learns is revealing some insights into the neural systems responsible for language acquisition. During the 1960s, Kenneth Dinklage (1971) at Harvard University was investigating why some of the brightest students at Harvard could not pass their second-language classes. The students were highly motivated and devoted enormous amounts of time and effort to studying their languages, but many were still failing. Furthermore, their anxiety over the situation only made the situation worse. After interviews and testing, Dinklage found that some of these students had been diagnosed with language disabilities that they had overcome with considerable effort and tutoring; others had undiagnosed language problems. Taking the university's language classes revealed these problems.

In an unorthodox experiment, Dinklage convinced native-language speakers with learning disabilities to teach the troubled students. Most students taught in this experiment passed their second-language classes. Dinklage's work highlighted the basic problem facing students with language disabilities in second-language classrooms: The problem is related to being learning disabled, not to any lack of motivation or effort or even to the anxiety produced by the situation. Anxiety was not the cause of failure but the result. Students not previously diagnosed as having language difficulties showed up as such in the second-language classroom. However, once the instructional methods addressed the language difficulties issues, the students could learn.

In the 1980s, Leonore Ganschow and Richard Sparks (1993 & 1995) studied Dinklage's work as well as related research that described language as having three component parts or linguistic codes: phonological, semantic, and syntactic. From this, they developed their own theory, called the Linguistic Coding Deficit Hypothesis. It states that difficulties with the acquisition of another language originate from problems in one or more of these linguistic codes in the student's native language system. These problems can result in mild to extreme deficiencies with specific oral and written aspects of language. Ganschow and Sparks further assert that most learners who experience difficulty with learning another language have problems with phonological awareness—the ability to recognize and manipulate the basic sounds of language (phonemes). Students who have difficulty recognizing phonemes will also have problems with the interpretation and production of language that is needed for basic understanding, speaking, and spelling.

> *Language deficits that arise when learning a first language are very likely to arise when learning a second language.*

Ganschow and Sparks (1995, 2001) maintain that individuals who are very strong in all three linguistic codes will be excellent language learners. Conversely, those who are weak in all three codes will be very poor language learners. In between these extremes lies a spectrum of students who may be very good at spoken language but poor at written language, and other students with the opposite characteristics, and still others with combinations of all the possible linguistic variations (Sparks, Philips, & Javorsky, 2003).

Because of these great variations in the capabilities of students with language deficits, the following question arises: What do we mean when we say they have *learned* the second language? Some students may become excellent readers of the language but not be able to carry on a simple conversation. Others may have difficulty reading the language but be very fluent in conversation and have a near-native accent. Still others may be able to speak correctly but with an accent that is not even close to that of native speakers.

The important point, nonetheless, is that the difficulties these students have in acquiring another language stem from deficits in their first language. Other studies have supported this notion (Arries, 1999; Palladino & Cornoldi, 2004; Scott & Manglitz, 2000). With this knowledge in hand, Ganschow and Sparks developed two approaches to second-language instruction that have been effective. See **Strategies to Consider** at the end of this chapter.

The Future of Speech-Language Disorders Research

Brain imaging technology continues to reveal more about the relationship between exposure to speech and language, brain development, and communication skills. Genetic studies are indicating that at least some language problems are inherited. Scientists are trying to distinguish those speech and language problems that may be overcome by maturation alone from those that may require some intervention or therapy. Researchers are focusing on characterizing dialects that belong to certain ethnic and regional groups. This knowledge will help professionals distinguish a language dialect from a language disorder. The success of these efforts would spare children who are merely slower in developing or speaking a dialect the embarrassment of unnecessary labeling, while concentrating treatment on those who really need it. Another area of intense study is the effect of speech and language development on later school performance, especially learning to read.

Finally, some studies are exploring how the brain acquires a second language either during or after learning one's native language. Understanding which neural systems are involved in learning native and second languages can guide the development of instructional practices that will make it easier for all students to speak and read more than one language.

WHAT EDUCATORS NEED TO CONSIDER

Educators should consider all of the following:

- Address any speech and language learning problems in young children quickly to take advantage of the brain's ability to rewire improper connections during this important period of growth
- Give more attention to the speech and language problems of adolescents
- Recognize that some speech and language delays are simply the result of delayed maturation and do not represent a permanent disorder
- Train secondary school teachers in identifying and addressing language weaknesses
- Accept the notion that students with language difficulties may still be able to learn a second language when taught with the appropriate instructional approaches
- Not assume that children with language learning problems are going to be limited in cognitive thought processes as well

Acquiring spoken language is a natural ability that comes more easily to some children than to others. Functional imaging technologies allow a more detailed study of the parts of the brain that are activated during the processing of spoken language. As research reveals more about the amazing process by which we learn to speak languages, parents and educators will be better able to help those with language learning problems.

STRATEGIES TO CONSIDER

Developing Oral Language Skills

Spoken language comes naturally to the young brain. But to master the language, the brain must first consistently *hear* it. Infants and young children hear the sounds of language and begin to make connections between words and objects or actions. At this point, speech is not necessary. The brain is acquiring vocabulary and making the associations that will give the child the words and patterns it will later need to speak the language. *Listening*, then, is the groundwork for speech and eventually for reading skills.

   Research confirms that the young brain is fully ready to learn through tactile (touch) interaction by nine months of age. The neural networks for abstract thinking, including math and logic, are set to begin shortly thereafter. Thus the ability to process language, sounds, music, and rhythms is functional before the age of one year. The parent is the first teacher, and what the parent does to nurture oral language skills in the early years may well set the stage for the child's future success in school. Because some language deficits are eventually overcome, the sooner the child's language skills are engaged and practiced, the greater the likelihood that the time required to correct the deficits will be reduced. Parents, teachers, and staff in early childhood centers can enhance the development of the child's oral language skills through the following activities suggested by Diamond and Hopson (1998) and the Learning Disabilities Association of America.

1. Talk to the child

- Talk to the child whenever you are together.
- Talk about the day's events, a book the child has read, a story the child has heard, or the traffic signs along the highway. Tell the child whatever you are doing.
- Ask the child to explain any activity you are doing at home, such as ironing, trimming bushes, or sorting laundry. Don't settle for single-word or short answers.
- Ask the child to point out objects in the environment and name them. Describe the characteristics of an object (long, yellow, and tasty), and ask the child to name it (banana).

2. Read to the child

- Read aloud at least 20 minutes every day while the child is sitting in your lap.
- Take turns talking about what was read.
- For a child with limited attention span, provide books with large, colorful pictures and few words.
- Ask the child to point out objects in the book as you read its name. Vary some of the phrases, like "cat in the hat" and "cat on the mat," to see if the child can hear the difference.

3. Reading books should be an interactive experience	• Discuss the book's pictures and paraphrase its story. • Let the child make up a version of what will happen next in the story. • If the story is familiar, allow the child to finish telling key events or to give the succeeding rhyme. • Give the child an opportunity to correct you by purposely misreading or omitting items and events. • Have the child point out words as you read them. • Act out the story or create a puppet show. • Reinforce sequential reading by starting at the beginning of the page and showing the direction of written text, from left to right and top to bottom of page.
4. Cultivate phonological awareness with auditory and visual word games	• Play rhyming games: If a child does not hear the rhyme, try a game with words that begin with the same sound. • Play the broken record game: Say a word very slowly and break it into syllables, then have the child repeat the word at a normal speed. • Pick a game the child enjoys, such as matching letters or copying the names of famous people. • Have the child draw pictures and make up a story while you write it down.
5. Learning starts with a one-to-one match, followed by patterns and sequence	• Children learn to count and learn the letters of the alphabet long before they make connections to arithmetic and reading. Use activities with the child that involve counting: "Bring me one cup and two plates. Put the napkin next to one plate." Have the child repeat the instructions and match the items to the number you requested. • Have the child match letters to items in the room that begin with that letter, such as *l* for lamp and *p* for pencil. Make sure the child repeats the letter and the word aloud and walks or points to the object. • Move on to activities that involve patterns and sequence. Posters, checkers, dominoes, and playing cards are strong symbols of patterns and sequence. The child doesn't have to learn the game to be able to identify patterns and sequences in the game pieces.
6. Provide a print-rich home and school environment	• Children with oral language difficulties are very likely to have problems learning to read. The sooner they can make connections between oral language and the written word, the better. Other media, such as videotapes, audiotapes, and the computer, can help with the effort of learning to read by making it fun and worthwhile. • Keep television watching to a minimum.

STRATEGIES TO CONSIDER

Teaching Other Languages to Students With Language Disabilities

Research studies are identifying the problems students with language disabilities have while acquiring another language. Armed with this knowledge, we can design instructional approaches that address the underlying causes and increase the chances for student success. Specifically, two successful approaches to second-language instruction for students with language disabilities emerged from the work of Ganschow and Sparks (1995).

　　1. The Phonological Deficits Approach. This approach springs from the notion that most students having difficulty in acquiring another language have phonological deficits in their native (first) language. Consequently, the following guidelines are suggested:

- **Teach the sound system of the second language explicitly.** The Orton-Gillingham method (explained in Ganschow and Sparks, 1995) is a particularly effective way to accomplish this. This method presents sounds in a highly structured fashion, accompanied by considerable visual, kinesthetic, and tactile practice and input. Studies using this method showed that students who were taught phonological skills in one language had improved their phonological awareness in English as well.

- **Teach the fundamentals of phonology in the student's native language before beginning instruction in the other language.** This step helps to address the students' native-language deficits, which we already noted as necessary for success in acquiring the other language. Here students are taught to recognize phonemes, to read words efficiently, and to apply the sounds to the written language. They are learning the sounds and components of language structure and how these sounds and components are manipulated for meaning.

- **Apply the fundamentals of phonology to the other language.** In this step, the sounds and components of the other language are identified. The students can then transfer the knowledge they have about phonology from their first language to the other language.

　　2. The Course Adaptation Approach. This approach adapts other language courses to conform to those principles of instruction suitable for students with learning disabilities. It can be done in two ways:

- **Changing the instructional strategies.** Teachers in these courses reduce the syllabus to the essential components, slow the pace of instruction, reduce the vocabulary demand, provide constant review and practice, and incorporate as many multisensory activities as possible.

o **Design courses to address specific deficits.** Courses can be adapted to respond to the specific requests of the students who are having difficulties in their second-language classes. For example, one course might be designed for students who are strong in listening and speaking skills but weak in reading and writing, while another course might be more appropriate for students whose skills are in the reverse order.

For either of these approaches to work effectively, students need to undergo a realistic assessment of their language learning problems. It becomes important to ensure that the learning environment is consistent with students' needs. For example, a student who is able to do oral language well should not be placed in a situation where passing grammar and translation tests is the main requirement. Nor should a student who reads and translates proficiently be placed with a teacher who values pronunciation and conversation. Reasonable accommodations need to be made.

It is perhaps unrealistic to assume that most high schools have the capacity or will to offer second-language classes solely to students with language disabilities. And even if the will were there, finding teachers who are trained in the methods of instruction for these students might be more of a problem. Nonetheless, the purpose of this book is to identify what current research is telling us about the learning process and to suggest ways of providing instructional settings that translate the research into educational practice.

Chapter 5

Reading Disabilities

Renewed emphasis in recent years on improving the basic skills of students has increased pressure to start reading instruction sooner than ever before. In many schools, reading instruction starts in kindergarten. Some neuropsychologists are now debating whether kindergartners are developmentally ready for this challenging task. Are we creating problems for these children by trying to get them to read before their brains are ready? Because boys' brains are physiologically one or two years less mature than girls' brains at this age, are boys at greater risk of failure? To answer these questions, let's examine what researchers have discovered about how the brain learns to read and the problems that can develop. Much of what follows in this chapter is a condensed version of the in-depth discussions of reading and reading difficulties that are explained in Sousa (2005), although new information and references have been added where appropriate.

LEARNING TO READ

Is Reading a Natural Ability?

Not really. The brain's ability to acquire spoken language with amazing speed and accuracy is the result of genetic hardwiring and specialized cerebral areas that focus on this task. But there are no areas of the brain that specialize in reading. In fact, reading is probably the most difficult task we ask the young brain to undertake. Reading is a relatively new phenomenon in the development of humans. As far as we know, the genes have not incorporated reading into their coded structure, probably because reading—unlike spoken language—has not emerged over time as a survival skill.

Many cultures (but not all) do emphasize reading as an important form of communication and insist it be taught to their children. And so the struggle begins. To get that brain to read, here's what we are saying, for example, to the English-speaking child: "That language you have been speaking quite correctly for the past few years can be represented by abstract symbols called the *alphabet*. We are going to disrupt that sophisticated spoken language protocol you have already developed and ask you to reorganize it to accommodate these symbols, which, by the way, are not very reliable. There are lots of exceptions, but you'll just have to adjust." Some children—perhaps 50 percent—make this adjustment with relative ease once exposed to formal instruction. It appears, however, that for the other 50 percent, reading is a much more formidable task, and for about 20 to 30 percent, it definitely becomes the most difficult task they will ever undertake in their young lives.

> *Reading is probably the most difficult task for the young brain to do.*

Spoken Language and Reading

Before children learn to read, they acquire vocabulary by listening to others and by practicing the pronunciation and usage of new words in conversation. Adult correction and other sources help to fine-tune this basic vocabulary (called the *mental lexicon*). Children with language impairments are at risk for problems when learning to read. A longitudinal study showed that children with language impairment in kindergarten were at high risk for reading disabilities in second and fourth grades. Figure 5.1 shows that the risk was higher for children with nonspecific language impairment (those with nonverbal and language deficits) than for children with specific language impairment (those with deficits in language alone). Children with language impairment in kindergarten who had improved their spoken language abilities by second and fourth grades had better reading outcomes than those with persistent language impairments (Catts, Fey, Tomblin, & Zhang, 2002).

Because the ability to read is so strongly dependent on the word forms learned during this period, a child's beginning reading will be more successful if most of the reading material contains words the child is already using. The phoneme-grapheme connection can be made more easily. Reading, of course, also adds new words to the child's mental lexicon. Consequently, there must be some neural connections between the systems that allow the brain to recognize spoken words and the system that recognizes written words.

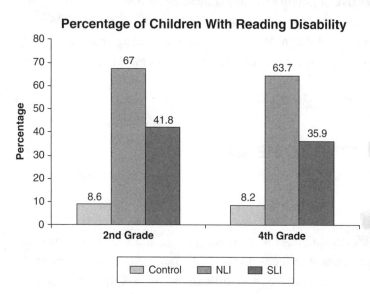

Percentage of Children With Reading Disability

Figure 5.1   The graph shows the percentage of children in the control, nonspecific language impairment (NLI), and specific language impairment (SLI) groups meeting the criterion for reading disability in second and fourth grades (adapted from Catts et al., 2002).

Late-Talking Toddlers

If spoken language ability is closely related to success in early reading, are late-talking toddlers (ages 24–32 months) likely to be slower in developing their reading skills? Probably so. Research studies seem to indicate that late-talking toddlers have average reading skills at age 6 or 7, but are slightly less skilled in reading at ages 8 and 9 (Rescorla, 2002). At age 13, late talkers also score lower than their peers in vocabulary, grammar, verbal memory, and reading comprehension (Rescorla, 2005). These findings suggest that slower spoken language development at an early age indicates a predisposition for slower acquisition of other language-related skills, including reading. The good news is that early intervention procedures while the late talker is age 2 appear to help language skill development (Kouri, 2005).

Decoding and Comprehension

Put very simply, successful reading involves two basic operations: *decoding* and *comprehension.* Learning to read starts with the awareness that speech is composed of individual sounds (phonemes) and a recognition that written spellings represent those sounds (called *the alphabetic principle*). Of course, to be successful in acquiring the alphabetic principle, the child has to be aware of how the phonemes of spoken language can be manipulated to form new words and rhymes. The neural systems that perceive the phonemes in our language are more efficient in some children than in others. Just because some children have difficulty understanding that spoken words are composed of discrete sounds doesn't mean that they have brain damage or dysfunction. The individual differences that underlie the efficiency with which one learns to read can be seen in the acquisition of other skills, such as learning to play a musical instrument, playing a sport, or building a model.

> *Put very simply, reading involves two basic operations: decoding and comprehension.*

Phonological and Phonemic Awareness

Phonological awareness is the recognition that oral language can be divided into smaller components, such as sentences into words, words into syllables and, ultimately, into individual phonemes. This recognition includes identifying and manipulating onsets and rimes as well as having an awareness of alliteration, rhyming, syllabication, and intonation. (Onsets are the initial consonants that change the meaning of a word; rimes are the vowel-consonant combinations that stay constant in a series. For example, in *bark, dark,* and *park,* the onsets are *b, d,* and *p;* the rime is *-ark.*) Being phonologically aware means having an understanding of all these levels. In children, phonological awareness usually starts with initial sounds and rhyming and a recognition that sentences can be segmented into words. Next comes segmenting words into syllables and blending syllables into words.

Phonemic awareness is a subdivision of phonological awareness and refers to the understanding that words are made up of individual sounds (phonemes) and that these sounds can be manipulated to create new words. It includes the ability to isolate a phoneme (first, middle, or last) from the rest of the word, to segment words into their component phonemes, and to delete a specific phoneme from a word. Children with phonemic awareness know that the word *cat* is made up of three phonemes, and that the words *dog* and *mad* both contain the phoneme */d/.*

Phonemic awareness is different from *phonics.* Phonemic awareness involves the auditory and *oral* manipulation of sounds. A child demonstrates phonemic awareness by knowing all the sounds that make up the word *cat.* Phonics is an instructional approach that builds on the alphabetic principle and associates letters and sounds with *written* symbols. To demonstrate phonics knowledge, a child tells the teacher which *letter* is needed to change *cat* to *can.* Although phonemic awareness and phonics are closely related, they are not the same. It is possible for a child to have phonemic awareness in speech without having much experience with written letters or names. Conversely, a child may provide examples of letter-sound relationships without ever developing phonemic awareness. In fact, simply learning these letter-sound relationships during phonics instruction does not necessarily lead to phonemic awareness (Chard & Dickson, 1999).

> *Simply learning letter-sound relationships during phonics instruction does not necessarily lead to phonemic awareness.*

Phonemic Awareness and Learning to Read

New readers must learn the alphabetic principle and recognize that words can be separated into individual phonemes, which can be reordered and blended into words. This enables learners to associate the letters with sounds in order to read and build words. Thus, phonemic awareness in kindergarten is a strong predictor of reading success that persists throughout school. Early instruction in reading, especially in letter-sound association, strengthens phonological awareness and helps in the development of the more sophisticated phonemic awareness.

Sounds to Letters (Phonemes to Graphemes)

To be able to read, the brain must memorize a set of arbitrary squiggles (the alphabet) and identify which symbols, called *graphemes,* correspond to the phonemes already stored in the mental lexicon. Many European languages use abstract letters (i.e., an alphabetic system) to represent their sounds so that the words can be spelled out in writing. The rules of spelling that govern a language are called its *orthography.* How closely a language's orthography actually represents the pronunciation of the phoneme can determine how quickly one learns to read that language correctly. Some languages, like Spanish, Italian, and Finnish, have a very close correspondence between letters and the sounds they represent. This is known as a *shallow* orthography. Once the rules of orthography in these languages are learned, a person can usually spell a new word correctly the first time because there are so few exceptions.

English, on the other hand, often has a poor correspondence between how a word is pronounced and how it is spelled. This is called a *deep* orthography. It exists because English does not have an alphabet that permits an ideal one-to-one correspondence between its phonemes and its graphemes. Consider that just when the beginning readers think they know what letter represents a phoneme sound, they discovers that the same symbol can have different sounds, such as the *a*'s in *cat* and in *father.* Consider, too, how the pronunciation of the following English words differs, even though they all have the same last four letters,

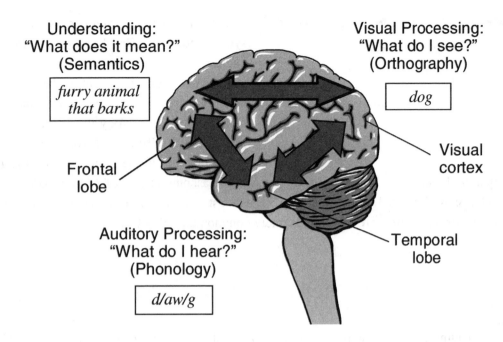

Figure 5.2 Successful reading requires the coordination of three neural systems: visual processing to see the word, auditory processing to hear it in the brain, and executive system processing for understanding.

and in the same sequence: *bough, cough, dough, rough* and *through*. This lack of sound-to-letter correspondence makes it difficult for the young brain to recognize patterns and affects the child's ability to spell with accuracy and to read with meaning. Eventually, the brain must connect the 26 letters of the alphabet (graphemes) to the 44-plus sounds of spoken English (phonemes) that the child has been using successfully for years. But it is not easy. You may be surprised to learn that because of the complexity of English orthography, there are more than 1,100 ways to spell the sounds of the 44 phonemes in English.

Learning to read, therefore, starts with phoneme awareness, a recognition that written spellings represent sounds and that this combination applies phonics to the reading and spelling of words. These skills are necessary but not sufficient to learn to read the English language with meaning. The reader must acquire vocabulary and also become proficient in grasping larger units of print, such as syllable patterns, whole words, and phrases. The ultimate goal of reading is for children to become sufficiently fluent to understand what they read. This understanding includes literal comprehension as well as more sophisticated reflective understandings, such as "Why am I reading this?" and "What is the author's point?" (Snow, Burns, & Griffin, 1998). It is no accident, then, that the National Reading Panel recommended that beginning reading programs include components that develop phonemic awareness, phonics, vocabulary, fluency, and comprehension (NRP, 2000).

The Neural Systems Involved in Reading

Successful decoding and comprehension in reading require the coordination of three neural networks (Figure 5.2): visual processing (orthography), phoneme recognition (phonology), and word interpretation (semantics). For example, in reading the word *dog*, the optic nerves send signals to the visual cortex, and the

> *Decoding and comprehension involve the coordination of three neural networks: visual processing, phoneme recognition, and word interpretation.*

visual processing system puts the alphabetic symbols together. The decoding process alerts the auditory processing system that recognizes the alphabetic symbols representing the sound "d/aw/g." Other brain regions, such as Broca's and Wernicke's areas, are coordinated by the frontal lobe for comprehension. If all systems work correctly, a mental image emerges in the mind's eye of a furry animal that barks (Gaillard, Naccache, Pinel, Clémenceau, Volle, Hasboun, et al., 2006; McCandliss, Cohen, & Dehaene, 2003; Shaywitz, 2003). Problems can occur almost anywhere in the system. Many variations of reading disorders exist, but here are some of the more common ones that teachers encounter.

DIFFICULTIES IN LEARNING TO READ

Difficulties in reading result essentially from environmental or physical factors, or some combination of both. Environmental factors are often social and cultural and include limited exposure to language in the preschool years (resulting in little phoneme sensitivity), clashes of language in the household, letter knowledge, print awareness, vocabulary, and reading comprehension. Physical factors include speech, hearing, and visual impairments and substandard intellectual capabilities. Any combination of environmental and physical factors makes diagnosis and treatment more difficult. Brain imaging technology, however, is showing great promise as a tool for diagnosing reading and language difficulties.

Social and Cultural Causes of Reading Problems

A large number of Black and Hispanic children who are performing poorly in reading display no signs of specific learning impairments. Clearly other factors are at work. Multiple studies have identified social conditions that have an impact on the achievement of children in inner-city schools. Limited teacher training, large class sizes, the absence of literature in the home, and poor parental support for schools have all been cited as causes for lack of student progress. Although these conditions cannot be ignored, schools need to focus more on the direct connections between what we are learning about how the brain learns to read and the *linguistic* barriers interfering with that learning.

Some researchers believe that these children are performing poorly on reading tests because their home language differs substantially from the language used in reading instruction (Labov, 2003). Black children, for example, were being immersed in a language dialect that has become known as African-American English (AAE). Residential desegregation has increased the impact of AAE (Bailey, 1993; Craig, Thompson, Washington, & Potter, 2003). Meanwhile, as Spanish-speaking populations increase, children are faced with learning to read English in school while speaking Spanish at home.

Consequently, some of the causes of poor performance by Black and Hispanic children can be attributed to impediments resulting from linguistic differences. That is, their native dialect or language is different in significant ways from what is being taught in school. They come to school with a mental lexicon whose word representations often do not match what they are trying to decode on the printed page. Learning to read

involves determining which words *are* present in
their mental lexicon, what they represent, and
whether they can be comprehended in context. This
is not a physiological deficit; it is a social and cultural problem. For these children, we should not be
looking at what is wrong with them but how we can
alter instruction to make them more successful in
learning to read. Such alterations can be made when
teachers of reading are properly trained to recognize when a child's reading problems are the result of
linguistic clashes and not a pathology. Furthermore, that training should help teachers understand how they
can use some of the linguistic attributes of AAE and Spanish to help children pronounce, decode, and understand standard English.

> *Teachers of reading should be
> trained to recognize when a child's
> reading problems are the result of
> linguistic clashes and not a
> pathology.*

Physical Causes of Reading Problems

Recent research into the causes and nature of reading problems has revealed more about the neural
processes involved in reading. Recall that successful reading involves two basic processes—decoding and
comprehension—that are generated by three neural systems (Figure 5.2). Problems with any one or more of
these systems can cause reading difficulties. In some children, the problems occur during early brain development and affect their ability to process the sounds of language and, eventually, to decode written text. This
developmental deficit appears to be the most common cause of reading difficulties, and usually results in a
lifelong struggle with reading. Less common are problems with reading caused by impairments in hearing
and vision that can occur at any time in a person's life.

Most research studies on reading have focused primarily on developmental reading problems that scientists refer to as *developmental dyslexia.* In developmental dyslexia, the child experiences unexpected difficulty in learning to read despite adequate intelligence, environment, and normal senses. It is a spectrum
disorder, varying from mild to severe. Neuroimaging studies have established that there are significant differences in the way typical brains and brains with dyslexia respond to specific spoken and written language
tasks. Furthermore, there is evidence that these differences may weaken with appropriate instructional
interventions.

Scientists have long been searching for the causes of reading problems. This has not been an easy task
because of the large number of sensory, motor, and cognitive systems that are involved in reading. Struggling
readers may have impairments in any one or more of these systems, but not all struggling readers have
dyslexia. Specifically, dyslexia seems to be caused by deficits in the neural regions responsible for language
and phonological processing or by problems in nonlinguistic areas of the brain.

Linguistic Causes

Several potential linguistic causes of developmental dyslexia that have emerged from recent research
studies, including phonological deficits, differences in auditory and visual processing speeds, the varying
sizes of brain structures, memory deficits, genetics, brain lesions, and word-blindness. It is possible that
several of these causes are related to each other and can coexist in the same individual.

- **Phonological deficits.** The ability to sound out words in one's head plays an important role in reading familiar words and sounding out new ones. Phonological information is used by the working memory to integrate and comprehend words in phrases and sentences. Extensive evidence has existed for decades that phonological operations are impaired in many individuals with dyslexia (Harm & Seidenberg, 1999). But the causes of the impairment were not clear. Because many people with dyslexia have normal or above normal intelligence, researchers suspected that the phonological processing deficits appeared only when the brain was trying to decode writing. Exactly why that happens is not fully known. However, studies of the differences in auditory and visual processing speeds as well as fMRI scans of the brain during reading are shedding new light on the possible causes of the phonological impairments.

- **Differences in auditory and visual processing speeds.** One of the more intriguing explanations of some reading difficulties, including dyslexia, has come from research studies using magnetoencephalography (MEG), a technique for measuring the electric signals emitted during brain activation as a result of mental processing. These studies noted abnormal auditory activation but normal visual activation during reading (Helenius, Salmelin, Richardson, Leinonen, & Lyytinen, 2002; Renvall & Hari, 2002; Tallal, et al., 1996; Temple, et al., 2003). Sometimes referred to as *temporal processing impairment,* the differences in the processing speeds could explain some of the symptoms common to dyslexia.

The explanation goes like this: When reading silently, our eyes scan the words on the page (visual processing), and we sound out those words in our head. To read successfully, the visual and auditory processing systems have to work together, that is, be in synchrony. When a child begins to learn to read, it is essential that the letter (grapheme) the child sees corresponds to what the child hears (phoneme) internally. In Figure 5.3, the child with normal auditory processing (left) is looking at the letter *d* and the auditory processing system is simultaneously sounding out /d/ or *duh.* As the eye moves to *o,* the phoneme /ô/ or *awh* will sound out and then *g* produces the phoneme /g/ or *guh.* Later, when this child is asked to write *dog,* the /d/ phoneme will recall the letter *d,* and so on.

However, if the auditory processing system is impaired and lags behind the visual processing system, then the child's eye is already scanning the letter *g* while the phoneme /d/ or *duh* is still being processed in the auditory system. As a result, the child's brain incorrectly associates the letter *g* with the phoneme sound of /d/ or *duh.* Now, when we ask the child to write the word *dog,* the child hears the first phoneme /d/ or *duh* but incorrectly recalls letter *g,* perhaps eventually writing the word *god.*

If this notion is correct, then finding a way to bring the auditory and visual processing systems in closer synchrony should help to remedy the problem. That is exactly what several researchers

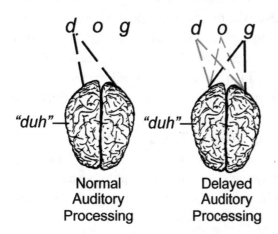

Figure 5.3 In normal auditory processing (left), the phoneme that the child hears correctly matches the letter that the eyes see—in this case, the sound "duh" corresponds to the letter "d." If the auditory processing system is delayed, however, the child's eyes are already on the letter "g" while the "duh" phoneme is still sounding in the child's head. The brain errs in matching "duh" with "g."

tried. They developed a computer program, known as *Fast ForWord,* designed to help poor readers slow down visual processing to allow the auditory processing sufficient time to recognize the sound of the initial phoneme. Using this program with children who had reading problems produced surprisingly successful results.

- **Structural differences in the brain.** Some MRI studies have found that the brains of people diagnosed with dyslexia are structurally different from typical brains. In one study, the researchers noted that the brains of 16 men with dyslexia had less gray matter (surface of the cerebrum) in the left temporal lobe, the frontal lobe, and cerebellum than the brains of 14 control subjects (Brown, et al., 2001). Having less gray matter (and thus fewer neurons) in the left temporal lobe (where Wernicke's area is located) and in the frontal lobe (where comprehension occurs) could contribute to the deficits associated with dyslexia.

- **Working memory deficits.** Skilled reading requires an ability to retain verbal bits of information (phonemes) in working memory. Recent studies have shown distinct deficits among poor readers in this component of working memory, called phonologic memory. The deficits more commonly involve serial tasks, such as holding a string of phonemes to make a word and a sequence of words to generate a sentence (Howes, Bigler, Burlingame, & Lawson, 2003). Studies also indicate deficits in visual-spatial memory, suggesting that poor readers have difficulty retaining the mental picture of the written word as well as the sounds (Gathercole, Alloway, Willis, & Adams, 2006).

- **Genetics and gender.** Studies of genetic composition have shown strong associations between dyslexia and genetic mutations in twins and families, and recent investigations seem to have actually identified some of the specific genes involved. Researchers have

> *Boys tend to be overidentified with reading problems; girls, on the other hand, tend to be underidentified.*

noted that a missing stretch of DNA in the gene called DCDC2 is strongly correlated with severe reading disability (Kaminen, et al., 2003; Schumacher, et al., 2006). Other genes are likely involved. Thus, dyslexia is a lifelong condition and not just a "phase." The genetic mutations could impede the development of systems that the typical brain utilizes to decode written text, forcing the brain to construct alternate and less efficient pathways. Nationwide, there are about three times more boys identified with reading problems than girls. Although this was once thought to be almost totally the result of genetic deficits, the true reason may be because boys are overidentified (often due to their rambunctious behavior) and girls are underidentified (sit quietly in class and obey the rules). Recent studies indicate that many girls are affected as well but are not getting help they need (Shaywitz, 2003).

- **Lesions in the word form area.** Researchers using PET scans have noticed that some people with developmental dyslexia have lesions in the left occipito-temporal area of the brain. This area is identified as the word form area most used by skilled readers to decode written text. Another discovery in these studies was that the amount of blood flowing to this brain region predicted the severity of the dyslexia (Rumsey, et al., 1999). Regardless of the cause, a lesion and reduced blood flow would likely hamper the ability of this patch of neurons to decode written text.

- **Word-blindness.** Word-blindness is the inability to read words even though the person's eyes are optically normal. Two forms exist: *Congenital word-blindness* involves a glitch in the wiring of neurons during embryonic development and is usually confined to those neural systems associated with reading. This disorder may go unnoticed for years, affecting reading and occasionally spoken language. *Acquired word-blindness* results from some traumatic event in the brain, such as a stroke or a tumor, occurring during a person's lifetime and interfering with already established systems. The damaged area is usually on the left side of the brain, causing weakness in the right side of the body and difficulty pronouncing words or naming objects (Shaywitz, 2003).

Nonlinguistic Causes

Some people, who are otherwise unimpaired have extreme difficulties in reading because of deficits in auditory and visual perception not related to linguistic systems. This revelation was somewhat of a surprise because conventional wisdom held that impairments in reading (and also in oral language) were restricted to problems with linguistic processing. The following are some possible nonlinguistic causes found in the research literature.

- **Perception of sequential sounds.** The inability to detect and discriminate sounds presented in rapid succession seems to be a common impairment in individuals with reading and language disorders. These individuals also have difficulty in indicating the order of two sounds presented in rapid succession. This particular deficit is related to auditory processing of sound waves in general and is not related directly to distinguishing phonemes as part of phonological processing. Hearing words accurately when reading or from a stream of rapid conversation is critical to comprehension (Wright, Bowen, & Zecker, 2000).

- **Sound-frequency discrimination.** Some individuals with reading disorders are impaired in their ability to hear differences in sound frequency. This auditory defect can affect the ability to discriminate tone and pitch in speech. At first glance, this may seem like only an oral language-related impairment. However, it also affects reading proficiency because reading involves sounding out words in the auditory processing system (Wright et al., 2000).

- **Detection of target sounds in noise.** The inability to detect tones within noise is another recently discovered nonlinguistic impairment. When added to the findings in the two deficits mentioned above, this evidence suggests that auditory functions may play a much greater role in reading disorders than previously thought (Wright et al., 2000).

- **Visual magnocellular-deficit hypothesis.** The interpretation of some research studies has led to a hypothesis that certain forms of reading disorders are caused by a deficit in the visual processing system, which leads to poor detection of coherent visual motion and poor discrimination of the speed of visual motion. This part of the visual system involves large neurons and so is referred to as the magnocellular system. Impairment in this system may cause letters on a page to bundle and overlap, or appear to move—common complaints from some struggling readers and those with dyslexia (Demb, Boynton, & Heeger, 1998). Other scientists, however, question this interpretation of the research mainly because it is not known how the visual impairments relate to the phonological impairments (Amitay, Ben-Yehudah, Banai, & Ahissar, 2002). Current evidence suggests that visual impairments by themselves are a very small part of dyslexia (Rayner, et al., 2001).

- **Motor coordination and the cerebellum.** Several imaging studies have shown that many readers with dyslexia have processing deficits in the cerebellum of the brain (Nicolson, Fawcett, & Dean,

2001). Another study determined that nearly 75 percent of the subjects with dyslexia had smaller lobes on the right side of the cerebellum than control participants (Eckert, et al., 2003). The cerebellum is located at the rear of the brain just below the occipital lobe (see Chapter 1). It is mainly responsible for coordinating learned motor skills. Deficiencies in this part of the brain could result, according to researchers, in problems with reading, writing, and spelling. Problems in reading may result if cerebellar deficits delay the time when an infant sits up and walks and begins babbling and talking. Less motor skill coordination can mean less articulation and fluency in speech. This, in turn, leads to less sensitivity to onset, rime, and the phonemic structure of language.

The possibility of deficits in visual and auditory perception and memory as well as in motor coordination on various reading tasks accounts for the wide range of individual differences observed among those with reading disorders. Analyzing these differences leads to a better understanding of the multidimensional nature of reading disorders and possible treatment.

Is Dyslexia Present in Readers of Other Languages?

Dyslexia appears in all languages, including those that are read from right to left, such as Hebrew and Arabic. People with dyslexia who speak highly phonetic languages, such as Spanish and Finnish, are identified with the disorder later than those who speak deep morphological languages such as English, where the linguistic demands of the language are more challenging. The key seems to be the degree to which there is a one-to-one correspondence between letters and sounds. Italians with dyslexia, for example, have an easier time because there are only 25 letters or combination of letters to represent Italian's 33 phonemes. French people with dyslexia have more difficulty because the 32 phonemes in French can be represented by about 250 letter combinations. But English, as we noted earlier, has more than 1,100 ways to spell its 44 phonemes and English speakers experience this complex phonetic structure early on in their schooling (Paulesu, et al., 2001).

Readers can also experience difficulties in logographic languages, such as Chinese, which use complex symbols to represent words. Brain imaging studies seem to indicate that readers of logographic languages use different neural regions to decode the meaning of symbols because of the added visual processing involved compared to alphabet-based languages. Deficits in these brain areas lead to visual confusion, probably due to poor visual-spatial memory. Chinese individuals with dyslexia thus have difficulty converting symbols into meanings, not letters into sounds. These findings imply that dyslexia may not have a universal origin in all humans, but that the biological abnormality of impaired reading is dependent on culture (Ho, Chan, Lee, Tsang, & Luan, 2004; Siok, Perfetti, Jin, & Tan, 2004).

Brain Imaging Studies and Dyslexia

Brain imaging technologies are of two kinds: those that look at the structure of the brain (e.g., MRI and CAT scans) and those that look at how the brain functions (e.g., PET and fMRI scans). In recent years, these scans have revealed differences in both the structure and function of brains with dyslexia compared to typical brains. Eventually, these types of investigations may lead to more accurate diagnosis and treatment.

Some Indicators of Dyslexia
(Few individuals exhibit all symptoms.)

- Difficulty recognizing written words
- Difficulty rhyming or sequencing syllables
- Difficulty determining the meaning or main idea of a simple sentence
- Difficulty encoding words—spelling
- Poor sequencing of letters or numbers
- Delayed spoken language
- Difficulty separating the sounds in spoken words
- Difficulty in expressing thoughts verbally
- Confusion about right- or left-handedness
- Difficulty with handwriting
- Possible family history of dyslexia

Studies of Brain Structure

MRI studies that have compared the brain structure of individuals with dyslexia to typical readers have found some interesting differences. These differences were more evident in individuals with dyslexia who had early spoken-language problems than in those with dyslexia whose speech progressed normally. The regions of the brain that showed structural variations were consistent across multiple MRI studies and were closely associated with those neural areas involved in spoken-language processing. The implication here is that an individual with atypical brain structures that hamper speech is likely to have difficulties in learning to read as well (Leonard, 2001).

Imaging studies also reveal that the brains of struggling readers are more likely to have fewer neural connections than typical readers in the white matter (the part below the surface's gray matter cortex) in an area spanning portions of the left temporal and parietal lobes. This region is activated during reading, and the decreased connectivity may lead to poorer reading ability (Beaulieu et al., 2005; Niogi & McCandliss, 2006).

Studies of Brain Function

Newer research in brain function is shedding more light on dyslexia. Because children with dyslexia often confused *b* and *d*, psychologists thought for many years that dyslexia was merely a vision problem. Researchers now believe that the letters can also be confused because they sound alike. This is the brain's inability to process what it hears, not what it sees. Other imaging studies show an imperfectly functioning system for dividing words into their phonological units—a critical step for accurate reading. Letter reversals can be the result of phonological missteps in the decoding of print to sound and back to print. It is likely that the learner has problems in assigning what he says or hears in his head (the phoneme) to the letters he sees on paper (the grapheme). Thus, remedial strategies should focus on reestablishing correct phonemic connections with intense practice.

Numerous functional imaging studies clearly indicate that poor readers use different brain pathways than typical readers. Good readers of all ages rely more on an area in the left rear of the brain called the occipito-temporal area. This region decodes word forms and requires only a little input from Broca's area (white area in left frontal lobe in Figure 5.4). By using just these three left-side areas, the ability of typical readers to recognize word forms, with practice, is automatic, and their reading becomes fluent.

The studies further show that readers with dyslexia at an early age do not use the word processing regions in the left rear part of the brain. Rather, they rely more on Broca's area for decoding text. This reliance increases with age so that, as adolescents, they are overactivating Broca's area and recruiting other

Reader With Dyslexia

Good Reader

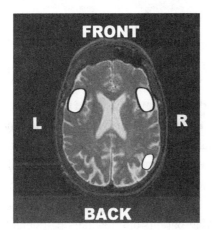 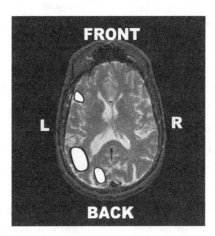

Figure 5.4 The brain regions that are activated during reading are shown as white areas in these representative fMRI scans. Readers with dyslexia (left) use different brain regions during reading than do good readers (right). Note that readers with dyslexia show little activation in the back of the brain but strong activation in the front regions, especially in Broca's area (front left hemisphere). Good readers, on the other hand, show strong activation in the back of the brain with lesser activation in the front (Shaywitz, 2003).

frontal regions as they try to read. Apparently, the increased use of frontal brain areas is an attempt to compensate for the disruptions in the rear of the brain. In the cross-sectional picture in Figure 5.4, note how during reading the brain of a reader with dyslexia activates an area in the right frontal lobe—used primarily for visual memory—in addition to Broca's area. But rote-based learning of words can get a reader only so far before the memory systems begin to fail. This overreliance on memory results in slow and laborious reading because the disruption in the rear brain areas prohibits automatic word recognition (Byring, Haapasalo, & Salmi, 2004; Richards, 2001; Shaywitz & Shaywitz, 2005; Simos, Breier, Fletcher, Mergman, & Papanicolaou, 2000). Functional imaging studies of adults with dyslexia, including high-achieving university students, reveal this same pattern of strong frontal area use during reading (Shaywitz, 2003).

The results of the numerous imaging studies seem clear: Good readers use left-side posterior areas of the brain for rapid, automatic decoding and reading. Readers with dyslexia, on the other hand, develop an alternative system that uses left and right frontal areas of the brain, often resulting in accurate but slow reading. Moreover, brains with dyslexia are working harder during reading—that is, employing more neurons—than the brains of good readers (Brun et al., 2003), and there are also differences in how they process phonemes (Stanberry et al., 2006). These different patterns between good readers and those with dyslexia are so consistent that neuroscientists believe that functional imaging may one day allow for early detection of dyslexia, perhaps even before a child begins to learn to read.

The different brain scan patterns between good readers and readers with dyslexia are so consistent that they may one day allow for early diagnosis, perhaps even before a child begins to read.

DETECTING READING PROBLEMS

In recent years, researchers have made significant progress using fMRI scans to understand how novice, skilled, and dyslexic brains read. Yet, despite these advancements, fMRI scans are not a practical tool at present for diagnosing dyslexia in a single individual. That is because the results of fMRI studies are usually reported for groups rather than for individuals. Researchers have found some variations in the activated areas of the brain among individuals within both the dyslexic and control groups. More research is needed to clarify these differences before fMRI or any other imaging techniques can be used for diagnostic purposes (Richards, 2001). Until that time, however, researchers can use the information gained from imaging studies to develop other kinds of diagnostic tests that more closely align with our new understanding of dyslexia.

For the moment, critical observation of a child's progress in learning to speak, and eventually in learning to read, remains our most effective tool for spotting potential problems. Most difficulties associated with reading do not go away with time. Therefore, the earlier that parents and teachers can detect reading problems in children, the better. The problems often begin to reveal themselves first in spoken language and later while children are learning to read.

Spoken Language Difficulties

Learning to read is closely connected to fluency in spoken language. Both speaking and reading rely on the proper functioning of the phonologic module, that brain region where sounds are combined to form words and words are broken down into their basic sounds. Consequently, difficulties that children have with spoken language are often clues to potential reading problems. Parents and teachers should remember that it is normal for all children to make occasional language errors while speaking. But frequent language errors, stemming from any one or a combination of the following conditions, could indicate that a child may run into trouble when beginning to learn to read. Some of the spoken language difficulties may involve any one or more of the following (IDA, 2003; NAEYC, 1998; Shaywitz, 2003):

- **Delay in speaking.** Children generally say their first words at about 12 months of age and follow with phrases when between 18 and 24 months old. Because learning to read is closely linked to a child's phonologic skills in spoken language, delays in speaking may be an early indication of potential reading problems, especially in a family that has a history of dyslexia.
- **Difficulties with pronunciation.** Children should have little difficulty pronouncing words correctly by 5 or 6 years of age. Difficulties in pronouncing words (sometimes referred to as "baby talk") may be an indication of future reading problems. Such trouble pronouncing long or complicated words could signal a snag in the parts of the brain that generate spoken language, causing a mix-up in the processing of the phonemes. Mispronunciations often involve mixing syllables within words (*aminal* for animal) and leaving off the beginning syllables (*luminum* for aluminum).
- **Difficulty in learning the letters of the alphabet.** Learning the names of the letters of the alphabet is an important, though not essential, step in learning to read. Marked difficulties in learning the letters could indicate a potential reading problem.
- **Recalling incorrect phonemes.** A child looks at a picture of a donkey and recalls the word *doggie,* a word similar in sound but not in meaning. This recall of incorrect phonemes may cause a child to

talk about a word without actually recalling it. The child may get frustrated because of the inability to say the word. As these children get older, they may resort more to vague words in order to mask their difficulties in retrieving specific words. They use general words like things and stuff, making their conversations hard to follow. It is important to remember that the problem here is not with their thinking but with their ability to use expressive language, that is, to recall a word on command.

- **Insensitivity to rhyme.** Part of a young child's enjoyment of spoken language is playing with rhyme. Hearing and repeating rhyming sounds demonstrates how words can be separated into smaller segments of sound and that different words may share the same sound. Children with good rhyming skills are showing their readiness for learning to read. Those with little sensitivity to rhyme, on the other hand, may have reading problems because they are unable to detect the consonant sound that changes the meaning of closely rhyming words.

- **Genetics.** Looking at the family tree for signs of dyslexia in close relatives is a clue because about 25 to 50 percent of the children born to a parent with dyslexia will also carry the trait (Kaminen et al., 2003; Schumacher et al., 2006; Shaywitz, 2003). Whether the child actually displays dyslexia depends somewhat on that child's environment. This revelation came from studies of identical twins. Because they share the same genes, if one twin has dyslexia, so should the other. But in reality, in 30 to 35 percent of the cases, one twin has dyslexia while the other does not (Fisher & DeFries, 2002). Apparently, even though these children had a genetic predisposition for dyslexia, differences in the home and school environments played important roles in determining how successful these children would be at reading.

Early Indicators of Reading Problems

Until the time that brain imaging becomes a standard diagnostic tool, researchers will continue to look for ways to accurately identify students with reading problems as early as possible. Multiple research studies have sought to find indicators of reading problems that are more valid than solely the professional judgment of the evaluating team. The obvious problem here is that the application of professional judgment is only as good as the training and competence of the team members. This approach can often lead to considerable variability in identification from district to district and even from state to state. Using more objective measures would reduce this variability. Research studies have found that letter fluency is a useful measure in kindergarten, while response to instruction can be a valuable measure in second grade.

Even though children have a genetic predisposition for dyslexia, differences in the home and school environment can determine how successful these children will be at reading.

Letter Fluency Tasks as Kindergarten Indicators

The earlier that children who are at risk for reading problems can be identified, the better. Trying to carry out such identification procedures in kindergarten is difficult because of the broad range of background experience these children bring to the classroom. Nonetheless, studies involving kindergarten children do seem to indicate that letter-name fluency and nonsense-word fluency can be valid indicators of early reading skills, such as oral reading fluency (ORF).

One study tested 39 kindergartners in the spring in several language skill areas, including receptive vocabulary, phonological awareness, letter-name knowledge, letter-sound knowledge, letter-name fluency, and nonsense-word fluency (Speece & Mills, 2003). These same children were again tested one year later in first grade in similar skills, plus oral reading fluency. Nonsense-word fluency and letter-word fluency, respectively, were the highest predictors of oral reading fluency. In fact, the fluency measures were more accurate at predicting ORF than national normed measures of reading and phonological awareness, which identified only 33 percent of the poor readers in this study.

Using Response to Instruction as an Indicator in Second Grade

Another technique for avoiding the misidentification or nonidentification of students with reading problems is to place increased emphasis on measures of school performance. The response-to-instruction model (like the responsiveness to intervention model discussed in Chapter 2) identifies students based on low achievement, application of certain criteria for exclusion, and their response to interventions. Those who would be identified as having reading problems are children who did not respond to treatment and still display low achievement in reading, especially where the primary cause is not considered to be a social or economic disadvantage, mental deficiency, or linguistic and cultural diversity (Foorman & Ciancio, 2005).

Studies that tested this approach provided children in primary grades with incremental periods of instruction and moved them out when they made adequate progress. The instruction included fast-paced lessons that focused on phonemic awareness, phonics, fluency, comprehension, and spelling, with correction and feedback and many opportunities for reading practice. Students were tested periodically to determine if they met the exit criteria. Those who met the criteria were removed from the program, and those who did not received another round of supplemental instruction (Torgesen, 2001; Vaughn, Linan-Thompson, & Hickman, 2003).

The researchers suggested that using response to instruction (1) helps identify children who might be missed through other referral approaches, (2) provides supplemental instruction to a large number of at-risk students, (3) requires consistent monitoring of student progress, and (4) reduces the many biases inherent in the traditional referral systems that rely heavily on the interpretations and perceptions of classroom teachers. A longitudinal study of the response-to-instruction approach supports its validity (Case, Speece, & Molloy, 2003).

Persistent Reading Difficulties

Remember that all children make errors in spoken language and while reading. But the number of errors should decrease with time, and there should be clear evidence of growth in vocabulary and reading comprehension. Determining whether a child has consistent problems with reading requires careful and long-term observation of the child's fluency in speaking and reading. Most children display obvious improvements in their speaking and reading skills over time. Researchers, clinicians, and educators who study dyslexia and who work with poor readers look for certain clues that will show whether a child's reading ability is progressing normally.

WHAT EDUCATORS NEED TO CONSIDER

Because reading does not come naturally to the human brain, most children learning to read have to put much effort into associating their spoken language with the alphabet and with word recognition. If they are to do this successfully, their phonemic awareness is essential. Educators should give second thought to reading programs that delay phonemic awareness or that treat it as an ancillary skill to be learned in context with general reading. (For a comparison of the components of eight popular programs that address phonemic awareness, see Santi, Menchetti, & Edwards, 2004.) All teachers are teachers of reading, and thus should have the training to strengthen the reading skills of students at every grade level.

What Teachers Should Know About Teaching Reading

- How the brain learns to read
- The relationship between spoken language and reading
- Direct instruction in phonics
- Direct instruction in the alphabetic principle
- How to diagnose spelling and reading skills
- How to build vocabulary
- How to develop fluency and comprehension
- How to use a variety of reading intervention strategies

What Beginning Readers Need to Learn

- Phonological awareness: Rhyming, alliteration, deleting and substituting sounds, sound patterns
- Phonemic awareness: Segmenting words into individual sounds, manipulating phonemes
- Alphabetic principle: Correlating letter-sound patterns with specific text
- Orthographic awareness: Understanding spelling rules and writing conventions
- Comprehension monitoring strategies: Identifying the main idea, making inferences, using study skills that assist reading

Some Effective Reading Intervention Programs

Using Phonemic Awareness to Rewire Brains

Building Phonemic Awareness in Young Readers. Perhaps the most exciting news from neuroscience about reading has been the studies to determine whether such rewiring can occur as a result of using reading interventions. These imaging studies looked at children with difficult reading problems before and after they were subjected to an extensive phonologically based reading program. Figure 5.5 shows representative fMRI images before the interventions. Note the activation in the frontal areas of the brain typical of readers with

Changes in Brains of Struggling Readers

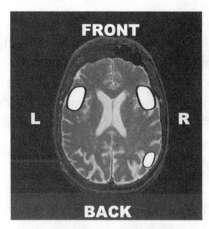

Before Reading
Interventions

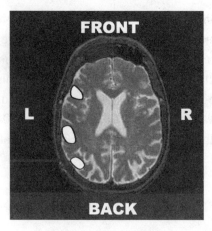

After Reading
Interventions

Figure 5.5   These representative scans show the changes evident in the brains of struggling readers about one year after their involvement with effective reading interventions. Note that the interventions have helped the children develop reading areas (shown in white) that more closely resemble the areas used by typical readers, as shown in Figure 5.4 (Shaywitz, 2003).

dyslexia. In a study sponsored by Syracuse University, specially trained teachers provided second-grade and third-grade struggling readers with 50 minutes of individualized tutoring daily in activities related to the alphabetic principle. The tutoring, which lasted eight months (105 hours) was in addition to the students' regular reading instruction. At the end of the yearlong intervention, all of the children improved their reading in varying degrees. The fMRI images taken immediately after the program showed the emergence of primary processing systems on the left side of the brain (like those used by good readers) in addition to the auxiliary pathways on the right side common to readers with dyslexia. Furthermore, one year after the program intervention, fMRIs indicated there was additional development of the primary neural systems on the left rear side of the brain while the right front areas were less prominent (Figure 5.5). In other words, the program intervention appeared to have rewired the brains of struggling readers to more closely approximate the reading circuitry in the brains of typical readers, resulting in accurate and *fluent* readers (Shaywitz, 2003; Shaywitz & Shaywitz, 2005).

Studies using fMRI indicate that intensive research-based interventions can change the brain processing of struggling readers to more closely match that of typical readers.

These and subsequent studies seem to indicate that research-based reading programs that use computers to help students build phonemic awareness can substantially—and perhaps permanently—benefit struggling readers. The changes due to remediation brought the brain function of children with dyslexia closer to that seen in children without reading problems. Apparently, the commonly observed dysfunction in the brains of children with dyslexia can be at least partially improved through programs that focus on auditory processing and oral language training, resulting in improved language and reading ability. Three effective computer programs are *Earobics* by Cognitive Concepts, Inc., *Fast ForWord* by the Scientific Learning Corporation, and the *Lindamood Phoneme Sequencing Program (LiPS)* by the Lindamood-Bell Learning Processes Company. See the **Resources** section for more information.

Reading Recovery

Started in 1984, Reading Recovery in the United States has served nearly 1.5 million children. This program is designed for the lowest-achieving readers in first grade. Specially trained teachers meet with the children individually for 30 minutes daily for 12 to 20 weeks. Instruction focuses on developing phonemic awareness, practicing learning letter-sound relationships through phonics, strategies for enhancing text comprehension, and teaching for fluency and phrasing. The children are tested before entering the program, at the end of the Reading Recovery instruction, and at the end of first grade. Their scores are compared with a random sample of their peers. A Spanish version is available.

Numerous studies and research reports over the past 15 years have documented the effectiveness of Reading Recovery for the lowest-performing first graders. Cumulative 17-year results show that 81 percent of children who have the full series of lessons can read at the class average. A recent meta-analysis of 36 research studies on Reading Recovery has confirmed this success rate. Furthermore, most of these children maintain and improve their gains in later grades (D'Agostino & Murphy, 2004).

Success for All—Reading First

Based on the widely used Success for All comprehensive reform model introduced in 1987, this adaptation is a core reading program for grades K to 3 designed to strengthen the students' phonemic awareness, phonics, vocabulary, fluency, and comprehension. Students have a 90-minute reading period daily with specially trained teachers. The program uses proven instructional strategies, such as cooperative learning, partner reading, a rapid pace of instruction, frequent standards-based assessments, and effective classroom management techniques to engage each student. Also included are activities that build on existing textbooks to emphasize comprehension of narrative and expository texts, metacognitive comprehension strategies, writing, study skills, and home reading. Children are assessed every eight weeks in decoding, reading comprehension, and fluency. Based on these assessments, teachers regroup the children across grade lines so that each teacher can work with children at one reading level. This program is also available in Spanish.

Since the inception of the basic program, Success for All has been evaluated in grades K to 3 through several major experimental studies. Independent studies have found that, in comparison to matched control schools, students in Success for All schools read significantly better, are promoted regularly from grade to grade, are less often referred to special education, and attend school more regularly (Borman, Hewes, Overman, & Brown, 2003). A recent three-year randomized study, sponsored by the U.S. Department of Education, found that primary students in this program showed a half-year gain in their reading skills over the control group and scored in the 64th percentile on a standardized test compared with the 50th percentile of the other students (AIR, 2005).

The READ 180 Program

Improving Reading Skills in Older Readers. Significant progress is being made in understanding the connection between the visual and auditory processing systems during reading. Research-based reading programs that use computers to coordinate these systems have substantially benefitted older struggling readers.

Among the commercial programs available to help older struggling readers, the READ 180 program, now published by Scholastic, Inc., has yielded some impressive results. The research behind this program began in 1985 at Vanderbilt University, where computer software was developed that used student performance data to adjust and differentiate the path of reading instruction. The software program continued to be revised and was eventually field-tested with more than 10,000 students in the Orange County, Florida, schools from 1994 through 1997. Designed for low-achieving readers in grades four through 12, the software program emphasizes direct, explicit, and systematic instruction in word analysis, phonics, spelling, reading comprehension, and writing.

Because of its success in raising the reading scores of older struggling readers in Orange County, the Council of Great City Schools piloted the program during 1998–1999 in the Department of Defense schools and in some of its largest urban schools, including Boston, Columbus, Dallas, Houston, and Los Angeles. Most students in the pilot schools who participated in the program showed significant improvements in reading and overall school performance as well as the development of more positive attitudes and behaviors. The program is now used in 6,500 classrooms in the United States.

STRATEGIES TO CONSIDER

Strategies for Teaching Students With Reading Problems

It is usually the regular classroom teacher who works the most with struggling readers and who helps them learn to read. The following strategies may make the instructional process somewhat easier and more successful for all students (DITT, 2001).

General Strategies

- Make your classroom expectations clear.
- Ensure that classroom procedures are orderly, structured, and predictable.
- Remember that many struggling readers *can* learn to read. They just need different kinds of instructional strategies.
- Be constructive and positive. Labeling can often be disabling when you label the child rather than the behavior. Avoid labels and sarcasm, which undermine the instructional environment and adversely affect the child's self-concept and performance.
- Recognize that struggling readers will take up to three times longer to complete work and will tire quickly.
- Avoid appeals to "try harder." The brains of struggling readers are already expending extra effort while decoding print, and these appeals will not improve performance. What is needed is slower speed with clearer comprehension.
- Determine and then compliment these children's abilities, and teach through their strengths. Plan lessons so the students experience a sense of accomplishment rather than failure.

In the Elementary Classroom

- Get a complete explanation of the child's history of problems encountered when learning to read.
- Select scientifically researched reading strategies and use a multisensory approach.
- Recognize the frustration that these students feel as they struggle to read.
- Show concern and understanding.
- Recognize that performance may be well below the child's potential.
- Remember that this child learns in different ways, but can learn.
- Realize that the child may have behavioral and self-esteem problems.
- Develop student-teacher rapport.

- Maintain contact with the child's parents and give them periodic progress reports. Make suggestions of what they can do with the child at home to complement your classroom strategies.
- Ensure that other classmates understand the nature of dyslexia so that the child is not bullied or mocked.
- Assign a buddy to help the struggling reader in the class and school.
- Encourage the child to point out talents and strengths.

In the Secondary Classroom

- Get a complete explanation of the student's history of reading problems.
- Use a multisensory approach in classroom instruction.
- Recognize the compounded frustrations of a teenager with dyslexia.
- Remember that students with dyslexia learn in different ways, but they *can* learn.
- Realize that these teenagers may have problems with their self-esteem.
- Recognize that these students may have behavior or truancy problems.
- Realize that these students often have a significant gap between their performance and their potential.
- Show concern and understanding.
- Use diagrams and graphic organizers when teaching. Advanced organizers that contain important notes about the lesson are also very helpful and can help prevent failure.
- Develop student-teacher rapport.
- Maintain contact with the student's parents and give them periodic progress reports. Make suggestions of what they can do with the student at home to complement your classroom strategies.
- Ensure that these students' legal rights are adhered to when they take tests.
- Students with mild dyslexia often develop coping strategies in elementary school. Be aware that these strategies may be inadequate for the complex and multifaceted secondary curriculum.
- Ensure that any remedial materials are relevant to the maturity and not the academic level of the student.
- Be aware that struggling readers can have great difficulty reading an unseen text aloud in class. Asking them to do this can adversely affect their self-esteem.

STRATEGIES TO CONSIDER

Developing Phonological Awareness

Training in phonological awareness needs to be more intense for children with reading disabilities. Reading programs are filled with activities for separating words into phonemes, synthesizing phonemes into words, and deleting and substituting phonemes. Research suggests that the development of phonological awareness is more likely to be successful if it follows these general principles (Chard & Osborn, 1998; Oudeans, 2003; Santi, Menchetti, & Edwards, 2004):

- **Continuous Sounds Before Stop Sounds.** Start with continuous sounds such as /s/, /m/, and /f/ that are easier to pronounce than the stop sounds of /b/, /k/, and /p/.

- **Modeling.** Be sure to model carefully and accurately each activity when it is first introduced. Modeling should start with the teacher demonstrating the desired behavior, so that students hear what is expected of them. Then the teacher and students perform the behavior together.

- **Simple to Complex Tasks.** Move from simpler tasks, such as rhyming, to more complex tasks, such as blending and segmenting. Blending helps children decode unfamiliar words. Segmenting words into phonemes helps children in spelling unfamiliar words and retaining those spellings in memory.

- **Larger to Smaller Units.** Move from the larger units of words and onset-rimes to the smaller units of individual phonemes.

- **Teacher Feedback.** Teacher feedback is important and should be explicit for both correct and incorrect responses. For incorrect responses, the teacher should model the correct response and ask the student to say the response with the teacher. The teacher should then ask the student to make the response alone.

- **Additional Strategies.** Use additional strategies to help struggling readers, such as concrete objects (e.g., bingo chips or blocks), to represent sounds.

STRATEGIES TO CONSIDER

Phonemic Awareness and Guidelines

Research studies clearly indicate that early phoneme awareness is a strong indicator of later reading success (NRP, 2000). Further, the research on interventions clearly demonstrates the benefits of explicitly teaching phonemic awareness skills. No students benefit more from this instruction than those already burdened with reading problems. The development of phonemic awareness occurs over several years. It is the last step in a developmental continuum that begins with the brain's earliest awareness of rhyme. Figure 5.6 illustrates the continuum from rhyming to full phoneme manipulation (Chard & Dickson, 1999).

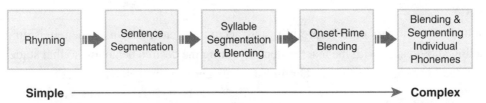

Figure 5.6   The development of phonological awareness is a continuum that begins with simple rhyming and ends with the manipulation of individual phonemes.

The first four steps, from rhyming to onset-rime blending, can occur during the preschool years in the appropriate environment. If the parent sings rhyming songs and reads to the child from rhyming books, the child's brain begins to recognize the sounds that comprise beginning language. However, many children begin school with a very weak phonological base. Teachers must then assess where students lie on the phonological continuum and select appropriate strategies to move them toward phoneme awareness. Here are some guidelines to consider when selecting strategies to help students recognize and successfully manipulate phonemes (Edelen-Smith, 1998; Flett & Conderman, 2002).

General Guidelines

- **Be specific.** Identify the specific phonemic awareness task and select the activities that are developmentally appropriate and that keep the students engaged in the task. Select words, phrases, and sentences from curricular materials to make this meaningful. Look for ways to make activities enjoyable so students see them as fun and not as monotonous drills.

- **Avoid letter names.** Use the phoneme sounds of the alphabet when doing activities and avoid letter names. Letters sounded as they are named can confuse the learner. Keep in mind that one sound may be represented by two or more letters. Target specific sounds and practice beforehand so students can hear them clearly.

- **Treat continuant and stop sounds differently.** Continuant sounds are easier to manipulate and hear than the stop sounds. When introducing each type, treat them differently so students become aware of their differences. Exaggerate continuant sounds by holding on to them: *sssssing* and *rrrrrun*. Use rapid repetition with the stop consonants: */K/-/K/-/K/-/K/-/K/-/K/-/K/-athy*.

- **Emphasize how sounds vary with their position in a word.** Generally, the initial position in the word is the easiest sound. The final position is the next easiest, and the middle position is the most difficult. Use lots of examples to make this clear, such as *mop*, *pin*, and *better*.

- **Be aware of the sequence for introducing combined sounds.** When introducing the combined sounds, a consonant-vowel pattern should come first, then a vowel-consonant pattern, and finally, the consonant-vowel- consonant pattern. For example: first *tie*, next *add*, and then *bed*.

- **Teach nursery rhymes.** Including nursery rhymes helps children develop the ability to rhyme. Read them aloud or say them in groups in songs and chants. Set up a listening station that includes nursery rhymes on audiotape.

- **Create a sound box in the classroom.** When discussing a new sound, have the students bring in objects from home that begin with the new sound and place them in the box. For instance, if introducing the */b/* sound, students may bring in a ball, a toy boat, or a balloon.

- **Draw attention to rhyming words in classroom activities.** Take advantage of rhyming words in normal classroom activities. If a student says "ball" and "fall" in the same sentence, have the students identify the rhymes and think of additional rhyming words, such as "tall" and "wall."

Onset and Rime

The brain's awareness of onsets, rimes, and syllables develops before an awareness of phonemes. Onsets are the initial consonants that change the meaning of a word; rimes are the vowel-consonant combinations that stay constant in a series. For example, in *bend*, *lend*, and *send*, the onsets are *b, l,* and *s*; the rime is-*end*. Using literature, word families, and direct instruction are strategies that focus on word play designed to enhance onset and rime recognition (Edelen-Smith, 1998).

- **Literature.** Books with rhyming patterns (like many books by Dr. Seuss) are easily recalled through repeated exposure. Almost any literary source that plays with word sounds is valuable. Books that particularly develop awareness of sound patterns associated with onset and rime are those using alliteration (the repetition of an initial consonant across several words, e.g., *Peter Piper picked a peck of peppers*) and assonance (the repetition of vowel sounds within words, e.g., *The rain in Spain stays mainly in the plain*).

- **Word Families Charts.** Using words from a story or book, construct a chart that places a different beginning letter in front of a rime. For example, start with the rime *-at* and add *f, h, b,* and *s* to form *fat, hat, bat,* and *sat*. Have the students make up a storyline whenever the word changes, e.g., "The fat cat chased a hat." Encourage the students to make their own charts with different rimes and to keep them for future reference.

- **Direct Instruction.** Students who have difficulties distinguishing the sounds among rhyming words need more direct instruction. Model rhyming pairs (e.g., *sun-fun* and *hand-band*), using flash cards so students match what they see with what they hear. Be sure they repeat each rhyming pair several times to reinforce auditory input. Another activity includes three cards, only two of which have rhyming words. Ask students to pick out and say the two that rhyme or the one that doesn't. Later, change the rhyming words to two rhyming pictures out of three (e.g., a nose, a rose, and a horse).

STRATEGIES TO CONSIDER

Simple Phonemic Awareness

Young students are usually unaware that words are made of sounds that can be produced in isolation. This leaves it up to the teacher to find ways to emphasize the concept of speech sounds through *systematic* and *direct* instruction. An effective reading program should include activities that help children manipulate phonemes. Here are some ways to do this (Edelen-Smith, 1998):

- **Recognizing Isolated Sounds.** Associate certain speech sounds with an animal or action that is familiar to the students. For example, the buzzing sound of a bee or snoring in sleep is *zzzzzzzz–,* the hissing of a snake, *sssssss–,* the sound of asking for quiet, *shhhhhhhh–,* or the sound of a motor scooter or motor boat, *pppppppp–.* Alliteration also helps with this task. Talking about Peter Piper picking a peck of peppers affords the valuable combination of sound recognition, storytelling, and literary context. It also provides self-correcting cues for initial-sound isolation and for sound-to-word matching.

- **Counting Words, Syllables, and Phonemes.** It is easier for a child's brain to perceive words and syllables than individual phonemes. Thus word and syllable counting is a valuable exercise for sound recognition that can lead later to more accurate identification of phonemes. Start with a sentence and say it aloud. Do not write it out because the students should focus on listening. Ask the students to count the number of words they think are in the sentence. They can use markers or tokens to indicate the word number. Then show or write the sentence, and have the students compare the number of words to their own count. Syllable counting can be done in many ways. Students can count syllables in the same way they identified the word count. Also, they can march around the room while saying the syllables; they can clap hands, tap pencils, or do any overt activity that indicates counting.

- **Synthesizing Sounds.** Sound synthesis is an essential yet easily performed skill for phonemic awareness. Start with using the initial sound and then saying the remainder of the word. For example, the teacher says, "It starts with *b* and ends with *-and;* put it together, and it says *band.*" The students take turns using the same phrasing to make up their own words. Variations include limiting the context to objects in the classroom or in the school, or to a particular story that the class has recently read. Guessing games can also be productive and fun activities for playing with sounds. One game involves hiding an object in a bag or other place and giving clues to its name sound-by-sound or syllable-by-syllable. When a student guesses the word correctly, you reveal the object. Songs can also be used. Blending the music with the sounds of words increases the chances that the phonemes will be remembered.

- **Matching Sounds to Words.** This activity asks the learner to identify the initial sound of a word, an important skill for sound segmentation. Show a picture of a kite and ask, "Is this a *dddd-ite,* or a *llll-ite,* or a *kkkk-ite?*" You could also ask, "Is there a *k* in *kite?*," or "Which sound does *kite* start with?" This allows students to try three onsets with three rimes and to mix and match until they get it correct. Consonants are a good beginning because they are easier to emphasize and prolong during pronunciation. Have students try other words in threes. Be sure to use the phoneme sound when referring to a letter, not the letter name.

- **Identifying the Position of Sounds.** Segmenting whole words into their components is an important part of phonemic awareness. This ability is enhanced when learners recognize that sounds occur in different positions in words: initial, medial, and final. Edelen-Smith (1998) suggests explaining that words have beginning, middle, and end sounds just like a train has a beginning (engine), middle (passenger car), and end (caboose). Slowly articulate a consonant-vowel-consonant (CVC) word at this time, such as *c-a-t,* and point to the appropriate train part as you sound out each phoneme. Then have the students sound out other CVC words from a list or recent story, pointing to each train part as they say them.

- **Segmenting Sounds.** One of the more difficult phonemic tasks for children is to separately pronounce each sound of a spoken word in order. This process is called sound segmentation. Developing this skill should start with isolating the initial phonemes. The previous activities—matching sounds to words and identifying the position of sounds—help the learner identify and recognize initial phonemes. Visual cues can also play an important part in segmenting sounds. Select words that are familiar to the students (or have the students select the words) so that they can use contextual clues for meaning. After sufficient practice, eliminate the cards so that students can perform the sound segmenting task without visual cues.

- **Associating Sounds With Letters.** For successful reading, the brain must associate the sounds it has heard during the prereading years of spoken language with the written letters that represent them. This is particularly difficult for students with disabilities that hamper the learning of reading. Consequently, extensive practice is essential. Nearly all of the activities mentioned above—especially those involving visual cues—can be modified to include associations between sounds and letters. As the students master individual sounds, their corresponding letter names can then be introduced. A type of bingo game can also be used to practice sound-with-letter association. Each student gets a card with letters placed into a bingo grid. Draw a letter from a container and call out the phoneme. Students place tokens on the letter that corresponds to the phoneme. The student who first gets "phoneme bingo" names the letters aloud. Teachers can devise all types of variations to this fun bingo game.

STRATEGIES TO CONSIDER

Compound Phonemic Awareness

In compound phonemic awareness, the learner must hold one sound in memory and match it to a second sound. For example, "Do *dog* and *deer* begin with the same sound?" Two activities that develop compound phonemic awareness involve matching one word to a second word and the deleting of sounds in a word.

- **Matching One Word to Another Word.** Byrne (1991) has suggested three games for developing phonemic word matching skills. The words and pictures used in each of these games should relate to themes and readings done in the classroom. One involves making a set of dominoes that have two objects pictured on each tile. The students have to join the tiles that share the same beginning or ending sounds.

  A second game uses picture cards that are placed face down in a pile. Each student draws a card from the pile and places it face up. Students continue to draw cards and place them in the face-up pile. The first student to match the beginning or ending sound of a drawn card with the top card on the face-up pile says the match aloud and collects the pile.

  The third game is a variation of bingo. Each bingo card contains pictures, which the students mark when their picture has the same beginning or ending sounds as the word said by the caller (student or teacher).

- **Deleting Sounds.** Deleting sounds from words and manipulating phonemes within words are more difficult tasks for the young brain to accomplish. Studies show that most children must attain the mental age of seven years before this task can be accomplished adequately (Cole & Mengler, 1994). Furthermore, segmentation skills and letter names must be mastered before sound-deletion tasks can be successfully learned.

  Three tasks seem to be particularly important to mastering this skill: deleting parts of a compound word, identifying a missing sound, and deleting a single sound from a word.

  - *Deleting parts of a compound word.* To illustrate deleting parts of a compound word, point to a picture or an object that is a compound word and demonstrate how each word can be said with one part missing. For example, "This is a classroom. I can say *class* without the *room*. And this is a farmhouse (or greenhouse). I can say *farm* (*green*) without *house*. Now you try it. This is a playground." Use other common examples, such as *lighthouse, airplane, grandmother, seashore, sandbox, toothpaste,* and *night-light.*

  - *Identifying the missing sound.* In this task, focus on deleting the initial and final sounds instead of the medial sounds, which is the first step to master for the young brain. Take word pairs, such as *ate-late,* and ask "What's missing in *ate* that you hear in *late*?" Other examples are *ask-mask, able-table,* and *right-bright.* After a few trials, have the students make up their own word pairs, preferably from lesson material.

o *Deleting a single sound from a word.* This task should begin with segmentation practice. First, separate the sound for deletion. For example, separate *g* from *glove.* "Glove. It starts with *g* and ends with *love.* Take the first sound away and it says *love.*" Use words for which a sound deletion results in another real word. Other examples are *spot-pot, train-rain, scare-care,* and *snap-nap.* After practicing this skill, say a word aloud and ask students to say the word with the initial sound missing: "Say *mother* without the *m.*" Visual clues can help those who have difficulty saying a word with the deleted sound.

STRATEGIES TO CONSIDER

Reading Strategies for Fluency and Comprehension

Studies have shown that children with reading problems are able to master the learning strategies that improve reading comprehension skills. For students with learning problems, learning to use questioning strategies is especially important because these students do not often spontaneously self-question or monitor their own reading comprehension.

Here are three strategies that researchers and teachers have found particularly effective. Some of the strategies have been around for over 20 years, but their fundamental premises have been reaffirmed by recent research (NRP, 2000).

Questioning and Paraphrasing: Reciprocal Teaching

Reciprocal teaching is a strategic approach that fosters student interaction with the text being read (Palincsar & Brown, 1984). In reciprocal teaching, students interact deeply with the text through the strategies of questioning, summarizing, clarifying, and predicting. Organized in the form of a discussion, the approach involves one leader (students and teacher take turns being the leader), who, after a portion of the text is read, first frames a question to which the group responds. Second, participants share their own questions. Third, the leader summarizes the gist of the text, and participants comment or elaborate on that summary. At any point in the discussion, either the leader or participants may identify aspects of the text or discussion that need to be clarified, and the group joins together to clarify the confusion. Finally, the leader indicates that it is time to move on and solicits predictions about what might come up next in the text.

The value of paraphrasing, self-questioning, and finding the main idea are well-researched strategies. Students divide reading passages into smaller parts, such as sections, subsections, or paragraphs. After reading a segment, students are cued to use a self-questioning strategy to identify main ideas and details. The strategy requires a high level of attention to reading tasks because students must alternate their use of questioning and paraphrasing after reading each section, subsection, or paragraph. Furthermore, it incorporates all modes of communication, including reading, writing, speaking, and listening. Consequently, students are more likely to find meaning in what they are reading, thereby increasing the likelihood they will remember it. Although paraphrasing for comprehension does not have to be used in every reading situation, it is another effective strategy designed to increase students' understanding of text (Fisk & Hurst, 2003).

Questioning to Find the Main Idea

This self-questioning strategy focuses primarily on identifying and questioning the main idea or summary of a paragraph. Here's how it works. Students are first taught the concept of a main idea and how to do self-questioning. Students then practice, asking themselves questions aloud about each paragraph's main idea.

They can use a cue card for assistance. Following the practice, the teacher provides immediate feedback. Eventually, following successful comprehension of these short paragraphs, students are presented with more lengthy passages, and the cue cards are removed. Continuing to give corrective feedback, the teacher finishes each lesson with a discussion of students' progress and of the strategy's usefulness. Studies show that students with learning disabilities who were trained in a self-questioning strategy performed significantly higher (i.e., demonstrated greater comprehension of what was read) than untrained students (Idol, 1987).

Story Mapping

In this strategy, students read a story, generate a map of its events and ideas, and then answer questions (Idol, 1987). Figure 5.7 is one example of a story map. In order to fill in the map, students have to identify the setting, characters, time, and place of the story; the problem, the goal, and the action that took place; and the outcome. The teacher models for students how to fill in the map, then gives them many opportunities to practice the mapping technique for themselves and receive corrective feedback. The map is an effective visual tool that provides a framework for understanding, conceptualizing, and remembering important story events. The reading comprehension of students can improve significantly when the teacher gives direct instruction on the use of the strategy, expects frequent use of the strategy, and encourages students to use the strategy independently. The story map in Figure 5.7 focuses on story content, but some story maps are to designed to also help students with reading difficulties enhance their understanding of story grammar (Boulineau, Fore, Hagan-Burke, & Burke, 2004).

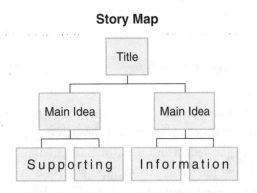

Story Map

Figure 5.7 This is just one example of a story map. By filling in the information, students get a vivid visual representation that helps them to understand, conceptualize, and remember important aspects of the story.

STRATEGIES TO CONSIDER

Teaching for Reading Comprehension

Students with reading disorders often have difficulty deriving meaning from what they read. If little or no meaning comes from reading, students lose motivation to read. Furthermore, meaning is essential for long-term retention of what they have read. Strategies designed to improve reading comprehension have been shown to improve students' interest in reading and their success.

The PASS Process

One such successful strategy, suggested by Deshler, Ellis, and Lenz (1996), is a four-step process called by the acronym **PASS** (**P**review, **A**sk, **S**ummarize, and **S**ynthesize). The teacher guides the students through the four steps, ensuring that they respond orally or in writing to the activities associated with each step. Grouping formats, such as cooperative learning, can be used to encourage active student participation and reduce anxiety over the correctness of each student's response.

1. **P**review, Review, and Predict:
   o Preview by reading the heading and one or two sentences.
   o Review what you already know about this topic.
   o Predict what you think the text or story will be about.

2. **A**sk and Answer Questions:
   o Content-focused questions:
      Who? What? Why? Where?
      How does this relate to what I already know?

   o Monitoring questions:
      Does this make sense?
      Is my prediction correct?
      How is this different from what I thought it was going to be about?

   o Problem-solving questions:
      Is it important that it make sense?
      Do I need to reread part of it?
      Can I visualize the information?
      Does it have too many unknown words?
      Should I get help?

3. *Summarize*:
   o Explain what the short passage you read was all about.

Preview	
Ask	
Summarize	
Synthesize	

4. **S***ynthesize*:
   - Explain how the short passage fits in with the whole passage.
   - Explain how what you learned fits in with what you knew.

If students have difficulty with any particular step, they can go back to the previous step to determine what information they need in order to proceed.

Collaborative Strategic Reading

Another excellent technique for helping students comprehend what they read and build vocabulary is called collaborative strategic reading (CSR). It is particularly effective in classrooms where students have many different reading abilities and learning capabilities. The strategy is compatible with all types of reading programs. Longitudinal studies show that students in CSR classrooms improved significantly in reading comprehension compared to students in control groups (Klingner, Vaughn, Arguelles, Hughes, & Leftwich, 2004).

CSR uses modified reciprocal teaching and the collaborative power of cooperative learning groups to accomplish two phases designed to improve reading comprehension (Klingner, Vaughn, & Schumm, 1998). The first phase is a teacher-led component that takes students through four parts of a reading plan: Preview, Click and Clunk, Get the Gist, and Wrap-Up. The second phase involves using cooperative learning groups to provide an interactive environment where students can practice and perfect their reading comprehension skills (Klingner, Vaughn, Dimino, Schumm, & Bryant, 2001).

PHASE ONE
Teacher-Led Activities

- **Preview the reading.** Students know that previews in movies give some information about coming events. Use this as a hook to the new reading. The learners preview the entire reading passage in order to get as much as they can about the passage in a just a few minutes' time. The purpose here is to activate their prior knowledge about the topic and to give them an opportunity to predict what they will learn.

  Refer to student experiences about a movie, television program, or a prior book that might contain information relevant to the new reading. Also, give clues to look for when previewing. For example, pictures, graphs, tables, or call-out quotes provide information to help predict what students already know about the topic and what they will learn.

- **Click and clunk.** Students with reading problems often fail to monitor their understanding while they read. Clicks and clunks are devices to help students with this monitoring. Clicks are parts of the reading that make sense; clunks are parts or words that don't.

  Ask students to identify clunks as they go along. Then the class works with the teacher to develop strategies to clarify the clunks, such as

  - Rereading the sentences while looking for key words that can help extract meaning from the context o Rereading previous and following sentences to get additional context clues

   o Looking for a prefix or suffix in the word that could help with meaning

   o Breaking the word apart to see if smaller words are present that provide meaning

- **Get the gist.** The goal of this phase is twofold. First, ask the readers to state in their own words the most important person, place, or thing in the passage. Second, get them to tell in as few words as possible (i.e., leaving out the details) the most important *idea* about that person, place, or thing. Because writing often improves memory, occasionally ask the students to write down their gists. Students can then read their gists aloud and invite comments from the group about ways to improve the gist. This process can be done so that all students benefit by enhancing their skills.

- **Wrap-up.** Wrap-up is a closure activity that allows students to review in their minds what has been learned. Focus students on the new learning by asking them to generate questions whose answers would show what they learned from the passage. They should also review key ideas.

    Start with questions that focus on the explicit material in the passage, such as who, what, where, and when. Afterward, move to questions that stimulate higher-order thinking, such as "What might have happened if . . . ?" and "What could be another way to solve this problem?" Writing down the response will help students sort out and remember the important ideas.

PHASE TWO

Cooperative Learning Groups

This phase puts the students into cooperative learning groups to practice CSR in an interactive environment. True cooperative learning groups are usually made up of about five students of mixed ability levels who learn and perform certain roles in the group to ensure completion of the learning task (Johnson & Johnson, 1989). The roles rotate among the group members so that every student gets the opportunity to be the leader and use the various skills needed to perform each task. Although there are many roles that students can perform, here are the most common (assuming four members per group):

   o **Leader.** Leads the group through CSR by saying what to read next and what strategy to use.

   o **Clunk Expert.** Reminds the group what strategies to use when encountering a difficult word or phrase.

   o **Announcer.** Calls on different group members to make certain that everyone participates and that only one person talks at a time.

   o **Gist Expert.** Guides the group toward getting the gist, and determines that the gist contains the most important ideas but no unnecessary details.

Other suggestions for using the cooperative learning groups with this strategy are as follows:

- **Cue Sheets.** Giving all group members a cue sheet to guide them through the CSR provides a structure and focus for the group. The cue sheet should be specific for each role. For example, the leader's sheet contains statements that steer the group through each step of CSR (e.g., "Today's topic is . . ." "Let's predict what we might learn from this." "Let's think of some questions to see if we really understand what we learned.") and also direct other group members to carry out their role (e.g., "Announcer, please call on others to share their ideas." "Encourager, tell us what we did well and what we need to do better next time.").

- **CSR Learning Logs.** Recording in logs helps students keep track of what was learned. Students can keep separate logs for each subject. The log serves as a reminder for follow-up activities and can be used to document a student's progress as required by the individualized education plan.

- **Reading Materials.** CSR was originally designed for expository text, but has also been used successfully with narrative text. For the strategy to be successful, select reading passages that are rich in clues, that have just one main idea per paragraph, and that provide a context to help students connect and associate details into larger ideas.

Chapter 6

Writing Disabilities

Once the enormous challenge of learning to read is undertaken, the brain is faced with the daunting task of directing fine muscle movements to draw the abstract symbols that represent the sounds of language. For many years, researchers thought that the mental centers responsible for speech and writing were located in the same (left) side of the brain. Imaging studies, however, indicate that these two processes are related yet separate, sometimes residing in different cerebral hemispheres (Gazzaniga, Ivry, & Mangun, 2002). This finding, which suggests that spoken and written language develop differently, is not surprising when we realize that human beings have been speaking for well over 10,000 years but writing for only about 5,000 years. Thus spoken language has become innate and usually develops with ease, but writing usually does not develop without instruction.

LEARNING TO WRITE

Learning to write consists of integrating two components: the consolidation of mental functions that select the content of the writing (the writing process) with the physical act of moving a writing instrument across a surface to form words (handwriting). This is not an easy accomplishment, especially for young children whose executive thought processes and fine motor skills are at early stages of development.

Writing is a highly complex operation requiring the coordination of multiple neural networks. It involves the blending of attention, fine motor coordination, memory, visual processing, language, and higher-order thinking. When an individual is writing, the visual feedback mechanisms are at work checking the output, adjusting fine motor skills, and monitoring eye-hand coordination. Meanwhile, kinesthetic monitoring systems are conscious of the position and movement of fingers in space, the grip on the pencil, and the rhythm and pace of the writing. Cognitive systems are also busy, verifying with long-term memory that the symbols being drawn will indeed produce the sounds of the word that the writer intends. Accomplishing this task

119

requires visual memory for symbols, whole-word memory, and spelling rules. Hence, the phoneme-to-grapheme match is a continuous feedback loop ensuring that the written symbols are consistent with the oral language protocols the writer has previously learned.

Front of Brain

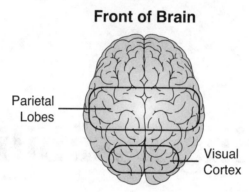

Figure 6.1 In a right-handed individual, writing involves mainly the left parietal lobe. For a left-handed person, the right parietal lobe is the area of main activation. Regardless of which hand is used, the visual cortex involvement is the same.

Brain imaging studies have shown the labor-intensive nature of writing. The parietal lobe, which includes the motor cortex, and the occipital lobe, where visual processing occurs, were the areas of highest activity (Figure 6.1) when an individual was writing (Menon & Desmond, 2001; Wing, 2000). Not surprising was the discovery that spoken-language areas in the left hemisphere were also activated. Writing relies heavily on speech because most of us sound out words in our head as we write them down.

After reviewing numerous scanning studies on the writing process, Alan Wing (2000) pieced together a complex flow diagram illustrating the relationships between the neurological networks responsible for both speech and writing. Figure 6.2 is a simplified version of Wing's diagram. The visual systems analyze the spelling and grammar as it is written out on paper (orthography) and adjust the motor output to form the letters correctly. Simultaneously, the auditory system is sounding out the words in the brain (phonological output), associating and converting the sounds to letters (phoneme-to-grapheme conversion) for writing (motor output).

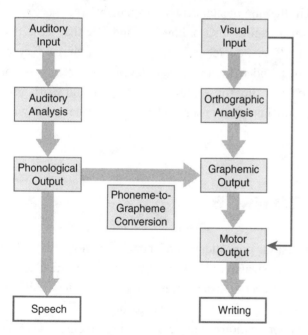

Figure 6.2 The diagram shows the relationship between speech and handwriting. The writer hears the word (phonological output) and converts the sounds to the appropriate letters (graphemes). The dotted arrow shows how motor adjustments are made as the visual system judges the legibility of the writing (adapted from Wing, 2000).

At a minimum, the ability to write requires a properly functioning central nervous system, intact receptive and expressive language skills, and the related cognitive operations. To write accurately and clearly also requires emotional stability; application of the concepts of organization and flow; an understanding of the rules of pronunciation, spelling, grammar and syntax; visual and spatial organization; and simultaneous processing.

When all these operations fall into place, writing becomes a valuable tool for learning. Writing encourages mental rehearsal, reinforces long-term memory, and helps the mind sort and prioritize information. However, for some students, the process of writing becomes an arduous task that actually interferes with learning.

DIFFICULTIES IN WRITING

Environmental Causes

Difficulties with writing can be environmental—that is, too little time was spent in the child's early years on practicing correct writing—or they can stem from deficits within one or more of the neural networks needed for legible and clear writing to occur. Let's deal first with how the school environment may contribute inadvertently to writing problems.

Teachers of writing should realize that, like reading, the brain does not perceive writing to be a survival skill. That is, the brain has no "writing centers" comparable to those for spoken language. Instead, writing requires the coordination of numerous neural networks and systems, all of which have to learn new skills. Learning to write therefore requires direct instruction—it is not innate to the brain. Hard work and lots of practice are needed just to learn the fine motor skills for reproducing the printed and cursive letters of the alphabet. In some schools, little time is given

> *There are no areas of the brain specialized for writing.*

to formal instruction in handwriting. To conserve time, it is often taught as an activity ancillary to other learning tasks. Some of the difficulties students experience with writing may be due to an unfortunate combination of learning the difficult skills of writing with very little practice time. Furthermore, students are questioning the need to write well because they have access to computers at an early age and typing into a word processing program seems so much easier.

Invented Spelling

Is invented spelling a likely environmental cause of consistently poor writing? Spelling is closely linked to reading because it involves breaking apart a spoken word into its sounds and encoding them into the letters representing each sound. While learning to read words, children also learn how to spell those words. As children try to represent words in writing with the alphabet, they often encode words by their initial consonants, followed by their ending sounds. Middle sounds, usually vowels, are omitted at first. Thus, *horse* might be written as *hrs*, and *monster* as *mstr.* The pronunciation of this *invented spelling* is very close to that of the intended word. Invented spelling allows children to practice applying the alphabetic principle and gain in phonemic awareness. It serves as a transitional step and assists in the development of reading and writing.

> *Invented spelling allows children to practice applying the alphabetic principle and gain in phonemic awareness.*

Studies on early literacy development have shown that invented spelling is a reliable measure of early reading achievement. One study found that preschool and kindergarten children who were inventive spellers performed significantly better on word reading and on storybook readings. In a literacy study of four first-grade classrooms, two teachers encouraged invented spelling while the other two teachers encouraged traditional spelling. The inventive spellers scored significantly better than the traditional spellers on several measures of word reading that were administered during the second semester in first grade (Ahmed & Lombardino, 2000). Uhry (1999) found that invented spelling was the best predictor of how well kindergartners could match, through finger-point reading, spoken words to printed words in reading a sentence—a skill known as *concept of a word in text*. Other studies confirm that invented spelling is developmentally based and can increase a child's achievement in spelling ,reading, and writing (Bear, Invernizzi, Templeton, & Johnston, 2004; Kolodziej & Columba, 2005).

When their invented spelling is accepted, children feel empowered to write more and with purpose, communicating their messages from the very beginning of school. Writing slows down the process of dealing with text, allowing children more time to recognize and learn about sound-letter relationships. For some children, writing may be an easier way to literacy than reading. In reading, the process involves changing letter sequences to sounds, whereas in writing the process is reversed—going from sounds to letters. Accordingly, writing may be a simpler task because it involves going from sounds in the child's head that are already known and automatic, to letters, rather than from the unknown letters in reading to what is known.

Some educators and parents in the past have raised concerns about whether the persistent use of invented spelling leads to confusion and the formation of bad spelling habits. But research studies indicate that, with appropriate teacher intervention, the invented spellings gradually come closer to conventional forms. Consequently, spelling errors should not be seen as an impediment to writing but as an indication of the child's thought processes while making sense of letter-sound relationships. From that perspective, the errors could yield important information about a child's internal reading patterns (Sipe, 2001). On the other hand, remember that practice eventually makes permanent. The consistent repetition of incorrect spellings will, in time, lead to their storage in long-term memory. Therefore, teachers should use strategies that will help children transform invented spelling into conventional spelling.

Neurological Causes

Given that such a complex order of operations is necessary for accurate writing, difficulties can arise anywhere within the neural systems involved. Because writing is so dependent on the brain's parietal lobes, for instance, a lesion or stroke in this area would be especially significant. Another possible source of writing difficulty could result from problems with receptor cells located in the skin, muscles, tendons, and joints. These specialized cells, called *proprioceptors* (meaning "receptors for self") provide continuous information to the brain about the position of the limbs and head in space. Any deficits in the proprioceptor pathways could interfere with the intricate muscle coordination needed for legible and fluent writing (Purves, Augustine, Fitzpatrick, Katz, LaMantia, McNamara, et al., 2001)

Although researchers admit that eye problems could contribute to poor handwriting, there is little research evidence to support a connection between poor eyesight and persistently poor penmanship. It is more likely that any visual deficit results from problems in the visual processing system deep within the brain (Vlachos & Karapetsas, 2003).

Whatever the neurological cause of writing difficulties, some children struggle because so much time is spent on the transcribing *process* that they often lose track of the *content* they are working on. The persistent condition of not being able to put thoughts into writing or accomplish other parts of the writing process (such as letter formation) is known as *dysgraphia*.

Dysgraphia

Dysgraphia (also known as *agraphia*) is a spectrum disorder describing major difficulties in mastering the sequence of movements necessary to write letters and numbers. The disorder exists in varying degrees and is seldom found in isolation without symptoms of other learning problems.

Many students have difficulty with writing as

> ### Dysgraphia
>
> Symptoms:
> - Inconsistencies in letter formation; mixture of upper and lower cases, of print and cursive letters
> - Unfinished words or letters
> - Generally illegible writing (despite time given to the task)
> - Talking to self while writing
> - Watching hand while writing
> - Inconsistent position on page with respect to margins and lines
> - Slow copying or writing
> - Omitted words in writing
> - Inconsistent spaces between letters and words
> - Struggle to use writing as a communication tool
> - Cramped or unusual grip on pencil
> - Unusual body, wrist, or paper position

they progress through the upper elementary grades. But those with dysgraphia are inefficient at *handwriting* more than anything else, and this inefficiency establishes a barrier to learning. Their handwriting is usually characterized by slow copying, inconsistencies in letter formation, mixtures of different letters and styles, and poor legibility. Specific symptoms of the disorder are shown in the box titled *Dysgraphia*. Teachers must realize that dysgraphia is a disorder and is *not* the result of laziness, not caring, not trying, or just carelessness in writing.

What Causes Dysgraphia?

Dysgraphia is a neurological disorder that can stem from several causes. Although there are many individual variations, dysgraphia can be broadly classified into the following three types (Table 6.1) (Heilman, 2002; IDA, 2000; Rapcsak & Beeson, 2004).

Dyslexic Dysgraphia. Handwriting requires the ability to convert the sounds of language into the letters that represent them. The inability to make this phoneme-to-grapheme conversion usually results in poorly legible written text and severely abnormal spelling. Individuals with dyslexic dysgraphia may be able to write most simple words like *dog* or *hat*, but run into trouble writing words like *tomb*. If they had no prior exposure to *tomb*, they may write *toom*. However, these individuals can draw and copy written text adequately because little or no phoneme-to-grapheme conversion is required.

MRI studies have shown that individuals with dyslexic dysgraphia often have lesions in the brain's left parietal lobe. You may recall from Chapter 5 that this is the region actively involved in decoding and matching phonemes and graphemes.

Motor Dysgraphia. Problems with muscles controlling motor output to the hands, wrists, and fingers lead to a motor clumsiness that also produces poorly legible handwriting, drawing and copying. Students may also have memory deficits that interfere with their ability to remember the motor patterns of letter forms. Spelling, however, is generally good because the phoneme-to-grapheme systems are unaffected.

Spatial Dysgraphia. Sometimes, deficits in the spatial processing functions of the brain's right hemisphere cause poorly legible text, but with accurate spelling. Copying is poor to legible, depending on the spatial complexity of the original text.

Table 6.1	Different Types of Dysgraphia			
Type	**Symptoms**			**Possible Cause**
	Legibility	Spelling	Copying	
Dyslexic Dysgraphia	Poor	Poor	Satisfactory	Deficits/lesions in phoneme-to-grapheme conversion
Motor Dysgraphia	Poor	Satisfactory	Poor	Deficits in muscle control of motor output to fingers, wrist, and hand
Spatial Dysgraphia	Poor	Satisfactory	Satisfactory	Deficits/lesions in spatial processing systems of the brain's right hemisphere

Sources: Heilman, 2002; IDA, 2000

Diagnosing Dysgraphia

Dysgraphia cannot be diagnosed just by looking at a sample of handwriting. A qualified clinician must directly test the individual. Determining which type of writing disorder a child has requires the assessment of various factors, such as fine motor coordination, writing speed, organization, knowledge and use of vocabulary, spelling, and the degree of attention and concentration. Feifer and De Fina (2000) suggest that clinicians examining children for dysgraphia administer one test from each of the following eight categories:

1. **Intelligence Measures**

   - Cognitive Assessment System
   - Differential Ability Scales
   - Wechsler Intelligence Scales for Children
   - Woodcock-Johnson III

2. **Constructional Dysgraphia**

   - Bender Gestalt
   - Beery Visual-Motor Integration Test

- NEPSY (Design Copying)
- Process assessment of the learner (Copying)
- Rey Complex Figure Test
- Wide range assessment of visual motor abilities

3. **Working Memory**

- Children's Memory Scale
- Paced Auditory Serial Addition Test (PASAT)
- Planned Connections (Cognitive Assessment System)
- Test of memory and learning (Digits and letters backwards)
- Trailmaking Test (Halstead-Reitan)
- Wechsler Memory Scale (Visual reproduction and paired associate)
- Wide range assessment of memory and learning (Finger windows)
- WISC PI (Spatial span, arithmetic and sentence arrangement)
- Woodcock-Johnson III (Auditory working memory)

4. **Executive Functions**

- Booklet Category Test for Children
- BRIEF (Behavior Rating Inventory of Executive Functions)
- Brown ADD scales for children (3–12)
- Cognitive Assessment System (Planned Connections)
- Delis-Kaplan Executive Function Scale
- NEPSY (Tower)
- Stroop Test
- Wisconsin Card Sort Test
- WISC PI (Elithorn mazes)
- Woodcock-Johnson III (Planning)

5. **Writing and Spelling Skills**

- Informal writing assessment
- OWLS Written Expression Scale
- Test of Early Written Language, 2nd Edition (TWEWL-2)
- Test of Written Expression (TOWE)
- Test of Written Language, 3rd Edition (TOWL-3)
- Test of Written Spelling, 4th Edition
- Wechsler Individual Achievement Test, 2nd Edition
- Woodcock-Johnson III (Writing fluency)

6. **Phonological Awareness Tests**

- Comprehensive Test of Phonological Processing (C-TOPP)
- NEPSY (Phonological processing)
- Phonological awareness test
- Process assessment of the learner (Phonemes and pseudo-word decoding)

- Test of Word Reading Efficiency (TOWRE)
- Woodcock-Johnson III (Word attack)

7. Retrieval Fluency Measures

- Controlled Oral Word Association Test (COWAT)
- NEPSY (Verbal fluency and speeded coding)
- Process assessment of the learner (Expressive coding and sentence sense)
- Woodcock-Johnson III (Retrieval fluency and rapid picture naming)

8. Family History

We now know that the centers for processing spoken language and written language are separated in the brain. Teachers should not assume, therefore, that a student with symptoms of dysgraphia will have other language problems as well. In fact, students with dysgraphia but who are otherwise linguistically talented find enormous frustration when trying to convert their thoughts into written expression. Their frustration can eventually turn them away from writing. Teachers sometimes misinterpret this behavior as laziness, carelessness, or poor motivation. Administering assessment instruments will be useful in determining whether the cause of poor writing is of neurological or some other origin.

> *Students with dysgraphia have problems with the writing process. They are often frustrated and are not necessarily lazy or unmotivated.*

Associating Dysgraphia With Other Disorders

Students with dysgraphia sometimes have other learning difficulties as well. This condition is known as *comorbidity*. The following are the more common comorbid associations.

Dyslexia (Severe Reading Impairment). Studies show that many children with dyslexia often have poor handwriting and spelling. This strong correlation probably exists because deficits in the brain's angular gyrus (located in the left hemisphere) affect the child's ability to match phonemes to graphemes and vice versa. Successful interventions for dyslexia frequently result in improvements in handwriting and spelling (Mather, 2003; Shaywitz, 2003).

Sequencing Problems. Some individuals have a cerebral deficit that makes it difficult for them to process sequential and rational information. Students with this difficulty will have problems with the sequence of letters, numbers, and words as they write. Usually they slow down their writing to focus on the mechanics of spelling, punctuation, and word order. As a result, they may get so bogged down with the details of writing that they lose the thoughts they are trying to express.

Attention-Deficit Hyperactivity Disorder (ADHD). Students with ADHD (Chapter 3) often have difficulty with writing in general and with handwriting in particular. They are processing information at a very rapid rate and do not possess the fine motor skills needed to write down their thoughts legibly.

Auditory Processing Disorders. Students who have language disorders (Chapter 4) as a result of auditory processing deficits will usually have difficulty with writing. Those with expressive language disorder are particularly weak at writing because it is the most difficult form of expressive language.

Visual Processing Disorders. Most students with dysgraphia do not have visual processing problems. However, the small percentage of students who *do* will have difficulty with writing speed and legibility simply because they are not able to fully process the visual information as they are transferring it to paper.

WHAT EDUCATORS NEED TO CONSIDER

One of the main goals of writing is to help individuals express their knowledge and ideas. Students with dysgraphia have writing problems that lead to excessively rapid or slow writing, messy and illegible papers, and frustration. It is wrong to label them as lazy or unmotivated. Rather, educators should look for ways to help these students cope with their writing difficulties.

All teachers should emphasize that writing is more than *hand*writing. The notion of transferring thoughts and ideas from inside the brain to an outside device—paper or computer—requires teaching how to organize thoughts, analyze material, and sort out material differently, depending on whether students plan to relate an incident or persuade another person. To write an initial draft requires instruction in penmanship and learning the rules of written language, including spelling, capitalization, punctuation, and sentence structure. Unfortunately, complex rules in the English language are loaded with exceptions and require substantial practice for mastery. Even after the initial draft is written, students need to learn how to edit and revise their material for clarity.

The point here is that students who demonstrate difficulty with writing need a full assessment to determine whether their obstacles are environmental or systemic. Teachers should look first at the learner's background knowledge of writing and assess the type and degree of writing instruction that has been provided in the past. Simply by providing more and sustained practice of writing skills and written language rules, teachers can help many students to eventually overcome their writing difficulties.

Characteristics of Good Writing

Students with difficulties in the process of writing need help understanding what constitutes effective writing. The Northwest Regional Educational Laboratory in Portland, Oregon, developed a popular model in the early 1990s that identifies the following six common traits of good writing:

- *Ideas,* the main theme of the writing piece
- *Organization,* the internal structure of the piece
- *Voice,* the personal tone and message of the author
- *Word choice,* the vocabulary the writer chooses to convey meaning
- *Sentence fluency,* the rhythm and flow of the language
- *Conventions,* the mechanical correctness of the piece

Now used in many schools in North America, the model, originally called the *Six Traits Writing Project,* eventually added the seventh trait of *presentation,* which refers to how visual and verbal elements are combined in the piece. As a result, the model has been renamed *6+1 Trait Writing* (NWREL, 2006).

No formal research studies had been completed at the time of publication on the efficacy of this model with students who have writing difficulties. However, several anecdotal studies are on the Internet and in journals that attest to its effectiveness in improving the performance of struggling writers (James, Abbott, & Greenwood, 2001; Perchemlides & Coutant, 2004). For more information, see the **Resources** section.

Helping Students With Dysgraphia

Students with writing disorders often lack confidence in their ability to overcome the frustrations they experience when writing. Educators working with these students need to help them regain confidence. Regina Richards (1998) and Susan Jones (2000) suggest that educators develop three types of strategies for helping students with dysgraphia: accommodation (also called compensation) strategies, modification strategies, and remediation strategies. Accommodations bypass the problem by avoiding the difficulty and by reducing the impact that writing has on learning. Modification looks to change the types and the expectations of assignments. Remediation strategies focus on reteaching the concept or skill or providing additional structural practice that more closely matches the student's needs and learning style.

To help students, educators must first determine the point at which a student begins to struggle. Does the problem occur as the student begins to write, or does it appear later in the writing process? Is there a problem with organization of thoughts? Is the struggle more evident when the student changes from just copying material to generating complex ideas and trying to commit those to writing? Is the struggle because of confusion over printed and cursive letters, over grammar, or because of punctuation? Once the struggle area is identified, then it becomes a matter of selecting the appropriate combination of accommodation, modification, and remedial techniques for the student. See **Strategies to Consider** at the end of this chapter for ways to build confidence and for techniques that help students with writing difficulties.

STRATEGIES TO CONSIDER

Suggestions for Building Confidence in Students With Writing Disorders

Lack of confidence is one of the major difficulties of students with writing disorders. Here are a few suggestions to give to students with dysgraphia to help them regain confidence and overcome the frustrations they often experience when writing.

- **Organize Your Thoughts.** First try to get your major ideas down on paper. Then go back and fill in the details.

- **Use a Tape Recorder.** If you are feeling frustrated with your writing, stop and dictate what you want to write into a tape recorder. Listen to the tape later and write down your major ideas.

- **Use the Computer.** Even if you are not great at the beginning, it is important to practice your keyboarding skills. You will get better and faster at it once you have learned the pattern of the keys. Word processing programs can help you organize your thoughts, put them in the proper sequence, and even check your spelling. In the long run, it will be faster and clearer than handwriting.

- **Continue to Practice Handwriting.** No matter how frustrating handwriting is, you will need to be able to write things down in the future. Like any other skill, your handwriting will get better with continued practice.

- **Talk While Writing.** Talk to yourself while writing. This auditory feedback is a valuable tool for helping you monitor what and how you write.

- **Use Visual Aids.** Drawing a picture or filling in a diagram can help you organize your thoughts. Some computer programs, such as *Inspiration Software,* have the capability of producing all types of graphic organizers.

STRATEGIES TO CONSIDER

Prevention of and Intervention in Writing Difficulties

Students with writing difficulties need special attention to help them become good writers. Sometimes, instruction for these students focuses mainly on lower-level writing skills, such as handwriting and spelling, with few opportunities to actually write. Researchers believe that writing instruction must emphasize both prevention and intervention; respond to the specific needs of each child; maintain a healthy balance between meaning, process, and form; and employ both formal and informal learning methods. They suggest that such instruction consider the following six principles (Graham & Harris, 2005; Graham, Harris, & Larsen, 2001):

- **Provide effective writing instruction.** An important strategy in preventing writing difficulties, for children with and without learning disabilities, is to provide effective writing instruction. Such a program of instruction would contain the following features:
  - A welcoming and literate classroom environment where students' written work is prominently displayed, the room is filled with writing and reading material, and word lists adorn the walls
  - Daily writing assignments, with students working on a wide range of writing tasks for multiple audiences, including writing at home
  - Extensive efforts to make writing motivating by setting an exciting mood, creating a risk-free environment, allowing students to select their own writing topics or modify teacher assignments, developing assigned topics compatible with students' interests, reinforcing children's accomplishments, and specifying the goal for each lesson
  - Periodic teacher/student conferences about the writing topic the student is currently working on, including the establishment of goals or criteria to guide the child's writing and revising efforts
  - A predictable writing routine where students are encouraged to think, reflect, and revise
  - Overt teacher modeling of the process of writing and positive attitudes toward writing
  - Cooperative learning arrangements where students help each other plan, draft, revise, edit, or publish their written work
  - Group or individual sharing where students present work in progress or completed papers to their peers for feedback
  - Instruction covering a broad range of knowledge, skills, and strategies, including phonological awareness, sentence-level skills, text structure, the functions of writing, handwriting and spelling, writing conventions, and planning and revising. Follow-up instruction as needed
  - Integration of writing activities across the curriculum and the use of reading to support the development of writing
  - Frequent opportunities for students to self-regulate their behavior during writing, including working independently, arranging their own space, and seeking help from others
  - Teachers and students working together to assess writing progress, strengths, and needs
  - Periodic conferences with parents and frequent communications with home about the writing program and students' progress as writers

- **Tailor instruction to meet individual needs.** A critical aspect of tailoring writing instruction is finding the right balance between formal and informal instruction, and between meaning, process, and form. Each of these factors should be emphasized when developing a writing program. Teachers should adjust the emphasis placed on each, depending on an individual student's needs Tailoring instruction for individual students includes many different personalized strategies, such as:
  - o Devoting more attention to the development of critical skills, more explicit teaching of these skills, and more individually guided assistance
  - o Using scaffolding and guidance designed to help students refine and extend their writing skills— for example, with struggling writers receiving additional support with spelling, and extra time explicitly teaching letter-sound relationships
  - o Giving more attention to teaching handwriting, phonics for spelling, and punctuation and capitalization skills to weaker writers than to average writers
  - o Providing mini-lessons responsive to individual needs, and follow-up conferencing
  - o Using adult tutors or volunteers, or older and same-age peers (including collaborative planning, writing, or revising with a peer)
  - o Developing personalized spelling lists for weaker writers, directly helping them spell words they don't know, or providing resources (e.g., word banks) designed to facilitate correct spelling
  - o Allowing weaker writers to dictate their compositions or write with a keyboard
  - o Supporting the thinking and creative processes involved in writing by having weaker writers talk out their story before writing, using webs or graphic organizers to generate and sequence ideas, or drawing pictures depicting what would happen in the story
  - o Supporting the students' revising efforts by using revising checklists or through direct help from the teacher or a peer
  - o Providing additional personalized help by selecting writing topics, offering shorter or easier writing assignments, small-group instruction, additional homework assignments, and extra instruction on grammar and sentence writing skills

- **Intervene early.** Early supplementary instruction or intervention to prevent or alleviate writing difficulties yields more benefits than remediating problems in later grades. The basic goal is to help struggling writers catch up with their peers early, before their difficulties become more resistant to improvement. Such programs typically seek to accelerate the progress of struggling writers by providing them with additional instruction, either in a small group or through one-on-one tutoring.

  A few studies have examined the effectiveness of early intervention programs in writing. In each study, young children received extra instruction in either handwriting or spelling from an adult tutor, classroom aide, or a parent volunteer. The studies demonstrated that early intervention programs that provide instruction in either handwriting or spelling can have a positive effect on struggling writers' fluency of composition, as measured by the children's ability to either craft sentences or generate text when writing. These results have important implications for the prevention of writing problems because researchers have found that impaired compositional fluency in the primary grades may serve as the developmental origin of writing problems in later grades.

  Early intervention practices that are likely to be effective include allocating additional time for writing, providing individually guided assistance when writing, and supplying additional help in mastering critical skills, such as planning, revising, and sentence construction.

- **Expect that each child will learn to write.** Teachers sometimes set low expectations for students with writing and learning difficulties. These low expectations may lead to fewer interactions with the teacher, less attention and praise, more criticism, and less informative feedback. But many of these students can be taught to write, and recognizing that they are capable is a critical element for success. With this positive approach, teachers
  - Ignore negative expectations
  - Set high but realistic goals for each student's writing performance
  - Help students develop a positive attitude about their capabilities
  - Plan writing lessons so that all children can accomplish tasks successfully
  - Monitor and improve the quality of classroom interactions for struggling writers
  - Build a positive relationship with each child, accepting students as individuals and showing enthusiasm for their interests

- **Identify and address roadblocks to writing.** Another critical element in helping struggling writers is to identify and address obstacles that impede their success in learning to write. Children with learning disabilities may exhibit one or more inhibiting behaviors, including a low tolerance for failure, attention difficulties, and problems in activating and orchestrating the processes involved in learning. Other roadblocks include difficulties such as impulsivity, disorganization, inflexibility, lack of persistence, frequent absences, and poor home support. Teachers need to address these or any other roadblocks that might impede the writing development of struggling students. For example, not only teach students a planning strategy that will help them improve their written work, but also include a component that addresses their roadblocks. Students should be encouraged to attribute their success to their efforts as well as to the use of the planning strategy.

- **Take advantage of technological tools for writing.** A wide assortment of technological devices provides new options for minimizing the writing difficulties experienced by students with writing difficulties, allowing them to circumvent some problems and obtain support in overcoming others. These devices make the process of writing easier as well as more motivating. Thanks to word processing programs, for example, revising can be done without tedious recopying, the resulting paper can be presented in a wide range of professional-looking formats, and typing provides an inherently easier means for producing text.

  Technological tools can also provide support for planning and revising through the use of outlining and graphic mapping software, and multimedia applications. In addition, spell checkers, word prediction programs, grammar and style checkers, and speech synthesis all help to make text production easier. Finally, the use of computer networks allows students to collaborate and communicate easily with audiences that extend beyond their classroom.

  It is important to keep in mind that although technology can help students with learning difficulties to write, it does not make writing instruction superfluous. For instance, many of these students fail to take advantage of word processing when revising because they continue to revise in the same old way, mostly trying to correct mechanical errors. By teaching them to focus their attention on substantive changes when revising, students gain much greater use of the editing features of word processing and are more likely to make additions and rewrite parts of their text. Similarly, a spell checker will not eliminate spelling errors or the need for spelling instruction.

STRATEGIES TO CONSIDER

Accommodation Strategies for Students With Writing Disorders

Accommodation strategies help bypass writing difficulties and reduce the impact that writing has on the learning process so that students can focus more on the content of their writing. The accommodations can adjust the rate and volume of writing, the complexity of the task, and the tools used to create the final product. Here are some accommodation strategies in each of these areas (Jones, 2000; Richards, 1998).

Accommodating the Rate of Work Produced

- **Allow more time** for students to complete written tasks, such as note taking, written tests, and copying. Also, allow these students to begin written projects earlier than others. Consider including time in the student's schedule for acting as an aide, and then have the student use that time for making up or starting new written work.

- **Encourage developing keyboarding skills and using the computer.** Students can begin to learn keyboarding in first grade. Encourage them to use word processing programs. Teaching handwriting is still important, but students may produce longer and more complex writing with the computer.

- **Have students prepare worksheets in advance,** complete with the required headings, such as name, date, and topic. Provide a standard template with this information already on it.

Accommodating the Volume of Work Produced

- **Provide partially completed outlines** and ask students to fill in the missing details. This is a valuable, but not burdensome, exercise in note taking.

- **Allow students to dictate to another student.** One student (scribe) writes down what another student says verbatim and then allows the dictating student to make changes without help from the scribe.

- **Correct poor spelling in first drafts,** but do not lower the grade because of it. However, make clear to the students that spelling does eventually count, especially in assignments completed over time.

- **Reduce copying of printed work.** Avoid having students copy over something already printed in a text, like entire mathematics problems. Provide a worksheet with the text material already on it, or have the students just write down their original answers or work.

- **Allow students to use abbreviations** in some writing, such as *b/4* for *before,* *b/c* for *because,* and *w/* for *with.* These are also helpful shortcuts during note taking.

Accommodating the Complexity of the Work Produced

- **Allow students to use print or cursive writing.** Many students with dysgraphia are more comfortable with print (manuscript) letters. However, students should still be encouraged to use cursive writing. It eliminates the need to pick up a pencil and deciding where to replace it after each letter. Cursive has very few reversible letters, a typical source of confusion for students with dysgraphia. It eliminates word-spacing problems and allows the writing process to flow more easily.

- **Teach and model for students the stages of writing,** such as brainstorming, drafting, editing, and proofreading.

- **Encourage students to use a spell checker.** Using the spell checker decreases the demands on the writing process, lowering frustration and diverting more energy to thought production. For students who also have reading difficulties, concurrently using a computer reading program also decreases the demands on the writer.

- **Have students proofread after a delay in time** when they are more likely to catch writing errors. This way, they will see what they *actually* wrote rather than what they *thought* they wrote.

Accommodating the Tools of the Work Production

- **Allow students to use lined and graph paper.** Lined paper helps students keep their writing level across the page. Have younger students use graph paper for mathematics calculations to keep columns and rows straight. Older students can turned lined paper sideways for column control.

- **Allow students to use different writing instruments.** Students should use the writing instrument they find most comfortable. Some students have difficulty writing with ballpoint pens, preferring thin-line marker pens that have more friction with the paper. Others prefer mechanical pencils.

- **Have pencil grips available** in all styles. Even high school students enjoy these fun grips, and some like the big pencils usually associated with primary school.

- **Allow some students to use speech recognition programs.** For students with very difficult writing problems, using a speech recognition program within a word processing program allows them to dictate their thoughts rather than type them. However, this is not a substitute for learning handwriting.

STRATEGIES TO CONSIDER

Modification Strategies for Students With Writing Disorders

For some students, accommodation strategies will not remove the barriers that their writing difficulties pose. Teachers may need to make modifications in these students' assignments. Here are some suggested modifications in the volume, complexity, and format of written work (Richards, 1998; Jones, 2000).

Modifying the Volume of Work Produced

- **Limit the amount of copying that students do.** For example, to copy definitions, have the students rewrite and shorten them without affecting the meaning. Another option is to have them use drawings or diagrams to answer questions.

- **Reduce the length** of written assignments. Emphasize that students should be spending more time improving the quality of their work rather than increasing its length.

Modifying the Complexity of the Work Product

- **Prioritization of tasks.** Stress or de-emphasize certain tasks for a complex activity. For example, students could focus on complex sentences in one activity and on using descriptive words in another. Evaluate the assignment based on the prioritized tasks.

- **Use cooperative learning groups** to give students a chance to play different roles, such as brainstormer, encourager, information organizer, etc.

- **Provide intermittent deadlines** for long-term assignments. Work with other teachers when setting due dates, especially those involving writing assignments. Parents may also be able to monitor the student's work at home so that it can comply with deadlines.

- **Encourage graphic organizers.** Preorganization strategies such as the use of graphic organizers will help students get their main ideas in line before tackling the writing process. On the following page are just a few examples of the many different types of graphic organizers.

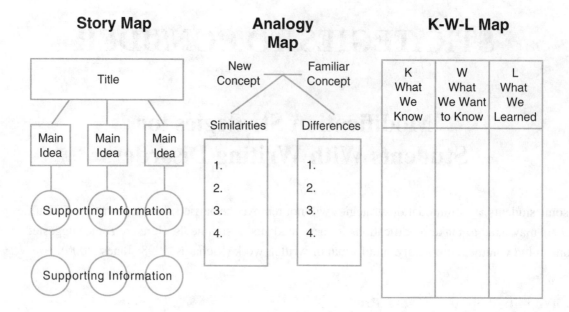

Modifying the Format of the Work Produced

- **Allow students to submit alternative projects,** such as an oral report or visual project. Ask for a short written report to explain or expand on the oral or visual work. However, these alternatives should not replace all writing assignments.

- **Allow students to use information directly from the Internet** in their term papers and other projects. Retrieved information still needs to be cited, but this method reduces the amount of copying.

STRATEGIES TO CONSIDER

Remediation Strategies for Students With Writing Disorders

Students should not be allowed to avoid the process of writing, no matter how severe their dysgraphia. Writing is an important skill that they will eventually use to sign documents, write checks, fill out forms, take messages, or make grocery lists. Thus they need to learn to write even if they can do so for just a short time.

Remediation strategies focus on reteaching information or a particular skill to help students acquire mastery and fluency. Substantial modeling of all strategies is essential for the students to be successful. Here are some suggested areas for remediation (Jones, 2000; Richards, 1998).

- **Teaching Handwriting Continuously.** Many students would like to have better handwriting. Build handwriting instruction into the students' schedule. Provide opportunities to teach them this, keeping in mind the age, aptitude, and attitude of each student.

- **Helping With Spelling.** Spelling difficulties are common for students with dysgraphia, especially if sequencing is a major problem. The students with dysgraphia who also have dyslexia need structured and specific instruction in learning to spell phonetically. This skill can help them use technical tools that rely on phonetic spelling to find a word.

- **Correcting the Pencil Grip.** Young children should be encouraged to use a proper pencil grip from the beginning of their writing experience. Descriptive research indicates that, for the best results, the grip should be consistently between 3/4 inch to 1 inch from the pencil tip. Moderate pressure should be applied, and the angle of the pencil to the paper should be about 45 degrees and slanted toward the student's writing arm. Accomplishing the proper slant will be difficult for left-handed writers.

  A poor pencil grip can be changed to the appropriate form by using plastic pencil grips, which are commercially available. Obviously, it is easier to encourage the correct grip as soon as the student begins writing; older students with poor grip posture find it very difficult to make changes. The teacher needs to consider whether it is worth the time and effort to get the student to change the grip to be more efficient. If not, identify compensatory strategies that are available for the student.

- **Writing a Paragraph.** Students can be taught this eight-step process for writing a paragraph.
  1. Plan the paper by thinking about the ideas that you want to include in it.
  2. Organize the ideas with a graphic organizer. Place the main idea in the center and supporting facts on lines coming out from the center, much like the spokes of a wheel.
  3. Analyze the graphic organizer to ensure that all your ideas have been included. Check your spelling.
  4. Write a draft of the paragraph, focusing on the main ideas.

5. Edit your work for punctuation, capitalization, grammar, and spelling.
6. Use the corrections made in Step 5 to revise the paragraph.
7. Proofread again, editing and revising as needed.
8. Develop a final product in written or typed form.

- **Increasing the Speed of Writing.** Many students with dysgraphia write very slowly. To identify the appropriate remediation strategy, teachers need to determine the cause of the slowness.
  - Is it the actual formation of the letters? If so, the students need more practice on this skill, perhaps by saying the letters aloud while writing. Air writing can be helpful because it uses many more muscles to form the letters. Also, have the students write large letters on a big surface, such as a chalkboard or dry-erase board.
  - Is it in the organization of ideas? If so, provide the students with graphic organizers to help them sort and prioritize their thoughts and facts.

- **Dealing With Fatigue.** Poor motor sequencing or an incorrect pencil grip can lead to fatigue with the writing process. The following can help students relieve the stress of writing and relax the writing hand.
  - Take writing breaks at regular intervals. Students should realize that it is permissible to stop occasionally and relax the muscles of the hand. This break also gives them a chance to review what has been written and to continue to organize their thoughts.
  - Shake the hands quickly to relax the muscles. This increases blood flow to the finger and hand muscles.
  - Rub the hands on some texture, like the carpet or clothes.
  - Rub the hands together and focus on the feeling of warmth. The rubbing also helps to restore blood flow to the area.

- **Giving Praise, Being Patient, and Encouraging Patience.** Genuinely praise the positive aspects of students' work. Be patient with their efforts and problems, and encourage them to have patience with themselves.

STRATEGIES TO CONSIDER

Expressive Writing for Students With Learning Disabilities

One of the goals of teaching writing is to help students express their thoughts and ideas in personal narratives and persuasive essays. Students whose learning disabilities include problems with writing often have great difficulty with this. Finding ways of helping these students has been the subject of considerable research.

A meta-analysis studied the effectiveness of research-based instructional approaches for teaching expressive writing to students with learning disabilities. The following three components of instruction consistently led to improving student success in learning expressive writing (Baker, Gersten, & Graham, 2003):

1. Adhering to a basic framework of planning, writing, and revision

Most of the successful interventions used a basic framework of planning, writing, and revision. Each step was taught explicitly, followed by multiple examples and the use of memory devices, such as prompt cards or mnemonics.

Planning. Planning results in better first drafts. One way of helping students develop a plan of action is to provide a planning think sheet that uses structured and sequential prompts. It specifies the topic and poses questions to guide the student's thought processes. See the sample sheet at the right.

Creating a First Draft. The planning think sheet helps students create first drafts by serving as a guide through the writing process. The guide also gives the student and teacher a common language for an ongoing discussion about the assignment. This student-teacher interaction emphasizes cooperative work rather than the recent method of writing mainly in isolation.

> **Planning Think Sheet**
>
> TOPIC: _____
>
> Who am I writing for?
>
> Why am I writing this?
>
> What do I already know about this?
>
> How can I group my ideas?
>
> How will I organize my ideas?

Revising and Editing. The skills of revising and editing are critical to successful writing. Some researchers found a peer editing approach to be particularly effective. Here's how it works:

- Pairs of students alternate their roles as student-writer and student-critic.
- The student-critic identifies ambiguities and asks the writer for clarification. The writer then makes revisions, with the teacher's help if needed.
- Once the clarifications are made, the student pair then moves on to correct capitalization, punctuation, and spelling.
- Throughout the process, the student writers have to explain the intent of their writings and continue revising their essays to reflect their intent accurately. These clarifying dialogues help the student pairs to understand each other's perspectives.

2. Teaching explicitly the critical steps in the writing process

Because different types of writing (e.g., personal narrative or persuasive essay) are based on different structures, explicitly teaching text structures provides the students with a specific guide to completing their writing task. For example, writing a persuasive essay requires a thesis and supporting arguments. Narrative writing focuses on character development and a story climax. Teach these structures, using explicit models of each text type.

3. Providing feedback guided by the information explicitly taught

The researchers found that successful interventions always included frequent feedback to the students on the quality of their overall writing, strengths, and missing elements. Combining feedback with instruction strengthens the dialogue between student and teacher, thereby helping students to develop a sensitivity to their own writing style. This sensitivity may lead students to reflect on, realize, and correct writing problems as well as perceive their ideas from another's perspective. The research studies also showed that student gains were more likely to occur when the teachers and other students provided feedback mainly in the areas of organization, originality, and interpretation.

> *Researchers found that frequent feedback was a powerful tool for improving students' writing.*

Chapter 7

Mathematical Disabilities

More researchers are beginning to accept the idea that humans are born with a number sense. Recent research has shown that toddlers have a sense of numbers and can already deal with limited arithmetic operations (e.g., simple adding and subtracting) before the age of one year (Diamond & Hopson, 1998). By the age of two years, most toddlers can recognize the greater-than and less-than relationships (the concept of *ordinality*) between numerical values as large as 4 and 5, even though they have not yet learned the numbers' verbal labels (Brannon & van der Walle, 2001).

Early numerical capability makes sense in terms of our past development as a species. In primitive societies, a youngster going for a stroll out of the cave needed to determine quickly if the number of animals in an approaching pack might spell danger or just an opportunity for play. Young hunters had to determine how *many* individuals would be needed to take down a large animal. Recognizing that three apples provide more nourishment than one was also a valuable survival asset. Numeration, then, persisted in the genetic code.

LEARNING TO CALCULATE

Brain imaging studies have revealed clues about how the brain performs different types of mathematical operations. Functional MRI scans indicate that the parietal and frontal lobes (Figure 7.1) are primarily involved in basic mental mathematics (e.g., counting forward or doing exact and approximate calculations). Activation intensifies as the number size increases. Approximate calculations require larger cerebral areas than exact calculations, presumably because approximation requires more number manipulation (Dehaene,

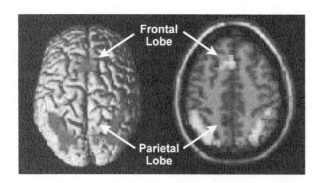

Figure 7.1 These scanning images show the regions of the brain that are activated during typical number calculation tasks. Most of the activity is in the frontal and parietal lobes. The activation increases with number size. Larger brain areas are needed for approximate calculations than for exact calculations (Dehaene et al., 2003; Molko et al., 2003).

Piazza, Pinel, & Cohen, 2003; Molko, Cachia, Rivière, Mangin, Bruandet, Bihan, et al., 2003). Other areas of the brain are recruited into action when dealing with more complex mathematics, such as in algebraic calculations and geometry (Qin, Carter, Silk, Stenger, Fissell, Goode, et al., 2004).

Numerical Reasoning Independent of Language

Research evidence continues to accumulate that casts doubt on a long-held belief that language underlies mathematical ability and other forms of abstract thinking. Brain imaging studies now seem to confirm that the brain areas responsible for calculations are different from those used in processing language. Some of the evidence comes from the following investigations.

- As mentioned earlier, most toddlers can recognize the greater-than and less-than relationships even though they do not yet have the vocabulary to label the integers.
- fMRI scans typically show more activation in the left temporal lobe during language processing (Figure 4.1), while numerical processing tends to activate the frontal and parietal lobes (Figure 7.1).
- Studies show that patients with severe damage to the language centers of their brains can still interpret mathematical formulas and solve problems involving numerical symbols (Varley, Klessinger, Romanowski, & Siegal, 2005).
- Observations from teachers and parents of children who are good with words but bad with numbers, and vice versa.

No matter how helpful language may be in developing mathematical ability, it is not necessary to calculation, and it is processed in different parts of the brain. The implication for schooling is to remember that students with mathematical difficulties may not necessarily have difficulties with language, and those with language problems may still be capable in mathematics.

Gender Differences in Mathematics

For decades, boys have consistently scored higher than girls on standardized mathematics tests, such as the SAT and the National Assessment of Educational Progress (NAEP). High school and college mathematics classes usually contain more males than females. Those seeking to explain this gender disparity have typically put the blame on outmoded social stereotypes. Recently, however, they have added discoveries in brain science as potential explanations. They say, for example, that males' brains are about 6 to 8 percent larger than females' brains. And brain imaging studies show that males seem to have an advantage in visual-spatial ability (the ability to rotate objects in their heads) while females are more adept at language processing. But whether these differences translate into a genetic advantage for males over females in mathematical processing remains to be seen and proved.

To some extent, the belief that boys are much better at mathematics than girls is out of proportion to the data. Recent test results indicate that the gender gap is narrowing. In the 2005 SAT, average mathematics scores for females rose by 3 points over the previous year to 504, while males' scores rose by 1 point to 538 over the same period (College Board, 2005). The 2004 NAEP mathematics test results showed an average score of 308 for high school males and 306 for females, a difference of only 2 points (NCES, 2004).

Although most neuroscientists will admit to gender differences in how the brain processes information, they are reluctant to support the concept that these differences offer a lifelong learning advantage for one sex over the other in any academic area. It is important, too, for educators to know about these gender differences and how they change through various stages of human development. The danger here is that people will think that if the differences are innate and unchangeable, then nothing can be done to improve the situation. Such ideas are damaging because they leave the student feeling discouraged, and they ignore the brain's plasticity and exceptional ability to learn complex information when suitably motivated. A variety of teaching approaches and strategies may indeed make up for these gender differences.

DIFFICULTIES IN MATHEMATICS

For many years, educators recognized that some children were very adept in mathematical calculations while others struggled despite much effort and motivation. But the percentage of school-age children who experience difficulties in learning mathematics has been growing steadily in the last three decades. Why is that? Is the brain's ability to perform arithmetic calculations declining? If so, why? Does the brain get less arithmetic practice because technology has shifted computation from brain cells to inexpensive electronic calculators?

In previous chapters, we have referred to the considerable amount of research that has been conducted to understand how the human brain learns. As a result, we also have a greater understanding of the diagnosis and remediation of learning disorders, especially in areas of language, reading, and writing. In addition, a few researchers have been studying why students have problems with learning early mathematics, despite normal intelligence and adequate instruction.

About 6 to 8 percent of school-age children have serious difficulty processing mathematics (Fuchs & Fuchs, 2002; Shalev, Auerbach, Manor, & Gross-Tsur, 2000). This is about the same number as children who have serious reading problems. However, because of the strong emphasis that our society places on the need to learn reading, many more research studies have focused on problems in this area than on mathematics. Nonetheless, the growing number of students who are having trouble learning mathematics has spurred research interest in how the brain does calculations and the possible causes of mathematical difficulties.

Dyscalculia

The condition that causes persistent problems with processing numerical calculations is referred to as *dyscalculia*. Dyscalculia is a difficulty in conceptualizing numbers, number relationships, outcomes of numerical operations, and estimation, that is, what to expect as an outcome of an operation. Dyscalculia manifests in a person as having difficulty:

- Mastering arithmetic facts by the traditional methods of teaching, particularly the methods involving counting
- Learning abstract concepts of time and direction, telling and keeping track of time, and the sequence of past and future events
- Acquiring spatial orientation and space organization, including left/right orientation, trouble reading maps, and grappling with mechanical processes
- Following directions in sports that demand sequencing or rules, and keeping track of scores and players during games such as card and board games
- Following sequential directions and sequencing (including reading numbers out of sequence, substitutions, reversals, omissions and doing operations backwards), organizing detailed information, remembering specific facts and formulas for completing their mathematical calculations

Dyscalculia can be (1) quantitative, which is a difficulty in counting and calculating, (2) qualitative, which is a difficulty in the conceptualizing of mathematics processes and spatial sense, or (3) mixed, which is the inability to integrate quantity and space.

Environmental Causes

Attitudes About Mathematics. Even individuals with normal abilities in processing numerical operations can display mathematical disorders. Because they have no inherent mathematical deficits, their difficulties most likely arise from environmental causes. In modern American society, reading and writing have become the main measures of a good student. Mathematics ability has been regarded more as a specialized function rather than as a general indicator of intelligence. Consequently, the stigma of not being able to do mathematics was reduced and became socially acceptable. Just hearing their parents say "I wasn't very good at math" allowed children to embrace the social attitudes that regard mathematics failure as acceptable and routine.

In recent years, schools have placed a heavy emphasis on raising standards in all curriculum areas. At the same time, the No Child Left Behind Act requirements include high-stakes assessments in reading and mathematics. Despite these initiatives, student attitudes about mathematics have not improved much. Surveys show that most students (including those who like mathematics) find making non-mathematical mistakes much more embarrassing than making mathematical mistakes (Latterell, 2005). Furthermore, regardless of the efforts toward gender equity, female high school students still rate themselves as less confident in mathematics than their male peers (Morge, 2005). These

> *Despite higher standards and high-stakes testing, student attitudes about mathematics have not improved much.*

findings are unsettling, especially because other research studies have shown that attitudes are formed by social forces and predict academic performance. Not surprisingly, students with positive attitudes about what they are learning achieve more than students with poor attitudes (Singh, Granville, & Dika, 2002).

Apparently, higher standards and increased testing are not sufficient as yet to improve how students feel about learning mathematics.

Fear of Mathematics. Some children develop a fear (or phobia) of mathematics because of negative experiences in their past or a simple lack of self-confidence with numbers. Mathematics anxiety conjures up fear of some type. Perhaps it is the fear that one won't be able to do the calculations, or the fear that it's too difficult, or the fear of failure, which often stems from having a lack of confidence. In people with mathematics anxiety, the fear of failure often causes their minds to draw a blank, leading to more frustration and more blanks. Added pressure of having time limits on mathematics tests also raises the levels of anxiety for many students.

Typically, students with this phobia have a limited understanding of mathematical concepts. They may rely mainly on memorizing procedures, rules, and routines without much conceptual understanding, so panic soon sets in. Mathematics phobia can be as challenging as any learning disability, but it is important to remember that these students have neurological systems for computation that are normal. They need help primarily in replacing the memory of failure with the possibility of success. Students with mathematical disorders, on the other hand, have a neurological deficit that results in persistent difficulty in processing numbers.

Quality of Teaching. One critical factor in how well students learn mathematics is the quality of the teaching. Studies show that student achievement in mathematics is strongly linked to the teacher's expertise in mathematics. Students of an expert teacher perform better on achievement tests than students of a teacher with limited training in mathematics (NSF, 2004). Presumably, the number of students being taught by teachers with expertise in mathematics will grow as the states take steps to meet the "highly qualified teacher" requirements of the No Child Left Behind Act.

Neurological and Other Causes

Because the parietal lobe is heavily involved with number operations, damage to this area can result in difficulties. Studies of individuals with Gerstmann syndrome—the result of damage to the parietal lobe—showed that they had serious problems with mathematical calculations as well as right-left disorientation, but no problems with oral language skills (Lemer, Dehaene, Spelke, & Cohen, 2003; Suresh & Sebastian, 2000).

Individuals with visual processing weaknesses almost always display difficulties with mathematics. This is probably because success in mathematics requires one to visualize numbers and mathematical situations, especially in algebra and geometry. Students with sequencing difficulties also may have dyscalculia because they cannot remember the order of mathematical operations or the specific formulas needed to complete a set of computations.

> **Mathematical Disorders**
>
> General Symptoms:
> - Inconsistent results with addition, subtraction, multiplication, and division
> - Inability to remember mathematical formulas, rules, or concepts
> - Difficulty with abstract concepts of time and direction
> - Consistent errors when recalling numbers, including transpositions, omissions, and reversals
> - Difficulty remembering how to keep score during games

Genetic factors also seem to play a role. For example, studies of identical twins reveal close mathematics scores. Children from families with a history of mathematical giftedness or retardation show common aptitudes with other family members. Girls born with Turner syndrome (a condition caused by the partial or complete absence of one of the two X chromosomes normally found in women) usually display dyscalculia, among other learning problems (Murphy, Mazzocco, Gerner, & Henry, 2006).

Types of Mathematical Disorders

The complexity of mathematics makes the study of mathematical disorders particularly challenging for researchers. Learning deficits can include difficulties in mastering basic number concepts, counting skills, and processing arithmetic operations, as well as procedural, retrieval, and visual-spatial deficits (Geary, 2000). As with any learning disability, each of these deficits can range from mild to severe.

Number Concept Difficulties. As mentioned before, the understanding of small numbers and quantity appears to be present at birth. The understanding of larger numbers and place value, however, seems to develop during the preschool and early elementary years. Studies show that most children with mathematical disorders nevertheless have their basic number competencies intact (Geary, 2000).

Counting Skill Deficits. Studies of children with mathematical disorders show that they have deficits in counting knowledge and counting accuracy. Some may also have problems keeping numerical information in working memory while counting, resulting in counting errors.

Difficulties With Arithmetic Skills. Children with mathematical disorders have difficulties solving simple and complex arithmetic problems. Their difficulties stem mainly from deficits in both numerical procedures (solving 6 + 5 or 4 × 4) and working memory. Moreover, deficits in visual-spatial skills can lead to problems with arithmetic because of misalignment of numerals in multicolumn addition. Although *procedural, memory,* and *visual-spatial* deficits can occur separately, they are often interconnected.

Procedural Disorders. Students displaying this disorder:

- Use arithmetic procedures (algorithms) that are developmentally immature
- Have problems sequencing the steps of multistep procedures
- Have difficulty understanding the concepts associated with procedures
- Make frequent mistakes when using procedures

The cause of this disorder is unknown. However, researchers suspect a dysfunction in the brain's left hemisphere, which specializes in procedural tasks.

Memory Disorders. Students displaying this disorder:

- Have difficulty retrieving arithmetic facts
- Have a high error rate when they do retrieve arithmetic facts
- Retrieve incorrect facts that are associated with the correct facts

Here again, a dysfunction of the left hemisphere is suspected, mainly because these individuals frequently have reading disorders as well (D'Amico & Guarnera, 2005). This association further suggests that memory deficits may be inheritable.

Visual-Spatial Deficits. Students with this disorder:

- Have difficulties in the spatial arrangement of their work, such as aligning the columns in multicolumn addition
- Often misread numerical signs, rotate and transpose numbers, or both
- Misinterpret spatial placement of numerals, resulting in place value errors
- Have difficulty with problems involving space in areas, as required in algebra and geometry

This disorder is more closely associated with deficits in the right hemisphere, which specializes in visual-spatial tasks. Some studies suggest that the left parietal lobe also may be implicated.

Many students eventually overcome procedural disorders as they mature and learn to rely on sequence diagrams and other tools to remember the steps of mathematical procedures. Those with visual-spatial disorders also improve when they discover the bene-fits of graph paper and learn to solve certain algebra and geometry problems with logic rather than through spatial analysis alone. However, memory deficits do not seem to improve with maturity. Studies indicate that individuals with this problem will continue to have difficulties retrieving basic arithmetic facts throughout life. This finding may

> *Children often outgrow procedural and visual-spatial difficulties, but memory problems may continue throughout life.*

suggest that the memory problem not only exists for mathematical operations but may signal a more general deficit in retrieving information from memory.

Associating Dyscalculia With Other Disorders

Reading Disorders. Some students with dyscalculia can also have developmental reading difficulties, or dyslexia, but these disorders are not genetically linked (Fletcher, 2005). Students with both disorders are less successful solving mathematics problems than those who have only dyscalculia, mainly because they have difficulty translating word problems into mathematical expressions. Computer programs are now available for elementary level students that address both weaknesses. For example, *Knowledge Adventure* has two software titles that focus on teaching basic mathematics and reading skills while adhering to national and state standards. Each program provides instruction at a student's own pace and includes automatic progress tracking for each student so teachers can provide additional instruction to those who need it.

Attention-Deficit Hyperactivity Disorder (ADHD). Because many children with ADHD have difficulty with mathematics, some researchers wondered if these two conditions had related genetic components, increasing the possibility that they would be inherited together. But studies show that these two disorders are transmitted independently and are connected to distinctly different genetic regions (Monuteaux, Faraone, Herzig, Navsaria, & Biederman, 2005). These findings underscore the need for separate identification and treatment strategies for children with both conditions.

Nonverbal Learning Disability (NLD). Individuals with NLD have difficulty processing nonverbal information but are very good at processing verbal information. They tend to be excessively verbal and expressive and show weaknesses in visual and spatial tasks. Although there is little evidence that NLD is directly associated with dyscalculia, NLD affects one's ability to manage and understand nonverbal learning assignments. Thus, students with NLD will have problems with handwriting, perceiving spatial relationships, drawing and copying geometric forms and designs, and grasping mathematics concepts and skills.

The Future of Research in Mathematics Disorders

Many questions remain unanswered regarding the environmental and innate causes of mathematical disorders. For example, we now believe that infants are born with an innate sense of number logic and the ability to perform simple arithmetic operations. Some researchers believe that toddlers can even communicate with each other about their counting through a form of "toddler arithmetic" (Diamond & Hopson, 1998). How do they do that? By learning more about exactly how infants' brains process arithmetic calculations, we can build on this foundation when exposing children to more complex mathematics. Likewise, researchers need to determine which types of mathematical disorders are simply delays in development and which may represent more fundamental problems. Other questions for research include the following: What genetic factors affect the neural networks and cognitive skills that support mathematical operations? To what degree does visual-spatial reasoning contribute to mathematical processing? What are effective ways for diagnosing mathematical disabilities in young children?

The ultimate goal of research is to develop remedies to help individuals deal with their problems. Remediation becomes difficult when a disorder is not well understood. Nonetheless, enough is now known to suggest some strategies that are likely to help those challenged by mathematical processing. Further research can only improve on this situation.

WHAT EDUCATORS NEED TO CONSIDER

Studies show that using intense tutoring with first graders who display problems with calculations significantly improved their end-of-year achievement in mathematics (Fuchs, Compton, Fuchs, Paulsen, Bryant, & Hamlett, 2005). The key, of course, is early detection so that interventions can begin as soon as practicable.

Determining the Source of the Problem

The first task facing educators who deal with children with mathematics disorders is to determine the nature of the problem. Obviously, environmental causes require different interventions than developmental causes. Low performance on a mathematics test *may* indicate that a problem exists, but tests do not provide information on the exact source of the poor performance. Standardized tests, such as the *Brigance Comprehensive Inventory of Basic Skills—Revised*, are available that provide more precise information on whether the problems stem from deficits in counting, number facts, or procedures.

Educators should examine the degree to which students with mathematics difficulties possess the prerequisite skills for learning mathematical operations. What skills are weak, and what can we do about that? They also should look at the mathematics curriculum to determine how much mathematics is being taught and the types of instructional strategies that teachers are using. Are we trying to cover too much? Are we using enough visual and manipulative aids? Are we developing student strengths and not just focusing on their weaknesses?

Prerequisite Skills. Examining the nature of mathematics curriculum and instruction may reveal clues about how the school system approaches teaching these topics. A good frame of reference is the recognition that students need to have mastered a certain number of skills before they can understand and apply the principles of more complex mathematical operations. Mathematics educators have suggested that the following seven skills are prerequisites to successfully learning mathematics (Sharma, 2006). They are the ability to

1. Follow sequential directions

2. Recognize patterns

3. Estimate by forming a reasonable guess about quantity, size, magnitude, and amount

4. Visualize pictures in one's mind and manipulate them

5. Have a good sense of spatial orientation and space organization, including telling left from right, compass directions, horizontal and vertical directions

6. Do deductive reasoning—that is, reason from a general principle to a particular instance, or from a stated premise to a logical conclusion

7. Do inductive reasoning—that is, come to a natural understanding that is not the result of conscious attention or reasoning, easily detecting the patterns in different situations and the interrelationships between procedures and concepts

Students, for example, who are unable to follow sequential directions will have great difficulty understanding the concept of long division, which requires retention of several different processes performed in a particular sequence. First one estimates, then multiplies, then compares, then subtracts, then brings down a number, and the cycle repeats. Those with directional difficulties will be unsure which number goes inside the division sign or on top of the fraction. Moving through the division problem also presents other directional difficulties: One reads to the right, then records a number up, then multiplies the numbers diagonally, then records the product down below while watching for place value, then brings a number down, and so on.

Diagnostic Tools for Assessing Learning Difficulties in Mathematics

Research studies over the last 15 years suggest that five critical factors affect the learning of mathematics. Each factor can serve as a diagnostic tool for assessing the nature of any learning difficulties students may experience with mathematical processing (Augustyniak, Murphy, & Phillips, 2005; Sharma, 2006).

- **Level of Cognitive Awareness.** Students come to a learning situation with varying levels of cognitive awareness about that learning. The levels can range from no cognitive awareness to high levels of cognitive functioning. The teacher's first task is to determine the students' level of cognitive awareness and the strategies each student brings to the mathematics task. This is not easy, but it can be accomplished if the teacher does the following:
  - o Interviews the students individually and observes how each one approaches a mathematical problem that needs to be solved
  - o Asks "What is the student thinking?" and "What formal and informal strategies is the student using?"
  - o Determines what prerequisite skills are in place and which are poor or missing
  - o Determines if a mathematics answer is correct or incorrect and asks students to explain how they arrived at the answer

Knowing the levels of the students' cognitive awareness and prerequisite skills will give the teacher valuable information for selecting and introducing new concepts and skills.

- **Mathematics Learning Profile.** Researchers agree that each person processes mathematics differently and that these differences run along a continuum from primarily quantitative to primarily qualitative.

Quantitative learners:

o Prefer entities that have definite values, such as length, time, volume, and size
o Prefer procedural approaches to problem solving and tend to be very methodical and sequential in all they do
o Approach mathematics as though following a recipe
o Prefer to break down problems into their parts, solve them, and then reassemble the components to deal with larger problems
o Are better at deductive reasoning, that is, reasoning from the general principle to a particular instance
o Learn best when mathematics is presented as a highly structured subject and with a continuous linear focus
o Prefer hands-on materials with a counting basis, such as base-10 blocks and number lines
o Stick with one standardized way of solving problems because alternative solutions are often perceived as uncomfortable and distracting

Qualitative learners:

o Approach mathematics tasks holistically and intuitively
o Describe mathematical elements in terms of their qualities rather than by separate parts
o Are social learners who reason by talking through questions, associations, and examples
o Learn by seeing relationships between concepts and procedures
o Draw associations and parallels between familiar situations and the current task
o Focus on visual-spatial aspects of mathematical information
o Have difficulty with sequences, algorithms, elementary mathematics, and precise calculations
o In their work, tend to invent shortcuts, bypass steps, and consolidate procedures with intuitive reasoning
o Often do not practice enough to attain levels of automaticity

Because both types of learning styles are present in mathematics classes, teachers need to incorporate multiple instructional strategies. Teaching to one style alone leaves out students with the other style, many of whom may do poorly in mathematics as a result. In fact, some may even exhibit the symptoms of mathematics disorders.

- **Language of Mathematics.** Mathematical disorders often arise when students fail to understand the language of mathematics, which has its own symbolic representations, syntax, and terminology. Solving word problems requires the ability to translate the language of English into the language of mathematics. The translation is likely to be successful if the student recognizes English language equivalents for each mathematical statement. For example, if the teacher asks the class to solve the problem "76 take away 8," the students will correctly write the expression in the exact order stated,

"76 - 8." But if the teacher says, "Subtract 8 from 76," a student following the language order could mistakenly write, "8 - 76." Learning to identify and correctly translate mathematical syntax becomes critical to student success in problem solving.

Language can be an obstacle in other ways. Students may learn a limited vocabulary for performing basic arithmetic operations, such as "add" and "multiply," only to run into difficulties when they encounter expressions asking for the "sum" or "product" of numbers. Teachers can avoid this problem by introducing synonyms for every function: "Let us *multiply* 6 and 5. We are finding the *product* of 6 and 5. The product of 6 *times* 5 is 30."

- **Prerequisite Skills.** As noted earlier, the seven prerequisite skills necessary to learning mathematics successfully are nonmathematical in nature. However, they must be mastered before even the most basic understandings of number concepts and arithmetic operations can be learned. Teachers need to assess the extent to which these seven skills are present in each student.

  Teachers might consider using this simple profile diagram to assist in their assessment. After assessing the student's level on each skill, they can analyze the results and decide on a plan of action that will address any areas needing improvement.

  Students with four or more scores in the 1 to 2 range will have significant problems learning the basic concepts of mathematics. They will need instruction and practice in mastering these skills before they can be expected to master mathematical content.

Prerequisite Skills Profile for Mathematics

Student's Name: _____ Date: _____

Directions: On a scale of 1 (lowest) to 5 (highest), circle the number that indicates the degree to which the student displays mastery of each skill. Connect the circles to see the profile.

Skill

Follows sequential directions	5	4	3	2	1
Recognizes patterns	5	4	3	2	1
Can estimate quantities	5	4	3	2	1
Can visualize and manipulate mental pictures	5	4	3	2	1
Sense of spatial orientation and organization	5	4	3	2	1
Ability to do deductive reasoning	5	4	3	2	1
Ability to do inductive reasoning	5	4	3	2	1

Action Plan: As a result of this profile, we will work together to _____

_____

by doing _____

- **Levels of Learning Mastery.** How does a teacher decide when a student has mastered a mathematical concept? Certainly, written tests of problem solving are one of the major devices for evaluating learning. However, they are useful tools only to the extent that they actually measure mastery rather than rote memory of formulas and procedures. Cognitive research suggests that a person must move through six levels of mastery to truly learn and retain mathematical concepts. For mastery, the student
  - Level One: Connects new knowledge to existing knowledge and experiences
  - Level Two: Searches for concrete material to construct a model or show a manifestation of the concept
  - Level Three: Illustrates the concept by drawing a diagram to connect the concrete example to a symbolic picture or representation
  - Level Four: Translates the concept into mathematical notation using number symbols, operational signs, formulas, and equations
  - Level Five: Applies the concept correctly to real-world situations, projects, and story problems
  - Level Six: Can teach the concept successfully to others, or can communicate it on a test

Too often, paper-and-pencil tests assess only level 6. Thus, when the student's results are poor, the teacher may not know where learning difficulties lie. By designing separate assessments for each level, teachers will be in a much better position to determine what kind of remedial work will help each student.

Other Considerations

Less Is More. Another lesson that research has taught us is that students with special needs are likely to be more successful if taught fewer concepts in more time. The notion that "less is more" can apply to all students, and is particularly important for those with learning problems. Studies of mathematics (as well as science) courses in the United States and other countries show that spending more time on fewer key concepts leads to greater student achievement in the long run. Yet our mathematics curriculum does not challenge students to study topics in depth. We tend to present a large number of ideas but develop very few of them. Students with special needs should focus on mastering a few important ideas and learn to apply them accurately.

Use of Manipulatives. Students with special needs who use manipulatives in their mathematics classes outperform similar students who do not. Manipulatives support the tactile and spatial reinforcement of mathematical concepts, maintain focus, and help students develop the cognitive structures necessary for understanding arithmetic relationships. In addition to physical manipulatives (e.g., Cuisenaire rods and tokens), computers and software help these learners make connections between various types of knowledge. For example, computer software can construct and dynamically connect pictured objects to symbolic representations (such as cubes to a numeral) and thus help learners generalize and draw abstract concepts from the manipulatives.

Search for Patterns. One of the more surprising research findings is that many children with learning disabilities—including those with mathematical disorders—can learn basic arithmetic concepts. What is needed for these children is an approach that relies less on intensive drill and practice and more on searching for, finding, and using patterns in learning the basic number combinations and arithmetic strategies.

Build on Students' Strengths. As obvious as this statement seems, teachers can often turn a student's failure into success if they build on what the student already knows how to do. Too often teachers get so focused on looking for ways to improve an area of weakness that they unintentionally overlook an individual's learning strengths. Yet many years of research into learning styles has demonstrated effective ways of recruiting style strengths to build up weaknesses.

Most people learn mathematics best in the context of real-world problems. School systems will increase all their students' chances for learning mathematics successfully if they plan curriculum content and instructional strategies that enhance prerequisite skills while developing knowledge and application of mathematical concepts and operations. Students are more comfortable with mathematics when they perceive it as a practical tool and not as an end unto itself. Integrated curriculum units provide opportunities for mathematics to be threaded through diverse and relevant topics. Finally, if the notion that babies are born with a sense of number logic continues to be supported by further research, then educators will need to reconsider how and when we teach mathematics in elementary schools.

STRATEGIES TO CONSIDER

General Guidelines for Teaching Mathematics

What we have learned about how students in general education learn mathematics can apply as well, with appropriate modifications, to students with mathematical disorders. Here are some recommendations gleaned from the research (Clements, 2000; Smith & Geller, 2004).

- **Help students develop conceptual understanding and skills.** These students need time to look at concrete models, understand them, and link them to abstract numerical representations. Allow them more time for mathematics study and for completing assignments.

- **Consider giving more oral and fewer written tests.** The stress of written tests increases the mental burden on these students, who often are better at telling you what they know than writing it.

- **Develop meaningful (relevant) practice exercises.** No one questions the value of practice—it makes permanent! But extensive practice that has little meaning for students is perceived as boring and may actually be harmful to students with special needs (Baroody, 1999). Practice solving problems that are purposeful and meaningful. Also, provide guided practice with feedback before independent practice so that students can understand what to do for each step and why.

- **Maintain reasonable expectations.** If we really want all students to have basic competencies in mathematics, then we must establish expectations that are reasonable. This should include problem-based learning, solving authentic problems, and showing the applications of mathematics to other subject areas, such as science. Similarly, setting expectations that are too low—explicitly or implicitly—increases the burden that children with all types of special needs may need to carry as adults.

- **Build on children's strengths.** In all areas of learning, teachers can often turn a student's failure into success if they build on what the student already knows how to do. Many years of research into learning styles has demonstrated effective ways of recruiting style strengths to build up weaknesses.

- **Use manipulatives appropriately.** Manipulatives can be valuable tools if students are able to connect what they are handling with what they are thinking. Have students explain aloud the connections they are making, and make sure they refer to the mathematical concepts and skills they are learning.

- **Help students make connections.** Students perceive meaning when they are able to connect what they are learning to prior knowledge or to future usefulness. Help students connect symbols to verbal descriptions. Find ways to link social situations to solving practical mathematical problems (e.g., splitting a restaurant check, determining an appropriate tip).

- **Determine and build on a student's informal learning strategies.** All learners develop informal strategies for dealing with their world. Determine what strategies the student is using and build on them to develop concepts and procedures.

- **Accommodate individual learning styles as much as is practicable.** Use as many multisensory approaches as possible. Include modeling, role-playing, demonstrations, simulations, and cooperative learning groups to provide variety and maintain student interest. Use mnemonic devices (Chapter 2) and games to help students remember number combinations and other important facts. Limit direct instruction (i.e., teacher talk) and use more interactive teaching strategies.

- **Use technology appropriately.** All students should have access to electronic tools. They can use them to understand mathematical concepts as well as how to benefit their adult lives. Using computer software that includes speech recognition and three-dimensional design, for instance, can be very helpful for students with special needs.

STRATEGIES TO CONSIDER

Teaching Strategies in Mathematics for Different Learning Styles

Cognitive researchers are suggesting that students approach the study of mathematics with different learning styles that run the gamut from primarily quantitative to primarily qualitative (Augustniak, Murphy, & Phillips, 2005; Farkas, 2003; Oberer, 2003; Sharma, 2006). The implication of this research is that students are more likely to be successful in learning mathematics if teachers use instructional strategies that are compatible with the students' cognitive styles. Tables 7.1 and 7.2 illustrate teaching strategies that are appropriate for the mathematical behaviors exhibited by quantitative and qualitative learners, respectively. Table 7.3 suggests a sequence for using inductive and deductive approaches when introducing a new mathematical concept.

Table 7.1 Teaching Strategies for Learners With Quantitative Style

Mathematical Behaviors	Teaching Strategies to Consider
Approaches situations using recipes	Emphasize the meaning of each concept or procedure in verbal terms.
Approaches mathematics in a mechanical, routine-like fashion	Highlight the concept and overall goal of the learning.
Emphasizes component parts rather than larger mathematical constructs	Encourage explicit description of the overall conceptual framework. Look for ways to link parts to the whole.
Prefers numerical approach rather than concrete models	Use a step-by-step approach to connect the model to the numerical procedure.
Prefers the linear approach to arithmetic concept	Start with the larger framework and use different approaches to reach the same concept.
Has difficulty in situations requiring multistep tasks	Separate multiple tasks into smaller units and explain the connections between the units.

Table 7.2 Teaching Strategies for Learners With Qualitative Style	
Mathematical Behaviors	**Teaching Strategies to Consider**
Prefers concepts to algorithms (procedures for problem solving)	Connect models first to the concept, and then to procedures before introducing algorithms.
Perceives overall shape of geometric structures at expense of missing the individual components	Emphasize how the individual components contribute to the overall design of the geometric figure.
Difficulties with precise calculations and in explaining procedure for finding the correct solution	Encourage explicit description of each step used.
Can offer a variety of approaches or answers to a single problem	Use simulations and real-word problems to show application of concept to different situations.
Prefers to set up problems but cannot always follow through to a solution	Provide opportunities for the student to work in cooperative learning groups. To ensure full participation, give the student one grade for problem approach and setup and one grade for exact solution.
Benefits from manipulatives and enjoys topics related to geometry	Provide a variety of manipulatives and models (e.g., Cuisenaire rods, tokens, or blocks) to support numerical operations. Look for geometric links to new concepts.

Tables 7.1 and 7.2 are meant to help teachers address specific mathematical behaviors that they identify in individual students. Such strategies target specific needs and, with practice, can strengthen a student's weakness. It is unrealistic, however, to expect teachers to identify and select individual strategies for problems encountered by all their students during a single learning episode.

Table 7.3 suggests an instructional sequence for introducing a new mathematical concept. The order first accommodates qualitative learners and then moves to techniques for quantitative learners.

Table 7.3	Inductive to Deductive Approach for Introducing a New Concept
Steps of the Inductive Approach for Qualitative Learners	• Explain the linguistic aspects of the concept • Introduce the general principle or law that supports the concept • Provide students opportunities to use concrete materials to investigate and discover proof of the connection between the principle and the concept • Give many specific examples of the concept's validity, using concrete materials • Allow students to discuss with each other what they discovered about how the concept works • Demonstrate how these individual experiences can be integrated into a general principle or rule that applies equally to each example
Steps for the Deductive Approach for Quantitative Learners	• Reemphasize the general principle or law that the concept relates to • Demonstrate how several specific examples obey the general principle or law • Allow students to state the principle and suggest specific examples that follow it • Ask students to explain the linguistic elements of the concept

By understanding the different approaches to the learning of mathematics, teachers are more likely to select instructional strategies that will result in successful learning for all students.

STRATEGIES TO CONSIDER

Teaching Mathematics to Students With Nonverbal Learning Disability

Students with nonverbal learning disability (NLD) have good verbal processing skills but will have problems comprehending the visual and spatial components of mathematics skills and concepts, especially when dealing with geometric shapes and designs. They generally learn verbal information quickly. But, for instance, when they look at a diagram for the first time, they look at a detailed piece. When they look a second time they see a different piece and then another piece when they look for the third time. Because there is no visual overview, the diagram may not make sense. Teachers of arithmetic and mathematics who work with students with NLD should consider the following strategies (Foss, 2001; Serlier-van den Bergh, 2006):

- Rely heavily on the student's verbal and analytic strengths. These students begin to work when speech is used, so use speech as the starting point.

- Gain a commitment from the student to collaborate to improve visual and spatial weaknesses.

- Use words to describe visual and spatial information. Ask the student to do the same while pointing to the corresponding places on the diagram or concrete model.

- Provide sequential verbal instructions for nonverbal tasks.

- Young students with NLD may feel awkward handling manipulatives because their tactile sense is not developed. However, manipulatives can help students develop mental images of geometric shapes and visualize spatial relationships as well as improve their visual memory skills. Ask them to touch objects first with their dominant hand, then with the nondominant hand, and finally with both hands at once.

- Encourage the student to slowly integrate sensory information: read it, say it, hear it, see it, write it, do it.

Chapter 8

Emotional and Behavioral Disorders

In recent years researchers have really begun to recognize the contribution that the emotions make to the development of the human brain and the impact they have on the learning process. Although these contributions are not always considered to be positive, understanding their impact can help parents and educators make appropriate decisions to meet the emotional needs of children and adolescents.

EMOTIONS, BEHAVIOR, AND LEARNING

The brain is genetically programmed to gather information and to develop skills that are likely to keep its owner alive. Among other things, human survival depends on the family unit, where emotional bonds increase the chances of producing children and raising them to be productive adults. Consequently, the human brain has learned over thousands of years that survival and emotional messages must have high priority when it filters through all the incoming signals from the body's senses.

The brainstem monitors and regulates survival functions, such as body temperature, respiratory rate, and blood pressure (Chapter 1). Emotional messages are carried through and interpreted in the limbic area, usually with the help of the frontal lobe (Figure 8.1). These survival and emotional messages guide the individual's behavior, including directing its attention to a learning situation. Specifically, emotion drives attention, and attention drives learning.

But even more important to understand is that emotional attention comes before cognitive recognition. You see a letter from the Internal Revenue Service in the mail, and within a few seconds your palms are sweating, your breathing is labored, and your blood pressure rises—all this before you even know what is in the letter. That's your amygdala acting up, the part of the limbic system responsible for emotional responses, and it can act without input from the cognitive parts of the brain (frontal lobe). In this instance, the brain is responding emotionally to a situation without the benefit of cognitive functions, such as thinking, reasoning, and consciousness (Damasio, 2003; LeDoux, 2002).

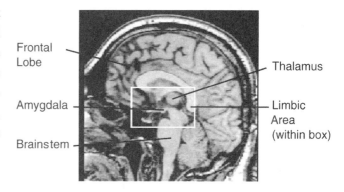

Figure 8.1 Survival functions are controlled from the brainstem. Emotional signals are processed and interpreted in the limbic area and frontal lobe.

Pathways of Emotional Signals

In Chapter 1, we learned that the thalamus receives all incoming sensory impulses (except smell) and directs them to other parts of the brain for further processing. Incoming sensory information to the thalamus can take two different routes to the amygdala. The quick route (called the *thalamic pathway*) sends the signals directly from the thalamus to the amygdala (pathway A in Figure 8.2). The second possibility (called the *cortical pathway*) is for the thalamus to direct the signals first to the cerebral cortex (in the cerebrum) for cognitive processing and then to the amygdala (pathway B).

The time it takes for signals to travel along the two pathways is different. For example, it takes sound signals about 12 milliseconds (a millisecond is 1/1,000th of a second) to travel pathway A and about twice as long to travel pathway B. Which pathway the signals take could mean the difference between life and death. If the sound from a car blasting its horn travels along pathway A, it will probably be fast enough to get you to jump out of the way even though you are not sure what is coming. Only later does your cerebral cortex provide the explanation of what happened. Survival is the first priority, an explanation second.

Disturbances in this dual pathway system can explain some abnormal behaviors. Anxiety disorders, for example, can result whenever a certain action, such as walking into a crowd, is associated with fear. If this activity always takes pathway A, then a phobia develops that cannot be easily moderated through rational discussion. This probably explains why psychotherapy alone is rarely successful in treating many phobias and anxiety disorders (Restak, 2000).

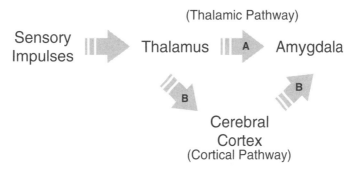

Figure 8.2 Sensory information travels to the thalamus, where it can be routed directly to the amygdala (thalamic pathway, A) or first to the cerebrum and then to the amygdala (cortical pathway, B).

Different Brain Areas for Different Emotions

Although the amygdala is the center of emotional response, neuroscientists now believe that different areas of the brain interpret specific emotions. The frontal cortex of the left hemisphere deals with positive emotions; the right frontal cortex is concerned with negative emotions (Figure 8.3). Damage to the front of the left hemisphere results in feelings of hopelessness and bouts of depression. However, if the front right side is damaged, the individual often expresses inappropriate cheerfulness, even denying the injury.

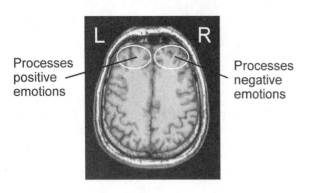

Processes positive emotions

Processes negative emotions

Figure 8.3   The left hemisphere's frontal cortex processes positive emotions. The right hemisphere's frontal cortex processes negative emotions and nuance.

People who normally have right hemisphere preference tend to have basically anxious and fearful approaches to life. Those with left hemisphere preference exhibit a more confident approach. The preference is probably caused by a number of factors, including genetics, experience, and the way an individual's brain is organized. Apparently, this hemispheric specialization begins at an early age. One interesting study using EEGs found that very young children with right-hemisphere activity were more likely to cry and be upset when separated from their parents than children with more dominant left-hemisphere activity (Davidson, 2000).

The Nature of Anxiety

Anxiety serves a useful purpose in that it signals us that something needs to be corrected in our environment. The anxious feelings you got when seeing the letter from the Internal Revenue Service were soon tempered when cognitive reflection reminded you that this is the time of year estimated-tax forms are sent out. This return to emotional stability is the result of the interactions between the emotion-generating amygdala and the emotion-inhibiting left frontal cortex. Both the amygdala and left frontal cortex need to be functioning properly for this balance to be maintained and, thus, for good mental health. If either one is malfunctioning, then the person's behavior likely will be abnormal.

First Survival and Emotions, Then the Textbook

The typical human brain is programmed to deal first with its owner's survival and emotional needs. Therefore, the brain is unlikely to attend to any other task until it is assured that these needs have been met and that the environment poses no threat. If we transfer this notion to schools, it means that students are not going to care about the curriculum unless they feel physically safe and emotionally secure.

Physical Safety. For students to feel physically safe, schools must be free of weapons and violence. A student will have trouble concentrating on the lesson if a nearby student displays a weapon or threatens physical harm. Physical safety also refers to the safe condition of the student's body. Has the student had enough sleep and an adequate breakfast? Rest and fuel are important requirements for attention and learning.

Emotional Security. Emotional security refers to the degree to which a student feels accepted as a valued member of a group. In my opinion, the emotional needs of children can be met in just three places:

> *Students must feel physically safe and emotionally secure before they can focus on the curriculum.*

- In the home (and those entities to which the family belongs, such as religious or community groups)
- In school, through the formal organization of educators and school groups
- Outside the school, from an informal organization of peers

The emotional needs of children and adolescents used to be met at home and in the neighborhood. The family dined together nightly, spending quality time to strengthen emotional bonds through reassurances, caring, and love. Neighbors watched out for each other's children at play, and it was a safer world.

In today's fast-paced lifestyle, many families dine together only once or twice a week. Hectic family schedules mean that parents and children have less time together. When the children *are* at home, they spend more time in their own bedrooms—playing computer games, calling on their cell phones, and watching television—than with their parents. According to surveys conducted in 2005 by America Online and Yahoo!, young people 13 to 19 years of age spend an average of about 14 hours a week watching televison and 17 hours a week on the Internet. When do they have time for meaningful conversation with their family?

Because the amount of quality time at home is so small, many students are not getting their emotional needs met. Consequently, they come to school looking for emotional support from the formal organization through teachers and other professionals in the school environment. Finding emotional support in the primary grades is easy because those teachers are trained to provide it. But it is an entirely different matter in secondary schools. High school teachers are trained to deliver curriculum efficiently and effectively. Few have had training in how to deal with the emotional needs of students, and even fewer ever believed that such training would be necessary. However, high school teachers are now well aware that they must meet the emotional needs of their students before they can be successful at presenting the curriculum.

If the students' emotional needs are not met in the home or in school, then some students resort to the third alternative—joining an informal organization of peers, commonly called a gang. These are family-like units that have a name, a set of values, and a system of rewards and punishments. Regrettably, their behavior is too often directed toward deviant, rather than socially acceptable, goals.

EMOTIONAL AND BEHAVIORAL DISORDERS

Because emotions and behavior affect each other and are so closely intertwined, disorders of these areas are usually discussed together. Although a few of these disorders can appear in early adulthood or later, many appear in childhood and adolescence. Some are more common than others, and conditions can range from mild to severe. Often, a person has more than one disorder. Nearly all of these disorders can seriously affect memory in children and adolescents, especially verbal memory (Günther, Holtkamp, Jolles, Herpertz-Dahlmann, & Konrad, 2004).

The causes of all the types of disorders can be biological, environmental, or a mixture of both. Biological factors include genetics, chemical imbalances in the body, and damage to the central nervous system, such as a head injury. Environmental causes can include exposure to violence, extreme stress, or the loss of an important person, such as by death or divorce.

An in-depth discussion of all types of emotional and behavioral disorders that afflict humans is beyond the scope of this book. Rather, the following describes those emotional and behavioral disorders that are most common among children and adolescents and that educators are likely to encounter in almost any school.

Anxiety Disorders

Most people experience feelings of anxiety before an important event, such as a business presentation, big test, or first date. But people with anxiety disorders have anxiety and fears that are chronic and unrelenting and that can grow progressively worse. Sometimes their anxieties are so bad that people become housebound.

> **Anxiety Disorders**
>
> - Phobias (social and specific)
> - Generalized anxiety disorder
> - Panic disorder
> - Obsessive-compulsive disorder
> - Post-traumatic stress disorder

Anxiety disorders are the most common of childhood disorders, affecting an estimated 13 percent of the 9- to 17-year-old population. These young people experience excessive worry, fear, or uneasiness that interferes with daily routines. Anxiety disorders include the following (NIMH, 2002a):

- **Phobias:** The two major types are *social phobia* and *specific phobia*. Children with social phobia (also called *social anxiety disorder*) have an overwhelming fear of scrutiny, embarrassment, or humiliation when with their peers. Their fear may be so severe that it interferes with schoolwork and other ordinary activities. Social phobia can be limited to only one type of situation, such as a fear of speaking, eating, or writing in front of others. In its most severe form, people experience symptoms almost anytime they are around others. Physical symptoms include blushing, profuse sweating, trembling, nausea, and difficulty talking. Social phobia usually begins in childhood or early adolescence, and there is some evidence that genetic factors are involved. Social phobia can be treated successfully with carefully targeted psychotherapy or medications.

  A specific phobia is an unrealistic and overwhelming fear of some situation or object that poses little or no actual danger. Some of the more common specific phobias are centered around closed-in places, heights, escalators, tunnels, highway driving, water, flying, dogs, and injuries involving blood. Such phobias aren't just extreme fear; they are an irrational fear of a particular thing. Specific phobias usually first appear during childhood or adolescence and tend to persist into adulthood. Specific phobias are highly treatable with carefully targeted psychotherapy.

- **Generalized anxiety disorder (GAD):** This disorder is a pattern of unrealistic and excessive worry not attributable to any recent experience, but disruptive to routine life and events. Those with GAD have incessant fears about the future and almost always anticipate the worst even though there is little reason to expect it. Their worries are accompanied by fatigue, headaches, muscle tension, muscle aches, difficulty swallowing, trembling, twitching, irritability, and sweating. Children with

GAD may seem unable to relax, and they may startle more easily than others. They tend to have difficulty concentrating, and often have trouble falling or staying asleep.

The disorder comes on gradually, though the risk is highest between childhood and middle age. Females are more than twice as afflicted as males, and there is evidence that genes play a modest role. GAD is commonly treated with medications.

- **Panic disorder:** Individuals with this condition experience repeated episodes of terrifying attacks of panic that strike without warning. They develop intense anxiety between episodes, worrying when and where the next one will strike. Physical symptoms include rapid heartbeat, chest pain, numb or tingling hands, nausea, abdominal distress, and dizziness. Panic attacks can occur at any time, even during sleep. An attack generally peaks within 10 minutes, but some symptoms may last much longer. Studies of twins indicate that the risk of developing panic disorder can be inherited. The risk falls off sharply with age and rarely appears after age 40 (Reilly, 2004).

  Panic disorder most often begins during late adolescence or early adulthood. People often avoid any situation in which they would feel helpless if a panic attack were to occur. When people's lives become so restricted, as happens in about one-third of those with panic disorder, the condition is called *agoraphobia.* Early treatment of panic disorder can often prevent agoraphobia.

- **Obsessive-compulsive disorder (OCD):** This disorder involves patterns of repeated thoughts and behaviors that are impossible to control or stop. Although rare in young children, the occurrence of the disorder increases in adolescents. Distinguishing OCD from developmentally normal childhood behavior involves assessing how often the child engages in the behavior, how much the behavior disrupts the child's daily routine, and how distressed the child becomes when the behavior is interrupted or prevented.

  Individuals with OCD may be obsessed with germs or dirt, so they wash their hands over and over, or they may be filled with doubt and feel the need to check things repeatedly. Some have frequent thoughts of violence and fear that people close to them will harm them. They may spend long periods touching things or counting or be preoccupied by order or symmetry. Children with OCD may not realize that their behavior is out of the ordinary.

  The course of the disorder varies in that symptoms may come and go, they may ease over time, or they can grow progressively worse. Research evidence suggests that OCD runs in families (Reilly, 2004). Depression or other anxiety disorders may accompany OCD, and some people with OCD also have eating disorders. OCD generally responds well to treatment with medications that regulate serotonin (called selective serotonin reuptake inhibitors), or carefully targeted behavioral therapy.

- **Post-traumatic stress disorder (PTSD):** A debilitating condition involving a pattern of flashbacks and other symptoms that occur in children who have experienced a psychologically distressing event (e.g., physical and sexual abuse, being a witness or victim of violence, or exposure to some other traumatic event, such as a hurricane, flood, or bombing). Nightmares, numbing of emotions, and feeling angry or irritable are common symptoms. PTSD can occur at any age. There is evidence that susceptibility may run in families, which would explain why only certain individuals exposed to similar traumatic events develop full-blown PTSD. In those who do develop PTSD, symptoms usually begin within three months of the trauma, and the course of the illness varies. Some people recover within six months; others have symptoms that last much longer. The disorder is often accompanied by depression, substance abuse, or one or more other anxiety disorders. PTSD can be treated with medications and carefully targeted psychotherapy.

Causes of Anxiety Disorders

Normal emotional behavior relies on the integrating balance between the emotions initiated by the amygdala and the mediating effect of our thoughts. If either one of these components malfunctions, problems arise. Brain imaging has helped neuroscientists gain a greater understanding of the source of these problems and thus the causes of anxiety disorders. For example, if a malfunction causes nonthreatening sensory signals to always take the thalamic pathway (Figure 8.2), panic attacks result because the signals are not benefiting from the mediating effect of cognitive thought. Here is an example: To most of us, the sound of a car backfiring is annoying, but we usually would not mistake it for a gunshot. However, to an adolescent brought up in a neighborhood where gunfire has killed a friend or family member, that backfiring could activate a full-fledged stress response. This post-traumatic stress response might send the adolescent diving for cover and in full panic. Apparently, the sounds of the backfiring went directly to the amygdala (thalamic pathway), triggering the panic behavior. No input from the cerebral cortex was present to curtail the post-traumatic response.

Treating Anxiety Disorders

For many years, psychiatrists thought that obsessive-compulsive disorder had psychological roots and attempted to treat it with psychoanalysis. Brain imaging studies, however, suggest that obsessive-compulsive behavior is the result of hyperactivity in a circuit of the brain that connects the frontal lobe to a part of the limbic area called the caudate nucleus. Activity in this circuit decreases between obsessive-compulsive episodes and after treatment. The disorder responds to a combination of drugs that increases the action of the neurotransmitter serotonin, followed by psychotherapy that addresses the specific nature of the behavior.

Depressive Disorders

Children and adolescents with learning disabilities are susceptible to chronic depression. About 6 percent of 9- to 17-year-olds have major depression. The onset of depressive disorders is occurring earlier in life today than ever before (NIMH, 2002b). Depressed children do not necessarily look like depressed adults. They are more often irritable, rather than sad and withdrawn.

The depressive disorders include major depressive disorder (unipolar depression), dysthymia (a less severe type of major depression), and bipolar disorder (manic-depression). All types can have far-reaching effects on the functioning and adjustment of young people. Children and adolescents with depressive disorders are at an increased risk for illness and interpersonal and social difficulties. These adolescents also have an increased risk for substance abuse and suicidal behavior.

Unfortunately, depressive disorders in adolescents often go unrecognized because their signs are interpreted as normal mood swings typical of this age group. For example, instead of communicating how bad they feel, they may act out and be irritable toward others, which may be interpreted simply as misbehavior or disobedience. Parents are even less likely to identify major depression in their adolescents than are the adolescents themselves.

Symptoms of Depressive Disorders

The symptoms of major depressive disorders are common to children, adolescents, and adults. Five or more of these symptoms must persist for an extended period of time before a diagnosis of depression is indicated. Because of the difficulty in diagnosing younger people using just the common symptoms, clinicians often look for other signs that are usually associated with the disorder.

Bipolar disorder, or manic-depression, in children and adolescents is marked by exaggerated mood swings between extreme lows (depression) and highs (excitedness or manic behavior). Periods of quiet may occur in between. The mood swings may recur throughout life. This illness is often confused with attention-deficit hyperactivity disorder.

Causes of Depressive Disorders

Depressive disorders can be caused by any of the following three conditions (or combination): genetics, events occurring in a person's environment, and events occurring inside the body (NIMH, 2000b).

Depressive Disorders

Depression: Symptoms common to all ages
- Persistent sad or irritable mood
- Loss of interest in activities once enjoyed
- Significant change in appetite or body weight
- Difficulty sleeping or sleeping too much
- Psychomotor agitation or retardation
- Loss of energy
- Feelings of worthlessness or inappropriate guilt
- Difficulty concentrating
- Recurrent thoughts of death or suicide

Bipolar Disorder: Symptoms for pre-teens and older
- Severe changes in mood
- Overly inflated self-esteem
- Increased energy
- Able to go without much sleep
- Talks too fast and too much, cannot be interrupted
- Excessive involvement in risk behaviors

Some types of depression run in families, suggesting that a biological vulnerability can be inherited. This seems to be the case with bipolar disorder. Studies of families in which members of each generation develop bipolar disorder found that those with the illness have a somewhat different genetic makeup than those who do not get ill (King, Knox, Henninger, Nguyen, Ghaziuddin, Maker, et al., 2006; Reilly, 2004). However, the reverse is not true: Not everybody with the genetic susceptibility to bipolar disorder will have the illness.

Apparently, environmental factors are involved in the disorder's onset. A serious loss, divorcing parents, accident, trauma, or any drastic change in life patterns can trigger a depressive episode. In a 10-year follow-up study, children who were raised in homes where they were exposed to high levels of parental depression and family discord had significantly higher rates of depressive disorders over the decade than their counterparts (Nomura, Wickramaratne, Warner, Mufson, & Weissman, 2002).

Physical changes in the body can be accompanied by mental changes as well. Medical illnesses, such as stroke, a heart attack, cancer, and hormonal disorders, can cause depressive illness, making the sick person apathetic and unwilling to care for physical needs. Very often, a combination of genetic, psychological, and environmental factors is involved in the onset of a depressive disorder.

Whether inherited or not, major depressive disorder is often associated with changes in brain structures or brain function. Below-normal concentrations of one or more neurotransmitters, such as serotonin, can be an underlying cause of depression.

Depressive Disorders

Signs associated with depressive disorders in children and adolescents
- Frequent, nonspecific complaints of headaches, tiredness, and stomach and muscle aches
- Frequent absences from school or poor performance in school
- Talking about running away from home
- Outbursts of crying, shouting, and complaining
- Being bored
- Lack of interest in playing with friends
- Alcohol or substance abuse
- Social isolation, poor communication
- Fear of death
- Extreme sensitivity to rejection or failure
- Increased hostility and irritability
- Reckless behavior
- Difficulty with relationships
- Self-mutilation

Treating Depressive Disorders

Treatment for depressive disorders involves short-term psychotherapy, medication, or the combination of both plus targeted interventions involving the home and school environment. Newer research shows that certain types of short-term psychotherapy, particularly cognitive-behavioral therapy (CBT), can help relieve depression in children and adolescents, as well as adults. CBT is based on the premise that people with depression have cognitive distortions in their views of themselves, the world, and the future. CBT, designed to be a time-limited therapy, focuses on changing these distortions. CBT targets higher-functioning areas in the frontal lobe, which in turn influence other brain regions (Kaufman, Rohde, Seeley, Clarke, & Stice, 2005).

Antidepressant medications act on the more primitive structures in the limbic area involved in mood and temperament. These in turn feed back to the frontal lobe through complex chemical pathways. Thus, CBT and antidepressant medications work differently in the brain. In Figure 8.4, representative PET scans show the changes that occur in the brain after treatment with CBT in the top image and the antidepressant medication paroxetine (brand name: Praxil) in the bottom image. Note that the CBT treatment primarily affected the frontal lobes, while the drug treatment centered on the limbic and more primitive areas (Seminowicz, Mayberg, McIntosh, Goldapple, Kennedy, Segal, et al., 2004).

Because different depression therapies affect the brain differently, more clinical practitioners now suggest using a combination of drug and psychotherapy rather than one or the other. However, only recently have studies shown antidepressant medications to be effective in treating children and adolescents with depression. Due to the potential side effects of antidepressant drugs, children given both therapies need to be monitored closely by a physician.

Other Emotional and Behavioral Disorders

A number of other emotional and behavioral disorders are found in the school population, such as the following:

Attention-Deficit Hyperactivity Disorder (ADHD). This disorder has received much attention from the media and from researchers. ADHD is discussed fully in Chapter 3.

Oppositional-Defiant Disorder. All children are occasionally oppositional by arguing, talking back, or defying their parents, teachers and other adults. However, persistent and openly hostile behavior that interferes with a child's daily functioning is called oppositional-defiant disorder. It is characterized by deliberate attempts to annoy others, excessive arguing with adults, frequent temper tantrums, and refusal to comply with adult requests. This disorder can look like ADHD, but these children are not only unruly, they harm animals, beat up on others, and destroy property. The cause is unknown, but treatment centers on psychotherapy. If the child does not respond to treatment, the behavior may worsen and become a general conduct disorder.

Conduct Disorder. This disorder usually begins with the appearance of hostile and defiant behavior during the preschool years, known as oppositional-defiant disorder. As the child gets older, conduct disorder may appear, causing children and adolescents to act out their feelings or impulses toward others in destructive ways. Young people with conduct disorder consistently violate the general rules of society and basic rights of others. The offenses they commit get more serious over time and include lying, aggression, theft, truancy, setting fires, and vandalism. However, most young people with conduct disorder do not have lifelong patterns of conduct problems or antisocial behavior.

Conduct disorder has a genetic link and seems to result from problems in the brain's limbic area (Haberstick, Smolen, & Hewitt, 2006). Studies using fMRI showed impairment in the systems that recognize emotional stimuli and cognitively

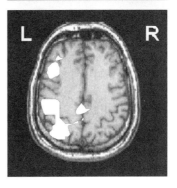

Figure 8.4 These images of representative PET scans show how different areas of the brain are affected after treatment with cognitive-behavioral therapy (top) and the antidepressant drug paroxetine (bottom).

control emotional behavior (Sterzer, Stadler, Krebs, Kleinschmidt, & Poustka, 2005). Males are more susceptible to this disorder than females. Researchers suggest that one genetic component related to aggression lies on the X-chromosome. Because males have only one copy of this X-chromosome gene, they are more vulnerable to its effects (Meyer-Lindenberg, Buckholtz, Kolachana, Hariri, Pezawas, Blasi, et al., 2006).

This is one of the most difficult behavior disorders to treat. Even so, progress can be made with family therapy, parent training, and the use of community support services. A recent study of adolescents with conduct disorder showed that their aggressive behavior also responded to treatment with a drug called olanzapine. Unlike the short-term effects of other drugs used to treat this disorder, the positive effects of the olanzapine treatment lasted from six to 12 months (Masi, Milone, Canepa, Millepiedi, Mucci, & Muratori, 2006).

Eating Disorders. Eating disorders involve serious

Conduct Disorder

Symptoms
- Shows aggressive behavior that harms or threatens to harm other people or animals
- Damages or destroys property
- Lying or theft
- Truancy or other violation of rules

---

disturbances in eating behavior, such as extreme and unhealthful reduction of food intake or severe overeating, as well as feelings of distress or extreme concern about body shape or weight. The main types of eating disorders are *anorexia nervosa* (the compulsive need to continually lose weight) and *bulimia nervosa* (the compulsion to eat large amounts of food and to take subsequent radical measures to eliminate it). A third type, binge-eating disorder, has been suggested but has not yet been approved as a formal psychiatric diagnosis.

Eating disorders frequently develop during adolescence or early adulthood, but some reports indicate their onset can occur during childhood or later in adulthood. People who suffer from eating disorders can experience a wide range of physical health complications, including serious heart conditions and kidney failure, which may lead to death. Females are much more likely than males to develop an eating disorder. Only an estimated five to 15 percent of people with anorexia or bulimia and an estimated 35 percent of those with binge-eating disorder are male (NIMH, 2001).

No generally accepted view of the causes of these disorders exists at present, although most experts believe the problem to be psychologically based. Adolescents displaying the symptoms of these disorders need immediate medical attention. Various forms of treatment are available, such as psychotherapy (individual, group, or family), counseling, self-help groups, and medication.

Autism. Autism is a spectrum disorder that usually appears before the child's third birthday. Children with autism have difficulty communicating with others and display inappropriate and repeated behaviors over long periods of time. Autism is discussed in Chapter 9.

Impact of Childhood Abuse

Child welfare agencies report over a million instances a year of childhood neglect and abuse. For years, mental health professionals thought that emotional, sexual, and physical mistreatment of children led to psychological problems that could be treated successfully with therapy. Yet, many children and adolescents did not respond to psychotherapy, and researchers wondered if the mistreatment led to more damaging changes in the developing brain. Brain-imaging studies and other experiments have confirmed that child abuse can cause permanent damage to the neural structure and function of the brain itself. Typically, the brains of adolescents with a history of abuse showed less blood flow to the cerebellum, a smaller corpus callosum, and reduced integration of activity between the left and right hemispheres. Researchers now suspect that the stress associated with childhood abuse triggered hormonal changes that rewired the child's brain to deal with a malevolent world (Teicher, 2002). This may explain why victims of child abuse can become abusers themselves as they age.

The consequences of childhood abuse can appear in many ways. Victims may suffer anxiety, depression, suicidal thoughts, or posttraumatic stress. Outwardly, they may display aggression, delinquency, hyperactivity, or impulsivity. During adolescence, they are at high risk for *borderline personality disorder* (BPD). Individuals with this disorder experience episodes of impulsive aggression, self-injury, and drug or alcohol abuse. They may feel unfairly misunderstood or mistreated, bored, empty, and have little idea who they are. Although they may form an immediate attachment and idealize another person, a slight conflict can cause them to switch unexpectedly to the other extreme and angrily accuse the other person of not caring for them at all. Suicide threats and attempts may occur along with anger at perceived abandonment and disappointments. Psychotherapy and medications have shown promise as treatments for this disorder.

The Future of Research in Emotional and Behavioral Disorders

As the number of children and adolescents with emotional and behavioral problems continues to increase, more resources will be devoted to searching out the underlying genetic and environmental causes of these disorders. Brain-imaging studies will give us more information on the neural and chemical mechanisms involved. New knowledge about causes often brings suggestions for new treatments. In the meantime, parents, educators, and clinicians need to work together to improve the identification and education of affected students.

WHAT EDUCATORS NEED TO CONSIDER

Researchers suggest that educators consider three areas for improving the identification and treatment of students with emotional and behavioral disorders (Forness, 2003). The first area is *developmental psychopathology,* which holds that the course of these disorders is determined by a variety of early genetic, biologic, and environmental factors. Parents and teachers may have noticed these earlier signs but did not necessarily view them as potential problems. Yet, early detection and prevention are more effective than just early identification and early intervention. Primary prevention or classroom-wide interventions in preschool can significantly improve both functional behavior and the symptoms in children at risk and possibly forestall the disorders in youngsters at highest risk (Serna, Nielsen, Mattern, & Forness, 2003). Training in early detection is essential for all personnel who work with these students.

The second area involves *psychiatric comorbidity,* the recognition that emotional and behavioral disorders may be preceded by other psychiatric problems. For example, children with disruptive disorders often have comorbid depression or anxiety disorders. Treatment for simple disruptive behavioral disorders does not work with children who have mixed disorders. Rather, differential treatment involving much more emphasis on cognitive-behavioral and emotional-regulation approaches will be more effective.

A third area for consideration is *psychopharmacology.* Special education teachers and general educators should be aware of how medication for psychiatric disorders has become an effective intervention, especially when combined with behavioral interventions. Selective serotonin reuptake inhibitors (SSRI), for example, can help up to 70 percent of cases on average. But collaboration among teachers, therapists, prescribing physicians, and families is critical for these medications to work effectively (Rosenberg, Davanzo, & Gershon, 2002).

STRATEGIES TO CONSIDER

Establishing a Positive Emotional Climate in the Classroom

All students—especially those with emotional and behavioral disorders—need to be in an emotionally secure setting before they can be expected to give attention to curriculum. The classroom climate is set by the teachers, and the school climate is set by the administration. Teachers and administrators need to recognize that many more students than ever come to school wanting to get at least some of their emotional needs met. Working together, faculty and staff should take **purposeful** steps to ensure that a positive emotional climate be established and maintained in the school and in all classrooms. Some ways to set a positive emotional climate are as follows:

- **Use humor, but not sarcasm.** Humor is a very effective device for getting attention and for establishing a warm climate. Laughter is common to us all, and it helps diverse people bond and feel good about being with each other. Sarcasm, on the other hand, is destructive. It hurts, no matter how familiar a teacher is with students. Occasionally, a teacher has said, "Oh, the student knows I was only kidding." In fact, we don't know that, and we need to wonder whether the student's sly grin means the brain is laughing or plotting revenge. Besides, there is so much good humor available that there is no need for sarcasm.

- **Insist on respect among students.** Not only is it important for teachers to respect students, and vice versa, but teachers must also ensure that students show respect for each other. This includes
  - listening to each other's class contributions (as opposed to just waiting for their turn to speak),
  - respecting different and opposing opinions,
  - acknowledging other students' comments,
  - complimenting and helping each other when appropriate,
  - asking others for their opinions, and
  - refraining from sarcasm.

- **Have just a few rules that all teachers enforce.** Students with emotional problems are very likely to get upset when they believe that they are not being treated fairly. Studies on school discipline show that schools with few discipline problems tend to be those with just a few rules (five to seven) that all teachers enforce uniformly. Keep in mind that secondary students usually see six to eight teachers during the school day. Perhaps one teacher allows gum chewing, but it drives the next period's teacher to distraction. An absent-minded, gum-chewing student going from the first to the second teacher's class may be headed for trouble.

- **Get training in how to handle emotional situations.** Most secondary teachers were not trained to deal with the emotional scenarios that appear in today's classrooms, mainly because emotional needs of adolescents are expected to be addressed in the family. But the reality is that more students are turning to the school setting for emotional fulfillment, and teachers must be trained to cope effectively with this situation.

- **Look for opportunities to teach students how to handle their emotions.** With training, teachers can use classroom and school opportunities to teach students how to handle their emotions. Look for ways to help them delay gratification, control impulses, express their feelings, and conduct themselves in their in-school relationships.

- **Use genuine praise.** Students with emotional problems often have low self-esteem. Genuinely praising their productive efforts can go a long way in helping them improve their self-image. Use "you" statements rather than "I" statements. For example, "You should be proud of the work you accomplished" is more effective for building self-esteem than "I am pleased with what you accomplished."

- **Reduce test anxiety.** Test anxiety affects many students, but it can be potentially serious when it leads to high stress in students who already have emotional and behavioral difficulties. Find ways to reduce test anxiety. Cognitive-behavioral treatments to reduce test anxiety have proven effective in several studies. With these treatments, students were less anxious about the tests and felt more confident about their academic work (Wachelka & Katz, 1999).

STRATEGIES TO CONSIDER

Interventions for Students With Behavioral Problems

Research on programs designed to help students with behavioral problems covers a wide variety of students, situations, and settings. As a result, there is a broad range of possible approaches that teachers and schools can take to make a difference in students' behavior. Here are some suggestions:

- **Identifying the cause of the misbehavior.** Problem behavior is obvious, but the reasons for it might not be. Schools need to investigate **why** the student is exhibiting undesirable behavior. As more is known about the cause, appropriate interventions can be identified and implemented.

- **Selecting classroom management and teaching strategies.** Blaming, punishing, and threatening students work only in the short term. Effective teachers rely instead on proactive strategies, such as reinforcing social behavior and teaching social problem solving. For difficult students, they use point or token systems, time-out, contingent reinforcement (reinforcement that is contingent on the display of acceptable behavior), and response cost (students lose points or tokens for unacceptable behavior) strategies.

- **Adapting curriculum and instruction.** Disruptive behavior is sometimes the result of inappropriate curriculum and ineffective teaching. When investigating the cause of student misbehavior, check whether curricular and instruction modifications have been made to accommodate these students. Are there visual aids to support lesson content? Are classes small enough so that there is sufficient teaching-student interaction?

- **Addressing social skills.** Students with behavioral problems often lack the social skills needed to maintain successful relationships with their peers and teachers. As a result, they experience teacher rejection, school failure, and social rejection. When teachers help students build social competence, they increase the likelihood that these students will succeed in school. Kathleen Lane and her colleagues suggest a six-step research-based method for designing, implementing, and evaluating a social skills intervention for elementary students (Lane, Menzies, Barton-Arwood, Doukas, & Munton, 2005). Schools using this approach have noticed fewer disruptive behaviors in the classroom, increased time on academic tasks, and improved social interactions on the playground. Here is a summary of the method.
  - *Step 1. Identify students for participation.* Use observations, behavioral instruments (e.g., Systematic Screening for Behavior Disorders), and rating scales (e.g., Student Risk Screening Scale) to select students who can best benefit from the interventions.

o *Step 2. Identify specific skill deficits and design the intervention program.* Use the data gathered from the first step to identify the skill strengths, skill deficits, performance deficits, and interfering problem behaviors for each student. Develop the social skills lessons, which will be presented as 30- to 60-minute sessions, two days a week, to groups of three to five students.

o *Step 3. Organize intervention groups.* Place students into intervention groups based on skill deficits, demographics (age or gender), or randomly (for larger groups).

o *Step 4. Prepare intervention leaders.* Initial and ongoing training of intervention leaders ensures that the intervention is implemented as intended and that best practices in social skills instruction are being followed.

o *Step 5. Implement the intervention.* Each lesson uses effective instructional strategies in a role-play format that contains five stages: tell, show, do, follow through and practice, and generalization. Use behavior checklists to monitor the extent to which the intervention plan is implemented as originally designed. Select rules for how the group functions so as to prevent problem behaviors from interfering with instruction.

o *Step 6. Monitor student progress.* Use teacher ratings, self-reporting, and direct observations to monitor and assess student progress.

- **Teaching social problem solving.** Effective programs for preventing discipline problems include the direct teaching of social problem solving. Although the interventions vary, they usually teach thinking skills that students can use to avoid and resolve interpersonal conflicts, resist peer pressure, and cope with their emotions and stress. The most effective programs also include a broad range of social competency skills taught over a long period of time.

- **Adopting schoolwide and districtwide programs.** School and district policies should make clear that appropriate behavior is a precondition to learning. Rules of behavior should be clear and communicated to staff, parents, and students. It is important that they be consistently enforced so students perceive the system as fair. The staff should also be trained to teach alternatives to vandalism and disruptive behavior.

- **Getting parental involvement.** Effective programs to control behavior almost always have a parental component. Parental management training and family therapy are two promising approaches for controlling student behavior. Parental management training teaches techniques such as strategic use of time-out, rewards, praise, and contingency contracting. Parents have ongoing opportunities to discuss, practice, and review these techniques. Family therapy is designed to empower parents with the skills and resources to solve their own family problems. Although parental management training and family therapy are very effective approaches, less intensive parental training should suffice for most children and adolescents.

  Such approaches include the Adolescent Transitions Program, a family-centered intervention strategy designed to reduce problem behavior and prevent drug use within a public school environment. Parent consultants provide interventions that enhance and support positive parenting practices known to reduce undesirable emotional behavior in adolescents. Despite significant variation in implementation across schools, this program has substantially reduced the growth in problem behavior over the course of the middle-school years (Stormshak, Dishion, Light, & Yasui, 2005).

- **Using auditory processing strategies.** Researchers have noted that students with behavior problems and low achievement in literacy may have *auditory processing* problems. Auditory processing is the ability to hold, sequence, and process accurately what is heard. Kathy Rowe and her colleagues in Australia have found that training teachers in strategies that support auditory processing resulted in a significant improvement in student attentiveness, behavior, and literacy (Rowe, Pollard, & Rowe, 2005). The training focused on five strategies:
  o Attracting the child's attention
  o Speaking slowly, using short sentences, eye contact, and visual cues
  o Pausing between sentences and repeating when necessary
  o Using visual cues, such as blank looks, and repeating instructions as needed
  o Creating hearing, listening, and compliance routines for students

STRATEGIES TO CONSIDER

Reducing the Risk of Antisocial Behavior

Behavior is the result of the interaction of environmental influences and genetic predispositions. Schools can do nothing to alter the genetic coding. But recent research seems to indicate that genes affecting personality traits are either activated or repressed by the individual's environment. Consequently, if schools undertake comprehensive efforts to provide supportive structures and reduce risk factors, then fewer children may fall victim to emotional and behavioral problems that can seriously interfere with their schooling and life. These efforts that will encourage prevention of problem behaviors fall into the broad areas of school organization and effectiveness, student achievement and early intervention, parent and community involvement, and professional development for staff (LDA, 2006b).

School Organization and Effectiveness	The school should • Have high expectations for learning and behavior for all students and help all children achieve them • Clearly communicate expectations for learning and behavior to all students • Include staff, students, parents, and community members in the decision-making process • Promote student engagement and attachment • Have a consistent system of reinforcement and recognition to shape student behavior • Provide alternatives to suspension and expulsion • Conduct risk assessment as part of safe schools improvement plans
Student Achievement and Early Intervention	The school should • Intervene early to identify and assist students who fail to meet expectations for learning and behavior • Evaluate students' social, emotional, and adaptive functions, as well as cognitive function • Include special education students in regular classrooms • Not disproportionately discipline students with disabilities

**Parent
and Community
Involvement**

The school should

- Work with parents and community groups to educate and care for children
- Involve parents and community groups in developing the safe schools improvement plan
- Provide information to parents about how to help their children learn and behave appropriately in school
- Collaborate with other agencies to meet family and community needs

**Professional
Development for
Staff**

The school should

- Train teachers to use a variety of instructional and classroom management strategies to prevent academic failure and problem behavior for all students
- Encourage preservice programs in teacher-training institutions to provide this training
- Encourage state departments of education to include this training in their inservice programs

Chapter 9

Autism Spectrum Disorders

E very 25 minutes, a child in the United States is diagnosed with an autism spectrum disorder (ASD). The Centers for Disease Control and Prevention in 2006 estimated that ASDs affect as many as 1 in 166 children. Four out of five of those affected are males. Researchers and clinicians still debate whether the rapid rise in the number of diagnosed cases is due to an actual increase in the incidence of ASD or to the broadened standards that physicians use to the make a diagnosis. Are more children developing ASD, or are we just getting better at finding those who already have it? Many experts say it is both.

This rapid increase in the number of cases of ASDs in recent years has prompted more research into their causes and into the effectiveness of past and newer treatments. It is not possible in this one chapter to explore in detail all the research pathways currently being pursued or to assess the efficacy of the many forms of treatment. Rather, my purpose here is to describe the conditions included in ASD,

Autism spectrum disorder affects as many as one in 166 people, and four out of five of those affected are males.

their diagnoses, possible causes, and considerations that educators should keep in mind when dealing with students who have ASD. Those who want to pursue this topic in greater depth will find support organizations and additional references listed in the **Resources** section at the end of this book.

PERVASIVE DEVELOPMENTAL DISORDERS

In previous chapters we discovered how the brain acquires language, learns to read and write, calculates, and generates the emotions to interact and communicate with other human beings. Different neural networks must work in harmony to carry out these activities successfully. When several networks malfunction early in a child's life, *pervasive developmental disorders (PDD)* appear. In this category of pervasive developmental disorders, the *Diagnostic and Statistical Manual of Mental Disorders, Fourth Edition-Text Revision* (DSM-IV-TR) includes five disorders: *autistic disorder* (classic autism), *Asperger syndrome, pervasive developmental disorder—not otherwise specified (PDD-NOS), Rett syndrome,* and *childhood disintegrative disorder.*

All these disorders are characterized by varying degrees of impairment in communication skills, social interactions, and restricted, repetitive, and stereotyped patterns of behavior. Each disorder is lifelong and can run the gamut from mild to severe. The severe form is called autistic disorder, and the milder form is referred to as Asperger syndrome. If a child has symptoms of either of these two disorders but does not meet the specific criteria for either, the diagnosis is called pervasive developmental disorder—not otherwise specified. The term *autism spectrum disorders* generally refers to these three disorders. They will be the focus of this chapter because Rett syndrome (occurring only in females) and childhood disintegrative disorder are rare.

Autism Spectrum Disorders

Autism spectrum disorders are more common in the child population than some better-known disorders, such as diabetes, spina bifida, or Down syndrome. This prevalence demonstrates the importance of early and more accurate screening for the symptoms of ASD. The earlier the disorder is diagnosed, the sooner the child can be helped through treatment interventions. Although early intervention has a dramatic impact on reducing symptoms and increasing a child's ability to grow and learn new skills, it is estimated that only 50 percent of children are diagnosed before kindergarten (NIMH, 2004).

Symptoms of Autism Spectrum Disorders

All children with ASD demonstrate deficits in (1) social interaction, (2) verbal and nonverbal communication, and (3) repetitive behaviors or interests. In addition, they will often have unusual responses to sensory experiences, such as certain sounds or the way objects look. Each of these symptoms will appear in individual children differently. For instance, a child may have little trouble learning to read but exhibit extremely poor social interaction. Each child will display communication, social, and behavioral patterns that are individual but fit into the overall diagnosis of ASD.

The symptoms usually appear before three years of age. In some children, parents may notice the hints of future problems from birth. Problems in communication and social skills become more noticeable as the child lags further behind other children the same age. Usually between 12 and 36 months old, the differences in the way they react to people and other unusual behaviors become apparent. Some parents report the change as being sudden, and that their children start to reject people, act strangely, and lose language and social skills they had previously acquired. In other cases, there is a leveling off of progress so that the difference between the child with ASD and other children the same age becomes more noticeable.

Other indicators of ASD. The following are possible indicators of ASD (NIMH, 2004):

- Does not babble, point, or make meaningful gestures by 1 year of age
- Does not speak one word by 16 months
- Does not respond to name

- Does not combine two words by 2 years
- Does not seem to know how to play with toys
- Excessively lines up toys or other objects
- Is attached to one particular toy or object
- Avoids eye contact
- Has poor language or social skills
- Rarely smiles
- Seems to be hearing impaired at times

Social symptoms. Typically developing infants are social beings. Early in life, they gaze at people, turn toward voices, grasp a finger, and even smile. In contrast, most children with ASD seem to have tremendous difficulty learning to engage in the give-and-take of everyday human interaction. Even in the first few months of life, many do not interact and they avoid eye contact. They seem indifferent to other people, and often seem to prefer being alone. They may resist attention or passively accept hugs and cuddling. Later, they seldom seek comfort or respond to parents' displays of anger or affection in a typical way. Research has suggested that although children with ASD are attached to their parents, their expression of this attachment is unusual and difficult to interpret. To parents, it may seem as if their child is not attached at all. Some children with ASD also tend to be physically aggressive at times, particularly when they are in a strange or overwhelming environment. Occasionally, they will break things, attack others, or harm themselves.

Communication difficulties. Some children with ASD remain mute throughout their lives. Others will only parrot what they hear (a condition known as *echolalia*). Those who do speak tend to confuse pronouns like "I," "my," and "you," and may use the same phrase, such as "milk and cookies," in many different situations. Some children only mildly affected may exhibit slight delays in language, or even seem to have precocious language and unusually large vocabu-laries, but have great difficulty in sustaining a conversation. The give and take of normal conversation is hard for them, although they often carry on a monologue on a favorite subject, giving no one else an opportunity to comment.

> **Autism Spectrum Disorders**
>
> Major Symptoms:
> - Social interaction impairments characterized by nonverbal behaviors, inappropriate peer relationships, failure to interact with others, and poor social or emotional reciprocity
> - Communication impairments characterized by a delay in, or lack of, spoken language development, stereotyped or repetitive language use or idiosyncratic language, and lack of developmentally appropriate spontaneous or social imitative play
> - Repetitive and restricted stereotyped patterns of behavior characterized by abnormally intense preoccupation with one or more restricted patterns, inflexible adherence to nonfunctional routines, repetitive motor movements, and persistent preoccupation with objects

It is very difficult to understand the body language of people with ASD. Most of us smile when we talk or shrug our shoulders when we cannot answer a question. But the facial expressions and movements of children with ASD rarely match what they are saying. In addition, their tone of voice does not usually reflect their feelings. Without meaningful gestures or the language to ask for things, these children are at a loss to communicate their needs. Consequently, they may simply scream or grab what they want.

Repetitive and obsessive behaviors. Most children with ASD appear physically normal and have good muscle control. But they can also exhibit repetitive actions, such as flicking their fingers, rocking back and forth, or running from room to room tuning lights on and off. Others demand consistency in their environment and develop fixations with certain objects, such as eating the same foods at the same time and sitting in the same place every day. Repetitive behavior sometimes takes the form of a persistent, intense preoccupation. For example, the child might be obsessed with learning all about refrigerators, train schedules, or lighthouses. Often there is great interest in numbers, symbols, or science topics.

Does this repetitive-obsessive behavior have the same underlying neurological cause as obsessive-compulsive disorder? In the first edition of this book, I wrote that this connection was possible but not likely, adding that researchers then favored the explanation that the obsessive behavior was a demand for consistency and stability in a world of sensory confusion. But subsequent research has altered this explanation. Several studies have found that children with ASD who have high rates of repetitive behaviors are significantly more likely to have one or both parents with obsessive-compulsive traits, suggesting a strong genetic link for this behavior (Hollander, King, Delaney, Smith, & Silverman, 2003). MRI scans have revealed that individuals with ASD and those with obsessive-compulsive behavior have the same abnormally enlarged structures in the brain's limbic area. This finding supports the notion that similar neurological deficits contribute to both the repetitive behaviors found in ASD and obsessive-compulsive disorder (Hollander, Anagnostou, Chaplin, Esposito, Haznedar, Licalzi, et al., 2005).

Sensory symptoms. When children's perceptions are accurate, they can learn from what they see, feel, or hear. On the other hand, if sensory information is faulty, the child's experiences of the world can be confusing. In ASD, the brain seems unable to balance the senses appropriately. Many children with ASD are highly attuned or even painfully sensitive to certain sounds, textures, tastes, and smells. For some children, even the feel of clothes touching their skin is almost unbearable. Loud and intrusive sounds, such as from a vacuum cleaner, a ringing telephone, or a sudden storm, will cause these children to cover their ears and scream.

Mental retardation. Many children with autistic disorder and pervasive developmental disorder—not otherwise specified have some degree of mental impairment. When tested, some areas of ability may be normal, while others may be especially weak. For example, a child with ASD may do well on the parts of the test that measure visual skills but earn low scores on the language subtests. Individuals with Asperger syndrome however, have average to above average intelligence.

Fragile X syndrome. This disorder is the most common inherited form of mental retardation. It was so named because one part of the X chromosome has a defective piece that appears pinched and fragile when viewed under a microscope. Fragile X syndrome affects about two to five percent of people with ASD. It is important to have a child with ASD checked for Fragile X, especially if the parents are considering having another child. If a child with ASD also has Fragile X, there is a one in two chance that boys born to the same parents will have the syndrome (Powers, 2000). Other members of the family who may be contemplating having a child may also wish to be checked for the syndrome.

Memory and recall. A few studies have looked at long-term memory and how well children with ASD learn information, encode it accurately, and retrieve it correctly. The results showed that most children with ASD had greater difficulty recalling verbal information compared to typically developing children. However, in studies involving working memory, individuals with high-functioning ASD (Asperger syndrome) solved problems involving spatial working memory at least as well as, or better than, the control group. These findings suggest that working memory deficits in ASD appear to affect verbal memory systems more than visual-spatial memory (Caron, Mottron, Rainville, & Chouinard, 2004; Williams, Goldstein, & Minshew, 2006).

> *Memory deficits in autism spectrum disorder affect verbal memory systems more than visual-spatial memory.*

Diagnosis of Autism Spectrum Disorders

No two children display ASD in exactly the same way. Further, some children can exhibit symptoms that look like ASD, but may indicate other disorders and not ASD. These possibilities also need to be investigated. The diagnosis requires a two-stage process. The first stage involves a screening process using parental questionnaires and clinical observations. Several screening instruments have been developed to quickly gather information about a child's social and communicative development within medical settings. If the screening process shows possible indicators of ASD, further evaluation is needed.

The second stage entails a comprehensive evaluation by a multidisciplinary team that includes a psychologist, a neurologist, a psychiatrist, a speech therapist, or other professionals who diagnose children with ASD. Specialists evaluate language and social behavior, talk with parents about the child's developmental milestones, and test for certain genetic and neurological problems. A hearing test should also be performed. Although hearing loss can occur with ASD, some children with ASD may be incorrectly thought to have such a loss.

Causes of Autism Spectrum Disorders

The exact causes of ASD are unknown. But researchers in the past 20 years have made impressive gains in understanding the impaired abilities of people with ASD and in using this understanding to develop theories about its causes. Most experts now agree that ASD is associated with abnormal brain developments that occur in part as a result of genetic factors. Here are some of the major areas of research looking into the causes of this complex set of disorders.

Brain structure studies. Brain imaging tools compare the structure and functioning of typical brains to those with ASD. Postmortem and MRI studies have shown that many major brain structures are implicated in ASD. This includes the cerebellum, cerebral cortex, limbic area, corpus callosum, basal ganglia, and brainstem (Akshoomoff, Pierce, & Courschesne, 2002).

Abnormal head size. Recent neuroimaging studies have shown that a contributing cause for ASD may be abnormal brain development beginning in the infant's first months. This is called the "growth dysregulation hypothesis" and it suggests that the anatomical abnormalities seen in ASD are caused by genetic defects controlling brain growth. Researchers found that the head measurements of 48 children with ASD were smaller at birth than the national norms (Figure 9.1). However, their heads grew dramatically during the first two months of infancy and between 6 and 14 months. Faster growth predicted greater impairment (Courchesne, Carper, & Akshoomoff, 2003).

The MRI scans of the children with ASD showed more brain tissue in both the cerebrum and cerebellum. By contrast, body weight and length developed normally in the children with ASD. The researchers also found that around the age of 5 years, the head size of a child with ASD was about the same as a typical teenage brain. However, by adulthood, the brain size was no different in those with or without ASD.

The unusually rapid increase in brain growth during infancy is particularly perplexing given the behavioral abnormalities that define ASD. One would assume that more brain tissue would lead eventually

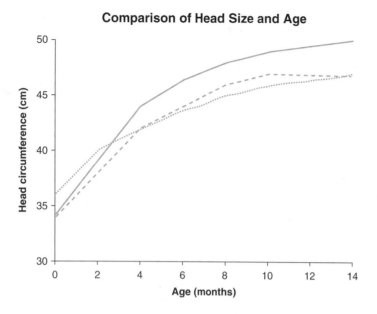

Comparison of Head Size and Age

Figure 9.1 The head sizes of children with ASD (solid and dashed lines) start out smaller than children without ASD (dotted line), but grow dramatically faster, with severe cases (solid line) growing fastest (adapted from Courchesne, Carper, & Akshoomoff, 2003).

to advantages rather than deficits. But white matter contributes disproportionately to this brain volume increase and in a non-uniform pattern. At some point it becomes impossible to interconnect so many extra brain cells, resulting in functional abnormalities (Herbert, 2005).

It is possible that sudden, rapid head growth in an infant may be an early warning signal that someday will lead to early diagnosis and effective biological intervention or possible prevention of ASD. But some scientists caution that rapid head growth could also indicate tumors, hydrocephalus, or nothing at all.

Parental similarities. MRIs of parents of children with ASD showed brain regions in the parent group that were either larger or smaller than in adults with no family history of ASD. For example, in the frontal lobes, the researchers found more gray matter but significantly less white matter. This is an executive-control area that plays a major role in understanding other people's mental states and acting accordingly. These findings offer hints at which brain abnormalities might be inherited with ASD.

Genetic studies. Studies of twins and families suggest that genetic factors play a dominant role in the causes of ASD (Korvatska, Van deWater, Anders, & Gershwin, 2002; Spence, 2004). Scientists are now hunting for the genes involved, but it is a difficult process. Unlike Down syndrome or Huntington's disease, in which a single gene or an entire chromosome is inherited, many gene mutations are involved in ASD. At the very least, anomalies on chromosomes 3, 7, 15, 17, and on the X chromosome appear to be implicated (Auranen, Vanhala, Varilo, Ayers, Kempas, Yisaukko-Oja, et al., 2003; Samaco, Hogart, & LaSalle, 2004). Researchers suspect that mutations in these genes may affect the activity of certain neurotransmitters as well as the brain's plasticity during development, thereby altering neural connections as a result of specific experiences. Various combinations of genetic mutations could also interact with unknown environmental factors resulting in the wide variety of symptoms that appear in children affected with ASD.

Gaze avoidance. One strategy for tracking down specific genes is to compare children with ASD to their unaffected family members and look for any overlap in behavior or brain function. Of particular interest to researchers was whether the siblings of children with ASD exhibited signs of *gaze avoidance.* This tendency to avoid eye contact is a key feature of ASD and often one of the earliest indications that a child may have the disorder. A few years ago, researchers thought that gaze avoidance resulted from deficits in the part of the brain associated with face perception, called the *fusiform gyrus.* These deficits, it was thought, led to less responsiveness to faces, a central cause of the social impairment observed in ASD. But subsequent studies indicate that this structure is normal in most individuals with ASD (Hadjikhani, Joseph, Snyder, Chabris, Clark, Steele, et al., 2004).

In a study using new technology that tracks a person's eyes when gazing at a photograph, researchers found that the unaffected siblings showed the same pattern of gaze avoidance for eyes as did the youths with

ASD (Figure 9.2). The low eye contact occurred even when they looked at pictures of family and friends, so the behavior did not reflect inherited shyness.

While the youths were looking at the photographs, MRI machines scanned the amygdala, because this brain structure is associated with emotions and the interpretation of facial expressions. The amygdala was smaller in both groups. Yet the smaller amygdala did not result in ASD symptoms. Apparently, other brain systems must compensate for this abnormality in the non-ASD siblings. Whenever the youths with ASD did gaze at the eyes in the picture, higher activity was detected in the amygdala, indicating the presence of negative feelings. When the individuals with ASD looked away from the image's eyes, they showed reduced activity in the amygdala. Gaze avoidance, then, may be serving the

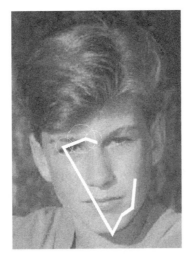

Figure 9.2 Children without ASD tend to look at another person's eyes and keep their gaze there, as seen by the representations of eye movements and fixations on the left. But children with ASD avoid looking into another person's eyes, as indicated on the right. The lines show the eye movements. Where the eyes stop is indicated by the circles, which grow larger the longer the eye gazes at a certain spot (adapted from Dalton, et al., 2005).

functional purpose of lowering the anxiety levels created by the stimulated amygdala (Dalton, Nacewicz, Johnstone, Schaefer, Gernsbacher, Goldsmith, et al., 2005; Schultz, 2005).

Assortative mating theory. ASD has an unusually high genetic component. About 90 percent of identical twins share the disorder compared to other highly genetic disorders where only 50 percent of identical twins are both affected. Why such a high incidence? One possible explanation is *assortative mating.* Assortative mating has been documented in other behavioral disorders. Studies show that people with alcohol and drug additions often chose mates with similar preferences. Individuals suffering from depression tend to find equally gloomy partners, and those with bipolar disorder often marry similarly moody people. Parents of children with ASD are twice as likely to be engineers as the general population. College graduates with degrees in mathematics, computer sciences, and physics score higher than others on tests of autistic thinking (Baron-Cohen, 2003). Assortative mating could increase the prevalence of a condition like ASD dramatically if it brings together people with less common, recessive genes who previously would not have mated.

Neurotransmitter studies. Numerous studies have looked at a wide array of neurotransmitters to determine how they may affect ASDs. These studies are complicated by the fact that ASDs vary over a broad spectrum and are often present with other behavioral problems. Of all the neurotransmitters studied, serotonin has the most empirical evidence for a role in ASD. Genetic studies of families with ASD reveal that they often have mutations within a specific gene on chromosome 17, called SERT, that regulates serotonin levels in the brain. About 25 percent of people with ASD have elevated serotonin levels. Drugs that are selective serotonin reuptake inhibitors (SSRIs) have eased the symptoms of ASD in some people (Scott & Deneris, 2005).

The "Theory of Mind" hypothesis and mirror neurons. One of the neurological signs of people with ASD is their failure to construe the mental states of others—a deficit in what has been called the "theory of mind." This theory refers to the everyday ability to infer what others are thinking or believing in order to explain and predict their behavior. Researchers are investigating how theory of mind develops in the brain,

> *Individuals with ASD have difficulty viewing situations from another person's perspective, and predicting other people's emotions and motives.*

but they suspect it is independent of other skills. Individuals with ASD have difficulty viewing situations from another person's perspective, and predicting other people's emotions and motives. This may explain why they have such difficulty with simple behaviors such as attending to a situation and playing games with others (Zimmer, 2003).

Some researchers are attempting to identify the brain structures associated with theory of mind, where fast intuitions are combined with slower, deliberate judgments. One idea centers around a type of neuron found in the cortex of the frontal and temporal lobes. Known as Von Economo neurons (named after their discoverer), these cells are distinguished by having larger and fewer dendrites extending from the cell body than typical neurons in the cortex. They develop after birth and are particularly vulnerable to dysfunction. Because these neurons have many receptors for dopamine and serotonin, they are believed to be strongly linked to the formation of social bonds, rewards and punishments, and intuitive responses to complex situations. MRI studies of individuals with ASD found that the brain region that contains the Von Economo neurons was reduced in volume compared to non-ASD controls. Furthermore, the areas in the white matter that carry these neurons' axons were in disarray. The failure of these neurons to develop normally may be partially responsible for the social impairments and faulty intuition typical of individuals with ASD (Allman, Watson, Tetreault, & Hakeem, 2005).

In Chapter 1 we discussed mirror neurons, which allow us to re-create the experience of others within ourselves, and to understand others' emotions and empathize. Researchers suspect that the inability of individuals with ASD to empathize may be due to deficits in mirror neuron systems. Studies using fMRI and EEG found little or no activity in the mirror neuron systems of individuals with ASD compared to the control participants (Dapretto, Davies, Pfeifer, Scott, Sigman, Bookheimer, et al., 2006; Oberman, Hubbard, McCleery, Altschuler, Ramachandran, & Pineda, 2005; Williams, Waiter, Gilchrist, Perrett, Murray, & Whiten; 2006). Mirror neurons are not located in the same brain areas as Von Economo neurons, and they are structurally different.

The extreme male brain theory of ASD. The observation that four out of five people with ASD are males has led some researchers to try to explain the reasons for this gender discrepancy. One possible explanation is that some of the genetic mutations associated with ASD may be located on the X chromosome. Because males inherit only one copy of this chromosome, they are more susceptible to the consequences of its defects.

Another explanation comes from Simon Baron-Cohen, a British researcher, who studies the differences between male and female brains. Baron-Cohen says males have a greater tendency than females to analyze,

> *Could individuals with ASD merely be displaying the extremes of normal male traits?*

construct, control, and predict the behavior of systems—a mental domain he calls "systemizing." Boys are more interested than girls in toy cars, building blocks and mechanical toys. They are better at reading maps, paying attention to relevant detail, judging the behavior of moving objects, constructing with building blocks, and converting 2-D diagrams into 3-D models. Females, on the other hand, have a greater tendency to identify other people's emotions and respond accordingly—a mental domain that Baron-Cohen calls "empathizing." He believes that genetics and culture drive systemizing and empathizing and that most people have components of both domains.

According to Baron-Cohen, people with ASD display the extremes of normal male systemizing traits. They are very poor at empathizing yet can show special abilities in mathematical calculations, music, chess, mechanical knowledge, and other areas involving systemizing. Not much is known about the neural circuits associated with systemizing, but research in this area may lead to greater understanding of ASD and treatment (Baron-Cohen, 2003).

Mercury toxicity. During the late 1980s and throughout the 1990s, some parents, researchers, and medical practitioners noted a correlation between a rise in ASD cases and the introduction of the measles, mumps, and rubella (MMR) combination vaccine. In 1998, a British physician reported that his study of 42 children with ASD revealed that they all had intestinal problems and autistic-like symptoms after receiving the MMR vaccinations. Subsequent articles compared these autistic-like symptoms to those of mercury poisoning, and suggested that they were caused by thimerosal, a mercury-based preservative contained in the vaccines (Bernard, Enayati, Redwood, Roger, & Binstock, 2001; Rimland, 2000).

Scientists are still debating whether a link between mercury and ASD exists. Several large studies, including those in Britain (103,000 children) and Denmark (537,000 children) have shown the rate of ASD about the same for both vaccinated and unvaccinated children. Despite these results, other scientists note that children with ASD often have higher levels of mercury in their bodies. Meanwhile, public health officials fear that parents worried over the potential link might not get their children vaccinated against these potentially fatal diseases. As a precaution, thimerosal-containing vaccines for children were phased out in the United States starting in 1999.

Some scientists suggest that children with ASD may also inherit a genetic fault that makes them far more susceptible to mercury poisoning. Mothers could pass mercury to the fetus during pregnancy from the heavy consumption of fish.

Unusual Abilities

About 10 percent of people with ASD display remarkable abilities and skills. At a time when other children are drawing lines or scribbling, some children with ASD can draw detailed, realistic pictures with proper dimensional perspective. Some begin to read before they speak or play musical instruments without being taught. Others can make mathematical calculations incredibly rapidly, or memorize enormous amounts of information, such as pages from a phone book, many years of sport scores, and entire television shows. Such abilities are known as *savant skills*, and the extreme forms are rare. Not all people with savant skills have ASD.

> *About 10 percent of people with ASD display remarkable abilities known as savant skills.*

Researchers have been trying to explain why certain people with ASD possess savant skills. The current theory is that one characteristic of ASD may provide both advantages and disadvantages. This characteristic is called *central convergence* and refers to the ability of the brain to process incoming information in its context, that is, to put parts together into a meaningful whole. Because this ability is weak in people with ASD, it may explain why they focus on details and parts at the expense of global meaning. It may also explain why they have difficulties in social situations and why their piecemeal processing of faces could hamper their recognition of emotions in others (Happé, 1997).

Savant skills may also be a result of the uneven development of the brain's hemispheres. Researchers have observed that savant skills in people with ASD are those associated with right hemisphere functions, while their deficits are associated with left hemisphere functions. The left hemisphere normally completes its development later than the right and is therefore subject to prenatal influences for a longer period. In the male fetus, excessively high amounts of circulating testosterone can slow growth and impair neural function in the more vulnerable left hemisphere. Consequently, the right hemisphere often compensates, becoming larger and more dominant in males (Treffert & Wallace, 2002).

Asperger Syndrome

Identified in 1944 by Austrian physician Hans Asperger, this syndrome is a developmental disorder with many of the same symptoms of autistic disorder. It is usually referred to as a mild form of ASD because people with Asperger syndrome generally have higher mental functioning than those with typical ASD, and they have better communication skills. Like all disorders of the autism spectrum, Asperger syndrome is a lifelong condition. The DSM-IV-TR classifies Asperger syndrome as a separate disorder, mainly because these individuals do not have language or cognitive delays. Their major impairments involve social interactions. However, researchers now question whether Asperger syndrome is indeed different from high-functioning autism. Recent studies found that clinicians have difficulty distinguishing Asperger syndrome from high-functioning autism based on the DSM-IV-TR criteria because a child can still be diagnosed with autism even without language and cognitive delays. Thus, some experts are suggesting that the next edition of the DSM remove Asperger syndrome and designate children with those symptoms as having high-functioning autism (Howlin, 2003; Tryon et al., 2006).

Treatment for Autism Spectrum Disorders

At present, there is no cure for ASD, nor do children outgrow it. Nonetheless, more than ever before, people with ASD can be helped. A combination of early intervention, special education support, and medication is helping children and adolescents with ASD lead more normal lives. Medications can alleviate some of the symptoms and therapy can help a child to learn, communicate, and interact with others in productive ways.

An effective treatment program builds on the child's interests, offers a predictable schedule, teaches tasks as a series of simple steps, actively engages the child's attention in highly structured activities, and provides regular reinforcement of desirable behavior. Parental involvement has emerged as a major factor in treatment success. Parents work with teachers and therapists to identify the behaviors to be changed and the skills to be taught. Recognizing that parents are the child's earliest teachers, more programs are beginning to train parents to continue the therapy at home.

One of the effective methods available for treatment of people with ASD is applied behavior analysis (ABA). Over 35 years of research have demonstrated the efficacy of applied behavioral methods in reducing inappropriate behavior and in increasing communication, learning, and appropriate social behavior in individuals with ASD. The goal of behavioral management is to reinforce desirable behaviors and reduce undesirable ones. This technique is tedious and time-consuming, calling for hours of daily instruction to break learning into very basic components and reward students for each positive step. If started at an early age, some experts believe, the process could actually help rewire the young brain (Simpson, 2001).

Elementary school. In elementary school, the child should receive help in any skill area that is delayed while being encouraged to grow in areas of strength. Where possible, the curriculum should be adapted to the individual child's needs. Many schools today have an inclusion program in which the child is in a regular classroom for most of the day, with special instruction for a part of the day. This instruction should include such skills as learning how to act in social situations and in making friends. Although higher-functioning children may be able to handle academic work, they too need help to organize tasks and avoid distractions.

The adolescent years. During middle and high school years, instruction should address such practical matters as work, community living, and recreational activities. This should include work experience, using public transportation, and learning skills that will be important in community living. Adolescence is a time of stress and confusion, and it is no less so for teenagers with ASD. The teenage years are also a time when children become more socially sensitive. At the age that most teenagers are concerned with acne, popularity, grades, and dates, teens with ASD may become painfully aware that they are different from their peers. They may notice that they lack friends, and unlike their schoolmates, they aren't dating or planning for a career. For some, the sadness that comes with such realization actually motivates them to learn new behaviors and acquire better social skills.

Medications used in treatment. Medications are often used to treat behavioral problems, such as aggression, self-injurious behavior, and severe tantrums, that keep the person with ASD from functioning more effectively at home or school. The medications used are those that have been developed to treat similar symptoms in other disorders. For example, selective serotonin reuptake inhibitors are the medications most often prescribed for symptoms of anxiety, depression, and/or obsessive-compulsive disorder. Antipsychotic medications have been used to treat severe behavioral problems. These medications work by reducing the activity in the brain of the neurotransmitter dopamine.

Seizures are found in one in four persons with ASD, most often in those who have low IQ or are mute. They are treated with one or more of the anticonvulsant medications, which usually reduce the number of seizures but cannot always eliminate them. Stimulant medications used in persons with attention-deficit hyperactivity disorder have also been prescribed for children with ASD. These medications may decrease impulsivity and hyperactivity, especially in higher functioning children.

The Future of Research on Autism Spectrum Disorders

Researchers and clinicians have launched an all-out effort to track down the causes and triggers for ASD. Medical researchers and physicians from leading medical centers in the United States have formed the Autism Treatment Network, a cooperative effort to develop reliable criteria for diagnosing ASD, to test medical treatments, and to prepare scientists and physicians for careers in ASD study and treatment. The Network is partially funded by a research support organization called Cure Autism Now. Meanwhile, the U. S. Centers for Disease Control and Prevention are supporting efforts to diagnose children with ASD earlier, by 18 months of age instead of age 3, hoping that earlier diagnosis and intervention will alter the disorder's course.

Another study funded by Cure Autism Now is aimed at characterizing subgroups of ASD. Currently, children with ASD may be labeled high functioning or low functioning, but little is known about what causes these functional variations. Discovering physiological differences could help physicians diagnose different subgroups of ASD and develop more effective and personalized forms of treatment for each child with ASD.

ASD has long been defined by its behavioral symptoms, but researchers are now focusing on what goes wrong in the brain to cause those behaviors. Research continues to look for genetic variants associated with ASD in the hope that this may provide a more accurate diagnostic tool for the future, at least in terms of estimating the chances that the children of siblings of a person with ASD may inherit the disorder. It may even lead to early interventions during infancy.

Another development is the Autism Tissue Program. Studies of the postmortem brain with imaging methods will help scientists learn why some brains are large, how the limbic system develops, and how the brain changes as it ages. Tissue samples can be stained and show which neurotransmitters are being made in the cells and how they are transported and released to other cells. Focusing on specific brain regions will make identifying susceptibility genes easier.

Scientists continue to explore the role that neurotransmitters may play in ASD. Individuals with ASD often show lower levels of neurotransmitters, such as acetylcholine, serotonin, and GABA, in several areas of the brain. These findings suggest that multiple neurotransmitter systems are affected in ASD. Researchers may be able to develop drugs that specifically target these neurochemical imbalances.

Because many fMRI studies have found the synchronization of brain activation consistently lower in people with ASD than in those without ASD, some researchers are proposing that ASD may be the result of poor interconnections between brain areas responsible for language and social behavior. This theory, known as *underconnectivity,* is consistent with other findings. For example, as explained earlier, larger brain size may interfere with critical connections between neuron networks. More study is needed, but researchers are hopeful that pursing underconnectivity will lead to improved treatments.

Other researchers are looking at whether abnormalities in the immune system contribute to ASD. About one third of children with ASD have unexplained gastrointestinal problems. Researchers have found that children with ASD have about one half the amount of glutathione (an antioxidant critical for the immune system) in their brain and stomach lining as children without ASD. Natural body chemicals that help make glutathione were also abnormal. Studies are investigating whether this glutathione abnormality can be reversed by administering certain vitamins, such as B_{12} and folic acid.

As researchers learn more about the development of the human brain, they will be better able to unlock the genetic, biochemical, psychological, and physiological mysteries of ASD.

WHAT EDUCATORS NEED TO CONSIDER

ASDs are neurological disorders that affect children's overall ability to communicate and interact socially. Their behavior may be difficult to control at times. Teachers should be adequately trained to use interventions that will preserve a positive educational climate in the classroom for these students and their peers.

Adolescents diagnosed with ASD have to bear both the burden of coping with the teenage years and the recognition that they are different from their peers. They typically lack friends and neither date nor plan for the future. Awareness of this often drives them to learn new and unacceptable behaviors. Success in school for students with ASD should be measured not so much by whether they succeed at algebra as by whether they acquire the knowledge and skills that will make them more self-sufficient as adults.

STRATEGIES TO CONSIDER

Enhancing Learning in Students With Autism Spectrum Disorders

The items listed here are for consideration by any educator responsible for helping students with ASD successfully cope with their situation and become self-sufficient adults.

- **Different learning style.** Students with ASD learn differently in that they have difficulty understanding the perceptions of others, experience sensory overload, and use intellect instead of emotion to guide their social interactions. Use visual aids whenever possible to help them organize their work and day.

- **Need for structure.** These students need structure. Their activities should

  o Organize their materials
  o Give clear instructions
  o Provide stability
  o Establish patterns
  o Provide consistency and predictability
  o Increase independence

- **Social interaction.** These students need to learn ways to interact socially with their peers and adults. When teaching them about social interaction, use

  o A predictable sequence of interactions (no surprises)
  o A planned set of conversational scripts
  o Lots of repetition
  o Messages linked to what the student is doing
  o Speech and visual cues simultaneously
  o Messages mixed with ongoing activities

STRATEGIES TO CONSIDER

Interventions for Young Children With Autism Spectrum Disorder

A 2006 study examined interventions conducted with young children with ASD to determine their effectiveness. The researchers found that interventions that included parent involvement, targeted various developmental areas, and extended over a long period of time (for 1 year or more) were the most effective (Levy, Kim, & Olive, 2006). Their findings are described in the six categories listed below.

- **Parent involvement.** Researchers have demonstrated the ability of parents to implement a variety of interventions, including a focus on areas such as language and behavior. Parents are effective intervention agents because they can increase the number of hours of intervention that children receive, and they can intervene throughout the child's life span. Furthermore, parents who serve as intervention agents often report that they have increased feelings of support and competence and fewer feelings of stress and depression. To be most effective, however, parents must be trained in how to implement the interventions properly. School districts could operate these parent-training workshops. Here are some interventions that worked:
  - Parents who implemented language and speech interventions with behavior modifications to their children for a period of 10 weeks found that the children mastered significantly more speech skills than prior to the intervention.
  - Parents trained to teach language, imitation, and preacademic skills by using structured teaching and visual aids to their children found that after 10 weeks the children scored better on subtests of a developmental profile.
  - Parents trained in behavior management had a significant reduction in their children's problem behaviors after 3 months of intervention.
  - Parents trained in language, social development, functional behavior assessment, and problem solving taught language and social skills to their children for 12 weeks. Children in the intervention group performed significantly better in language skills over time.

- **Intensive behavioral intervention.** Several studies in which children with ASD received intensive intervention (40 or more hours per week) in language, behavior, and social and emotional areas, ranging from 16 months to 2 years, all reported positive outcomes.

- **Multicomponent early intervention.** In these studies, children received multicomponent early intervention in language, social and emotional, cognitive, and behavior areas for periods of 43 weeks to 1 year. After the intervention, the children showed significantly improved scores in fine motor, cognitive, language (both receptive and expressive), and social and emotional areas. They also displayed a decrease in autistic behavior.

- **Language and speech treatments.** Children who received specific language training for periods of 1 to 2 years performed significantly better than the control group in auditory comprehension, non-verbal imitation, vocal imitation, and communicative speech.

- **Setting.** The presence of typically developing children was shown to significantly decrease autistic behavior as compared to the presence of other children with ASD.

- **Other interventions.** Other studies have shown some promise for the following interventions:
  - Touch therapy can improve social and communication skills and reduce autistic and negative classroom behaviors.
  - Children who received intensive behavioral interventions when under the age of 60 months had significantly better outcomes than those who received the interventions after the age of 60 months.
  - Children using a computer program with a teacher-directed behavior training on vocabulary acquisition significantly increased their learning of vocabulary as well as their attention and motivation scores.

STRATEGIES TO CONSIDER

Interventions for Children and Adolescents With Autism Spectrum Disorder

There are literally dozens of interventions and treatments currently being used or suggested for children and adolescents with ASD, ranging from behavior analysis to megavitamin therapy. Which are the most effective? Which have enough empirical evidence to be considered scientifically based practices? Simpson (2005) has reviewed many of these interventions and treatments, and found four that have been rigorously researched and that repeatedly yield significantly positive outcomes for students with ASD. Because every individual with ASD exhibits a unique combination of strengths and weaknesses in various areas, no one technique should be adopted at the exclusion of others. Here is a brief description of each:

- **Applied Behavior Analysis (ABA).** ABA emphasizes a proactive approach, using effective strategies for intervening after a behavior has occurred. It involves a comprehensive analysis of the student's environment, including adaptive and meaningful curriculum, appropriate instructional activities, appropriate stimulus control, and a positive classroom structure that increases the student's desired behaviors. The ABA techniques have been refined over more than 35 years to teach a variety of skills in multiple settings, including social skills in natural settings, one-to-one instruction, and group instruction. The effectiveness of ABA is enhanced because decisions related to this approach are driven by data collected through observation, either live or by videotaping. Researchers generally agree that starting ABA before age 5 increases the likelihood of successful outcomes.

  Because of the complexities involved in administering ABA, it is important that individuals who provide behavior analysis services be properly qualified and thoroughly trained. A national certification process has been established.

- **Discrete Trial Teaching (DTT).** DTT is related to applied behavior analysis and is a strategy for teaching new skills. The *trial* is a single teaching unit consisting of three components: an instructional piece, the student's response to the instruction, and the consequences. The teacher's instructions are given (e.g., "Tell me which of these objects is a cube"). Then comes the student's answer ("This one is the cube"), which is evaluated as correct ("That right. Good for you"), incorrect, or no response. As a consequence of the student's response, the teacher decides the next step, which may involve reteaching, modeling, prompting, or moving on. DTT uses techniques such as errorless learning, modeling, shaping, correction procedures, and reinforcement to promote skill acquisition. It can be used to teach new behaviors, such as motor skills, imitation and play skills, language skills, and emotional expression. DTT can also be used to reduce aggressive behaviors. Most educators can implement DTT with training and supervision, but special and extensive training is needed to develop DTT curricula and to supervise DTT programs.

- **Pivotal Response Training (PRT).** PRT focuses on pivotal areas that can improve other important areas and have a widespread impact on the child's development. It aims to provide individuals with ASD with the educational and social skills they need to function independently and successfully in inclusive settings. PRT uses the principles of applied behavior analysis (ABA) to help students respond to multiple cues and stimuli, improve motivation, increase response to natural cues in the environment, and improve self-management. PRT should be used in inclusive settings, such as general education classrooms and homes. This approach stresses the importance of inclusion as contrasted with the traditional ABA approach of one-on-one training.

- **Learning Experiences: An Alternative Program for Preschoolers and Parents (LEAP).** LEAP is an early childhood (ages 3 to 5) intervention approach that uses peer mediation and is designed to occur in inclusive preschool settings. A speech language therapist assists the children with ASD and their parents in the classroom and at home. Children without ASD are taught interventions that help them develop the social skills of their peers with ASD. The LEAP curriculum aims to develop language and communications abilities, increase choice making, facilitate independence in work and play activities, and generally enhance social and emotional growth. Family members receive training in teaching strategies and behavior management to ensure that the interventions are supported throughout the day. Studies have shown that students who attended LEAP schools for 15 hours per week and remained for two to three years improved in their social interaction, language and communication skills, cognitive function, and behavior, and a reduction in their autistic characteristics. Furthermore, the studies suggested that these improvements were maintained over time.

STRATEGIES TO CONSIDER

Helping Students With Asperger Syndrome

Children and adolescents diagnosed with Asperger syndrome usually have average or above average cognitive abilities. They tend to have excellent rote memory skills and often exhibit a precocious vocabulary. However, they have problems with abstract thinking. They frequently do not understand the logic of classroom instruction and discussion and are easily distracted. Educational structure and classroom management strategies become important. Instructional approaches have to be concrete and varied. Support and discipline strategies need to be clear and nonthreatening. Here are a few points to consider that could help students diagnosed with Asperger syndrome to succeed in the classroom (McAfee, 2002; Myles, 2005).

- **Educational Structure and Classroom Management**
  - Provide a predictable environment and routine, and prepare students for any upcoming changes
  - Ensure that each student is seated in a position of least distraction and close to the teacher or other source of information to which the student must respond
  - Be consistent and do not ask for an option if there is none
  - Avoid doing for the students what they can do for themselves
  - Give clear, precise, concrete instructions, and do not assume that mere repetition means that the student has understood
  - Find ways to tie new situations to old ones that students have experienced
  - State expectations clearly and allow each student time to process the information
  - Concentrate on changing unacceptable behaviors, and do not worry about those that are simply odd
  - Break tasks up into manageable segments, and plan a completion schedule with the student
  - Teach students how to complete a task, such as taking a multiple-choice test
  - Do not rely on emotional appeals by assuming students want to please you

- **Instructional Approaches**
  - Support verbal information with visual aids, such as blank graphic organizers, to help record and organize information
  - Incorporate 3-D models and manipulatives whenever possible
  - Consider tape recording information so students can take notes later at their own pace and refer back to the tape recording when needed
  - Model the action you want students to use, and maintain the behavior with visual cues
  - Use cooperative learning groups, but teach appropriate social responses to use in this activity
  - Minimize assigned written work because these students do not understand the logic of repetitive activities

o Use larger print on paperwork, and include only a few items on each page

o Assign enrichment activities related to the students' interests, as they will be more satisfied and productive gathering facts about a subject they like

o Avoid abstract language (e.g., metaphors and irony), and fully explain any constructions that you do use

o Work with students to determine the appropriate and interesting means for each to demonstrate knowledge of the topic (e.g., design and make a poster, give an oral presentation, write a story or poem, draw or paint a picture, make a collage, act out information, write a song, make a board game, or take a test)

- **Support and Discipline Strategies**
  o Have a strategy ready in case the students cannot cope due to overstimulation or confusion
  o Have a time-out area for discipline when needed, and make sure the time-out is not more appealing than the curricular activity
  o Look for stressors in their environment and try to reduce or eliminate them
  o Explicitly teach the rules of social conduct
  o Inform parents on a regular basis of the students' successes and failures, and ask for parental advice when appropriate
  o Give students some space, and avoid cornering or trapping them
  o Use an unemotional tone of voice when telling them what they need to do, and give sincere praise when they do it correctly
  o Try not to confuse lack of tact with rudeness
  o Protect them from teasing and bullying
  o Teach them how to meet someone, how to recognize when someone will not talk to them, and how to tell when someone is teasing them

Chapter 10

Putting It All Together

The preceding chapters have described some of the recent research on the human brain that sheds light on problems affecting learning. Some of the problems may result from genetic mutations, fetal brain injury during gestation, or environmental impact. Whatever the cause, teachers represent the essential link between the students with learning problems and the strategies and services selected to help them.

HELPING STUDENTS WITH LEARNING DIFFICULTIES

We know that students with learning problems *can* learn when teachers spend the time and use their expertise to find the appropriate ways to teach these students. To that end, let's look at four important areas that ought to be considered when working with students who have learning difficulties. Those areas are:

- Identification: How do we assess students for learning difficulties?
- Accommodation: How do we modify the instructional environment to help these students?
- Motivation: How do we encourage students with learning difficulties to achieve?
- Communication: How do we ensure that parents stay involved?

Identifying Students With Learning Difficulties

Very often, the regular classroom teacher is the first to recognize a potential learning problem. Although many students encounter learning problems at one time or another, these problems are usually temporary and

198

quickly overcome. For others, the problems persist and result in a lag in academic achievement compared to their learning potential. These students need help.

The question now is whether the learning problem can be addressed in the regular classroom. Asking older students to take an inventory similar to the one below will help you and them learn from their perceptions of how well they perform certain tasks. Working with a student on the comments section can provide useful insights on instructional approaches to consider. For younger students, a verbal discussion of these areas may be more effective than the written inventory.

Assessment Inventory			
Area	**Strengths**	**Challenges**	**Comments**
Attention			
Speaking			
Reading			
Writing			
Calculating			
Memory			
Emotional/Behavioral			

The results of the inventory, teacher observations, and student performance may indicate that a more formal assessment of the student's achievement is needed to determine if a learning disability exists. Many schools continue to use an ability (IQ)-achievement discrepancy model to identify the presence of a learning disability; that is, students with learning disabilities show an unexpected gap between their potential and achievement. As discussed in Chapter 2, the National Joint Committee on Learning Disabilities is suggesting that schools consider a Responsiveness to Intervention (RTI) method for identifying learning disabilities (NJCLD, 2005). In RTI, students who do not respond to intensive intervention would be identified as having a learning disability. Educators should carefully weigh the advantages and disadvantages of these and other identification methods.

The Ability-Achievement Discrepancy

Some educators still believe in the use of the discrepancy model, saying that it has a valid basis in that it provides psychometric evidence of the unexpected underachiever. It is a simple system that uses data from long-validated assessments. The model indicates the presence of underachievement but only the *possibility* of a disability and can thus serve as the first step in the identification process. Other educators say that even if the model is flawed, we should still use it but with greater integrity.

Arguments against the discrepancy method continue to surface. One argument is that the high number of students identified as learning disabled through this method is suspect. IQ tests, they say, can be biased against certain racial groups or those who are indigent. Furthermore, results are not consistent from state to state, or even from one school district to another: One district may have a high number of students with learning disabilities while another has few. Some research studies have shown that the same team using the discrepancy model will not identify the same students as having a learning disability. But proponents of the discrepancy approach say that these misidentifications are not because of a flawed model but due rather to the lack of rigor in its implementation (Kavale, 2005).

One of the most pressing arguments against the discrepancy model is what some critics see as its "wait-to-fail" aspect. Students must be in third or fourth grade to have a discrepancy large enough to be identified as having a learning disability (Vaughn & Fuchs, 2003). But supporters counter that this criticism is not really valid because early identification has long been a major focus. Schools do not wait for students to fail but attempt to find at-risk students as early as possible.

Responsiveness to Intervention (RTI)

With RTI, low achievers are identified as quickly as possible and provided intensive and validated instruction though the multiple-tier protocol described in Chapter 2. The model replaces traditional psychometric measures with an approach that emphasizes student outcomes rather than student deficits. At first glance, RTI seems to address the wait-to-fail issue. However, RTI also raises concerns. First, because we do not have effective measures for children in preschool, RTI can present its own version of wait-to-fail. Second, there is no guarantee that students who respond to interventions will continue to progress when they return to the general education classroom.

Other questions exist as to how RTI will be implemented. For example, how long should a child receive interventions and how extensive must nonresponsiveness be before a student is identified as learning disabled? It is possible that a student's nonresponsiveness is not at all due to a specific learning disability but to some other factor. Thus, critics argue, RTI should not stand alone as the primary means of identification because it also uses a single criterion (nonresponsiveness), the same criticism that has been leveled against the discrepancy model.

Another concern is that few intervention strategies exist for academic areas other than reading or for students at the middle or high school levels. Selecting intervention strategies will be challenging. For example, problem-solving interventions that allow special education teachers to individualize may compromise the program's integrity. With standard RTI protocol interventions, which involve a teaching package, teachers lose the ability to individualize instruction. Furthermore, teachers will need to teach, test, and keep data in ways they are neither accustomed nor trained to do. Finally, educators say, RTI is untested, and we don't know how to scale it to a national level.

RTI holds promise, and some of the screening procedures can help in identifying learning problems. But researchers are suggesting that there are not enough data at this time to support using RTI to replace the ability-achievement discrepancy model as the major means for identifying students with learning disabilities. Discrepancy remains a distinguishing characteristic of specific learning disabilities, and researchers argue that it should continue to be used, but not as the sole criterion for identifying learning disabilities.

The Neuropsychological Component

Some researchers are recommending that the RTI multitier model be expanded to a more complex framework that includes findings from neuroscience on how the brain develops and learns. They suggest, for example, that the expanded neuropsychological model could include a method for evaluating reading skills that also reveals whether the child can generalize learning or complete more abstract or inferential tasks. What do these evaluations tell us about the child's executive (frontal lobe) functions? This is important to know because the extent of executive function has implications for content courses, such as mathematics, science, and social studies.

The expanded model must also be able to differentiate among learners with different needs. The instruments should separate a child with reading difficulties due to attentional problems from one with reading difficulties due to problems with decoding. These two children need different interventions. With this approach, screening would include measures of attention, working memory, auditory processing ability, executive functions, processing speed, and other functions that affect learning (Semrud-Clikeman, 2005).

A Combined Model

Debate will likely continue for some time on the best methods for identifying whether a child has a learning disability. One possibility is to combine portions of several models into one that

- Recognizes the usefulness of the ability-achievement discrepancy
- Incorporates the advantages of a multitier framework
- Includes findings from neuroscience research about brain development and function

Kavale and Forness (2000) proposed a five-tier model that includes these components. In their model, the first level documents that a student has an ability-achievement discrepancy. It then progresses through the next four levels. The model in Figure 10.1 adapts the one proposed by Kavale and Forness (2000) to include some of the neuropsychological processes suggested by Semrud-Clikeman (2005). The advantages of this model are that it

- Starts with, but goes beyond, the ability-achievement discrepancy
- Ensures that the underachievement is occurring in a basic skill area
- Examines the student's ability to acquire and organize information
- Includes an assessment of neuropsychological processes associated with learning
- Eliminates other conditions that could be responsible for the underachievement

The identification process stops when the student cannot meet the criteria at any level. The designation of a *learning disability* occurs when the student passes successfully through each level.

Accommodating Students With Learning Difficulties

Here are some suggestions for teachers to consider when making accommodations for students with learning difficulties. Not all of these suggestions apply to every student, and individual strategies should be developed to address the needs of individual students. Implementing accommodations such as those listed here can improve the academic achievement of students with learning disabilities. In mainstreamed classrooms, take care to balance these accommodations so as not to appear unfair to the students who are not in need of these strategies.

Learn about learning. Educators in all areas can be empowered by updating their knowledge of what neuroscience is revealing about how the brain learns. These discoveries and insights can help explain

Level 5

> **Eliminate Other Conditions**
> Eliminating the following conditions leaves *learning disability* as the sole designation:
> **Cultural differences   Emotional or behavioral disorder**
> **Insufficient instruction   Mild mental retardation   Sensory impairment**

Level 4

> **Assess Neuropsychological Processes**
> The student is assessed in psychological processes to determine if any deficits exist. Those processes include:
> **Attention   Working memory   Linguistic processing**
> **Executive functions   Social cognition   Perception**

Level 3

> **Examine Learning Efficiency**
> This level examines the student's ability to structure and organize learning tasks as well as the rate of acquiring information. The goal is to determine the student's awareness about learning and whether tasks are being organized efficiently and efforts are being consistently sustained.

Level 2

> **Analyze Standard Achievement Test Scores in Major Academic Areas**
> To ensure that the discrepancy is based on a deficit in basic skill areas, analyze the student's total standardized achievement test scores in:
> **Language   Reading   Writing   Mathematics**

Level 1

> **Underachievement: Ability-Achievement Discrepancy**
> The student shows this discrepancy based on the most reliable total IQ and total standardized achievement test scores available to avoid a single, narrowly focused discrepancy.

Figure 10.1 This model combines the ability-achievement discrepancy with a multilevel approach that includes assessments of neuropsychological processes. Adapted from Kavale & Forness (2000) and Semrud-Clikeman (2005).

problems and improve instructional skills. Teachers should draw on the knowledge of special educators and researchers to address specific problems.

   Design a learning profile for each student with learning problems. For students with learning problems, keep a simple record of their

- Reasoning ability
- Learning style
- Classroom participation
- Comprehension
- Work level
- Progress

Design the profile to spot trends in each area. Use this information to build on students' existing strengths and identify areas needing improvement.

Use technology. Computers and other forms of advanced technology are useful tools for helping students with learning problems. Word processing programs with voice and handwriting recognition are just some examples of hardware and software components that can capitalize on students' strengths and minimize their weaknesses.

Modify the learning environment. Just a few changes in the learning environment can sometimes make a significant difference in student achievement. Consider which students might benefit if you

- Seat student in an areas free of distractions
- Consider using study carrels
- Keep the student's work area free of unnecessary materials
- Use a checklist to help get the student organized
- Stand near the student when giving directions
- Provide organizational strategies such as charts and time lines
- Assist in organizing the student's notebook
- Use materials that address the students' learning styles
- Provide opportunities for movement

Modify instructional strategies. Consider modifying instructional strategies to meet the various learning styles and abilities of students with learning problems. Here are some strategies to consider:

- Allow students to audiotape lectures
- Break assignment into shorter tasks
- Adjust the reading level of the classroom material
- Teach the concrete before the abstract
- Relate the new learning to students' experiences
- Reduce the number of concepts presented at one time
- Give an overview of the lesson before beginning
- Check the student's comprehension of the language used for instruction
- Monitor the rate at which you present material
- Require verbal responses from the student to check for comprehension
- Provide clear and concise directions for homework assignments
- Allow typewritten or word-processed assignments
- Consider the oral administration of tests and open book tests
- Provide practice test questions for study
- Allow use of dictionary or calculator during test
- Provide extra time to finish a written test

Modify the curriculum materials. Modifications to curriculum materials will vary depending on the nature of the student's learning problem.

For those with **spoken language** difficulties, you can:

- Paraphrase complex information
- Slow the rate of presentation
- Provide written directions to supplement verbal directions
- Keep sentence structures simple

- Avoid the use of abstract language such as puns, idioms, and metaphors
- Get the student's attention before expressing key points
- Use visual aids such as charts and graphs
- Call student by name before asking questions

For those with **written language** difficulties:

- Allow student to use cursive or manuscript writing
- Permit student to type, record, or give oral answers instead of writing
- Provide copies of class notes
- Avoid the pressure of speed and accuracy
- Reduce the amount of copying from the textbook or board
- Establish realistic standards for neatness
- Accept key word responses instead of complete sentences

For those with **organizational problems:**

- Establish clear rules and consistently enforce them
- Provide an established daily routine
- Consider making contracts with students and use rewards when the contract is completed
- Ensure that due dates are clearly understood
- Provide a specific place for turning in assignments

Get the reluctant starter going. Some students have difficulty getting started and need the teacher's guidance to move forward. For them, consider the following:

- Give a personal cue to begin work
- Check progress often, especially after the first few minutes of work
- Provide immediate feedback and reinforcers
- Divide work into smaller units
- Suggest time periods for each task
- Ensure that the student understands the instructions
- Present the assignment in sequential steps
- Provide a checklist for multitask assignments

Maintain attention. Because some students with learning problems can be easily distracted, look for ways to maintain attention during the lesson.

- Seat the students close to you
- Provide praise for correct answers
- Relate new learning to students' experiences
- Give an advance warning when a transition is going to occur
- Use physical proximity and appropriate touch to help student refocus

Use group instruction and peers. Although some students with learning problems do not always work well in groups, persistence and guidance can often result in a productive experience.

- Assign a peer tutor to record material dictated by the student

- Use cooperative learning strategies when appropriate
- Assign a peer helper to read important directions and information to the student and to check for understanding

Adjust time demands. Meeting time lines and deadlines is not always easy for some students with learning problems. Some get involved in minute details, while others dart from one idea to another and lose track of time.

- Increase time allowed for the completion of tests or assignments
- Reduce the amount of work or length of tests
- Introduce short breaks or change of tasks
- Follow a specific routine and be consistent
- Alternate active and quiet tasks
- Help students prioritize the steps needed to complete an assignment
- Set time limits for completing specific tasks

Deal with inappropriate behavior. Inappropriate behavior is not acceptable. But keep in mind that the misbehavior may not have been intentional.

- Provide clear and concise classroom expectations and consequences
- Enforce rules consistently
- Avoid confrontational techniques as they often escalate the situation
- Provide the student with alternatives
- Avoid power struggles
- Designate a cooling-off location in the classroom
- Ignore attention-getting behavior for a short time (extinction)
- Assign activities which require some movement
- Deal with the behavior and avoid criticizing the student
- Speak privately to the student about inappropriate behavior
- Check for levels of tolerance and be aware of signs of frustration

Modify homework assignments. Homework can be a valuable learning tool for students with learning problems if it is relevant and not excessive.

- Consider allowing student to work on homework in school
- Give frequent reminders about due dates
- Give short assignments
- Allow for extra credit assignments
- Develop an award system for in-school work and homework completed

Motivating Students With Learning Difficulties

Teachers are always looking for ways to motivate their students to learn. But motivating students with learning difficulties can be particularly challenging because these students have doubts about their abilities and often experience failure in the classroom. They get caught up in an unfortunate cycle where low expectations lead to poor performance, resulting in low motivation. The low motivation keeps their expectations low, and so the cycle continues. Eventually, these students can develop a negative self-concept, which can be frustrating for teachers to overcome. Waugh (2002) suggests that the low motivation among students is directly related to their fear of academic failure. He offers the following five basic strategies that teachers should consider to help motivate students with learning difficulties.

Structure activities for success. The old saying that nothing succeeds like success is appropriate for all students, but especially so for those who have not had the exhilaration that comes with successful academic experiences. Students are more likely to experience this success when teachers:

- Distribute an outline in advance of a lesson or unit that clearly describes assignments and the level of performance expected. This approach lowers the anxiety that often leads to poor performance.
- Break assignments into logical and sequential instructional steps and give feedback to the student regarding performance of each step. If the instructional goal is clear and the teacher provides guidance and encouragement, then students are more motivated to complete the task and less apt to go off course and get frustrated.
- Set assignments at the correct level of difficulty for each student. If the task is too easy, the student gets little satisfaction from completing it. However, if the task is too difficult, the student can become frustrated and give up.

Set realistic expectations. When students have few successful learning experiences, they have no way of knowing what skills are needed or how much effort to apply to accomplish a learning task. Consequently, they often set unrealistic goals, resulting in failure. Teachers can help students set realistic goals by:

- Discussing with the student a task which the student had performed poorly and determining the reasons for the poor performance. Point out that a little more effort may have made the difference. The goal is to identify the causes of failure so that the student can set realistic and attainable goals.
- Helping the student devise an action plan outlining how the student will use time and effort to accomplish a specific learning task.

Link success to effort. Students who generally experience failure in school tend to attribute their occasional successes to luck. Teachers should reinforce with students the notion that successful classroom work is the direct result of their effort and not luck. Give students genuine praise for their successful work, and congratulate them on completing the task.

Communicate positive expectations. Research studies have long shown that teacher expectations can have a powerful influence on a student's self-expectations and performance. For example, teachers communicate negative expectations when they call on and praise low-achieving students less often than high-achieving students, and when they smile and maintain eye contact more often with high-achieving students. Teachers are often unaware that they behave differently toward students of various ability levels. By occasionally asking themselves the following questions, they may become more conscious of their behavior and communicate positive expectations to all students:

- Do I give positive feedback to low-achieving students as often as I do to high-achieving students?
- Am I unduly critical of the performance of low-achieving students?
- Do I interact with low-achieving students as often as I do with high-achieving students?

Demonstrate noncontingent acceptance. Consistent failure in school erodes not only students' self-expectations but also their self-worth. Teachers can help these students improve their self-worth by:

- Telling them that their acceptance is not contingent on their levels of performance in the classroom
- Showing students that they genuinely care about their well-being
- Talking regularly with students about concerns and problems that are unrelated to their schoolwork
- Exhibiting an understanding of their students' problems and a willingness to listen and offer advice
- Helping students deal with their frustrations and reassuring them they have the ability to overcome difficult challenges

When teachers carefully structure classroom assignments and provide guidance and encouragement, students with learning difficulties can change their expectations from failure to success. Because the traditional approaches to understanding learning differences focus on detecting and fixing deficits, teachers can get so concerned about the students' problems that they miss the opportunity to capitalize on the students' latent talents and strengths. Many studies indicate that using an individual's strengths to mitigate areas of weakness results in improved motivation and performance and boost to that person's self-esteem.

Communicating With Parents

Raising a child with a learning disability can be stressful. Some families are more resilient than others in adapting to this stress. Many parents report benefits and positive outcomes for their families, including improved coping skills, family harmony, shared parental duties, spiritual growth, and better communications. Other parents, however, report that anger, guilt, blame, and frustration are often the cause of conflict in the home. The level of the child's disability, the type of family structure, family income, and ethnic and cultural factors all contribute to how a family adapts to raising a child with a learning disability (Ferguson, 2002).

School personnel can help ease parental stress by meeting personally with parents as soon as learning problems are detected. Several meetings may be needed before the parent gets past the emotional reactions and responds calmly and constructively. They should be encouraged to ask questions, which should be answered fully and openly. Some parents just need reassurance that they can overcome any feelings of helplessness and that they have there are resources available that can help them understand and manage their child's difficulties. Frequent communication with parents is important so that all are working together to assist the student in meeting expectations. Teachers can consider:

- Developing a daily and weekly journal and sharing it with the parents
- Scheduling periodic parent-teacher meetings
- Providing a duplicate set of textbooks that they can use at home during the school year
- Providing weekly progress reports to parents
- Mailing (or e-mailing) the parents a schedule of class and homework assignments
- Explaining clearly the school's grading policy and any adaptations that were made for the student. Surveys indicate that parents of students with learning difficulties want the grading system to be sensitive to an individual's progress and to communicate their children's strengths and needs, as well as offer suggestions for improvement (Munk, 2003).

Schools can also help by providing parents with contact information about local support groups, Internet sites, and organizations that assist parents of children with learning disabilities.

Glossary

Alphabetic principle. The notion that written words are composed of letters of the alphabet that intentionally and systematically represent segments of spoken words.

Amygdala. The almond-shaped structure in the brain's limbic system that encodes emotional messages to long-term storage.

Aphasia. The loss of language function.

Apoptosis. The genetically programmed process in which unneeded or unhealthy brain cells are destroyed.

Asperger syndrome. A disorder within the autism spectrum that results in social and communication, but not intellectual, impairments.

Attention-deficit hyperactivity disorder (ADHD). A syndrome that interferes with an individual's capacity to regulate activity level, inhibit behavior, and attend to tasks in developmentally appropriate ways.

Autism. A spectrum disorder that affects an individual's ability to communicate, form relationships with others, and relate appropriately to the environment.

Brainstem. One of the major parts of the brain, it receives sensory input and monitors such vital functions as heartbeat, body temperature, and digestion.

Broca's area. A region in the left frontal lobe of the brain believed responsible for generating the vocabulary and syntax of an individual's native language.

Cerebellum. One of the major parts of the brain, it coordinates muscle movement and is thought to play a role in long-term memory.

Cerebrum. The largest of the major parts of the brain, it controls sensory interpretation, thinking, and memory.

Comorbidity. The simultaneous appearance of two or more disorders within an individual, such as the co-occurrence of attention-deficit hyperactivity disorder and dyslexia. The association may reflect a causal relationship between one disorder and another, or reveal an underlying susceptibility to both disorders.

Computerized tomography (CT, formerly CAT) scanner. An instrument that uses X-rays and computer processing to produce a detailed cross section of brain structure.

Corpus callosum. The bridge of nerve fibers that connects the left and right cerebral hemispheres and allows communication between them.

Cortex. The thin but tough layer of cells covering the cerebrum that contains all the neurons used for cognitive and motor processing.

Dendrite. The branched extension from the cell body of a neuron that receives impulses from nearby neurons through synaptic contacts.

Dopamine. A neurotransmitter believed to control mood, behavior, and muscle coordination.

Dyscalculia. A condition that causes persistent problems with processing numerical calculations.

Dysgraphia. A spectrum disorder characterized by difficulty in mastering the sequence of movements necessary to write letters and numbers.

Dyslexia. Also known as severe reading disability, this is a learning disorder characterized by problems in reading and writing.

Frontal lobe. The front part of the brain that monitors higher-order thinking, directs problem solving, and regulates the excesses of the emotional (limbic) system.

Functional magnetic resonance imaging (fMRI). An instrument that measures blood flow to the brain to record areas of high and low neuronal activity.

Glial cells. Special "glue" cells in the brain that surround each neuron providing support, protection, and nourishment.

Gray matter. The thin but tough covering of the brain's cerebrum also known as the cerebral cortex.

Hippocampus. A brain structure that compares new learning to past learning and encodes information from working memory to long-term storage.

Limbic area. The structures at the base of the cerebrum that control emotions.

Magnetic resonance imaging (MRI). An instrument that uses radio waves to disturb the alignment of the body's atoms in a magnetic field to produce computer-processed, high-contrast images of internal structures.

Mirror neurons. Clusters of neurons in the brain that fire not only when experiencing a task or emotion but also when seeing someone else experience the same task or emotion.

Mnemonic. A word or phrase used as a device for remembering unrelated information, patterns, or rules.

Motor cortex. The narrow band across the top of the brain from ear to ear that controls movement.

Myelin. A fatty substance that surrounds and insulates a neuron's axon.

Neuron. The basic cell making up the brain and nervous system, consisting of a globular cell body, a long fiber, called an axon, which transmits impulses, and many shorter fibers, called dendrites, which receive them.

Neurotransmitter. One of about 100 chemicals stored in axon sacs that transmit impulses from neuron to neuron across the synaptic gap.

Orthography. The written system for a language.

Phonemes. The minimal units of sound in a language that combine to make syllables.

Phonemic awareness. The ability to deal explicitly and segmentally with sound units smaller than the syllable (i.e., the phoneme).

Phonological awareness. The ability to recognize the production and interpretation of the sound patterns (rather than the meaning) of language.

Positron emission tomography (PET) scanner. An instrument that traces the metabolism of radioactively tagged sugar in brain tissue producing a color image of cell activity.

Proprioceptors. Sensory cells in the skin, muscles, tendons, and joints that monitor the position of the limbs and head in space.

Prosody. The rhythm, cadence, accent patterns, and pitch of a language.

Rehearsal. The reprocessing of information in working memory.

Responsiveness to intervention. A method of determining whether students have learning difficulties by assessing their responses to the methods, strategies, curriculum, and interventions they encounter.

Retention. The preservation of a learning in long-term storage in such a way that it can be identified and recalled quickly and accurately.

Reticular activating system (RAS). The dense formation of neurons in the brainstem that controls major body functions and maintains the brain's alertness.

Synapse. The microscopic gap between the axon of one neuron and the dendrite of another.

Thalamus. A part of the limbic system that receives all incoming sensory information, except smell, and shunts it to other areas of the cortex for additional processing.

Transfer. The influence that past learning has on new learning, and the degree to which the new learning will be useful in the learner's future.

Visual magnocellular deficit. A disorder of the visual processing system that leads to poor detection of visual motion, causing letters to bunch up or overlap during reading.

Wernicke's area. A section in the left temporal lobe of the brain believed responsible for generating sense and meaning in an individual's native language.

White matter. The support tissue that lies beneath the cerebrum's gray matter (cortex).

Windows of opportunity. Important periods in which the young brain responds to certain types of input to create or consolidate neural networks.

Working memory. The temporary memory, wherein information is processed consciously.

References

Ahmed, S. T., & Lombardino, L. J. (2000). Invented spelling: An assessment and intervention protocol for kindergarten children. *Communication Disorders Quarterly, 22,* 19–28.

American Psychiatric Association (APA). (2000). *Diagnostic and statistical manual of mental disorders* (*DSM-IV-TR,* 4th ed., text revision). Washington, DC: Author.

Akshoomoff, N., Pierce, K., & Courchesne, E. (2002). The neurobiological basis of autism from a developmental perspective. *Development and Psychopathology, 14,* 613–634.

Allman, J. M., Watson, K. K., Tetreault, N. A., & Hakeem, A. Y. (2005, August). Intuition and autism: A possible role for Von Economo neurons. *Trends in Cognitive Sciences, 9,* 367–373.

American Institutes for Research (AIR). (2005). *CSRQ Center report on elementary school comprehensive school reform models.* Washington, DC: Author.

Amitay, S., Ben-Yehudah, G., Banai, K., & Ahissar, M. (2002). Disabled readers suffer from visual and auditory impairments but not from a specific magnocellular deficit. *Brain, 125,* 2272–2285.

Arries, J. (1999). Learning disabilities and foreign languages: A curriculum approach to the design of inclusive courses. *Modern Language Journal, 83,* 98–110.

Augustyniak, K., Murphy, J., & Phillips, D. K. (2005, December). Psychological perspectives in assessing mathematics learning needs. *Journal of Instructional Psychology, 32,* 277–286.

Auranen, M., Vanhala, R., Varilo, T., Ayers, K., Kempas, E., Yisaukko-Oja, T., et al. (2003). A genome wide screen for autism-spectrum disorders: Evidence for a major susceptibility locus on chromosome 3q25–27. *American Journal of Human Genetics, 71,* 777–790.

Bailey, G. (1993). A perspective on African-American English. In D. Preston (Ed.), *American dialect research* (pp. 287–318). Philadelphia: Benjamins.

Baker, S., Gersten, R., & Graham, S. (2003). Teaching expressive writing to students with learning disabilities: Research-based applications and examples. *Journal of Learning Disabilities, 36,* 109–123.

Barkley, R. A. (1998, September). Attention-deficit hyperactivity disorder. *Scientific American, 279,* 66–71.

Baron-Cohen, S. (2003). *The essential difference: The truth about the male and female brain.* New York: Basic Books.

Baroody, A. J. (1999). The development of basic counting, number, and arithmetic knowledge among children classified as mentally handicapped. In L. M. Glidden (Ed.), *International review of research in mental retardation* (pp. 51–103). New York: Academic Press.

Bartlett, C. W., Flax, J. F., Logue, M. W., Vieland, V. J., Bassett, A. S., Tallal, P., et al. (2002, July). A major susceptibility locus for specific language impairment is located on 13q21. *American Journal of Human Genetics, 71,* 45–55.

Bateman, B. Warner, J. O., Hutchinson, E., Dean, T., Rowlandson, P., Gant, C., et al. (2004). The effects of a double blind, placebo controlled artificial food colorings and benzoate preservative challenge on hyperactivity in a general population sample of preschool children. *Archives of Diseases in Childhood, 89,* 506–511.

Baumeister, R. F., Campbell, J. D., Krueger, J. I., & Vohs, K. D. (2005, January). Exploding the self-esteem myth. *Scientific American, 292,* 84–91.

Beatty, J. (2001). *The human brain: Essentials of behavioral neuroscience.* Thousand Oaks, CA: Sage Publications.

Bear, D. R., Invernizzi, M., Templeton, S., & Johnston, F. (2004). *Words their way: Word study for phonics, vocabulary, and spelling instruction* (3rd ed.). Upper Saddle River, NJ: Merrill Prentice Hall.

Beaulieu, C., Plewes, C., Paulson, L. A., Roy, D., Snook, L., Concha, L., et al. (2005, May). Imaging brain connectivity in children with diverse reading ability. *NeuroImage, 25,* 1266–1271.

Bernard, S., Enayati, A., Redwood, L., Roger, H., & Binstock, T. (2001). Autism: A novel form of mercury poisoning. *Medical Hypotheses, 56,* 462–471.

Biederman, J., & Faraone, S. V. (2005, July). Attention-deficit hyperactivity disorder (diagnosis and treatment). *Lancet, 366,* 237–248.

Bonifacci, P. (2004, September). Children with low motor ability have lower visual-motor integration ability but unaffected perceptual skills. *Human Movement Science, 23,* 157–168.

Borman, G. D., Hewes, G. M., Overman, L. T., & Brown, S. (2003). Comprehensive school reform and achievement: A meta-analysis. *Review of Educational Research, 73,* 125–230.

Boulineau, T., Fore III, C., Hagan-Burke, S., & Burke, M. D. (2004, Spring). Use of story-mapping to increase the story-grammar text comprehension of elementary students with learning disabilities. *Learning Disability Quarterly, 27,* 105–121.

Brannon, E. M., & van der Walle, G. (2001). Ordinal numerical knowledge in young children. *Cognitive Psychology, 43,* 53–81.

Brown, W. E., Eliez, S., Menon, V., Rumsey, J. M., White, C. D., & Reiss, A. L. (2001). Preliminary evidence of widespread morphological variations of the brain in dyslexia. *Neurology, 27,* 781–783.

Brun, M., Bouvard, M., Chateil, J., Bénichou, G., Bordessoules, M., & Allard, M. (2003). *Phonological treatment in dyslexic children: Neural network in fMRI.* Paper presented at the conference of the Organization for Human Brain Mapping, June, 2003, New York, NY.

Buckner, R. L., Kelley, W. M., & Petersen, S. E. (1999, April). Frontal cortex contributions to human memory formation. *Nature Neuroscience, 2,* 311–314.

Bush, G., Frazier, J. A., Rauch, S. L., Seidman, L. J., Whalen, P. J., Jenike, M. A., et al. (1999, June). Anterior cingulate cortex dysfunction in attention-deficit hyperactivity disorder revealed by fMRI and the Counting Stroop. *Biological Psychiatry, 45,* 1542–1552.

Byring, R. F., Haapasalo, S., & Salmi, T. (2004, November). Adolescents with learning disorders have atypical EEG correlation indices during reading. *Clinical Neurophysiology, 115,* 2584–2592.

Byrne, B. (1991). Experimental analysis of the child's discovery of the alphabetic principle. In L. Riehen and C. Perfetti (Eds.), *Learning to read: Basic research and its implications* (pp. 75–84). Hillsdale, NJ: Erlbaum.

Caron, M.-J., Mottron, L., Rainville, C., & Chouinard, S. (2004). Do high functioning persons with autism present superior spatial abilities? *Neuropsychologia, 42,* 467–481.

Case, L. P., Speece, D. L., & Molloy, D. E. (2003, Fall). The validity of a response-to-instruction paradigm to identify reading disabilities: A longitudinal analysis of individual differences and contextual factors. *School Psychology Review, 32,* 557–582.

Castellanos, F. X., Lee, P. P., Sharp, W., Jeffries, N. O., Greenstein, D. K., Clasen, L. S., et al. (2002, October). Developmental trajectories of brain volume abnormalities in children and adolescents with attention-deficit hyperactivity disorder. *Journal of the American Medical Association, 288,* 1740–1748.

Catts, H. W., Fey, M. E., Tomblin, J. B., & Zhang, X. (2002, December). A longitudinal investigation of reading outcomes in children with language impairments. *Journal of Speech, Language, and Hearing Research, 45,* 142–157.

Chard, D.J., & Dickson, S.V. (1999, May). Phonological awareness: Instructional and assessment guidelines. *Intervention in School and Clinic, 34,* 261–270.

Chard, D.J., & Osborn, J. (1998). *Suggestions for examining phonics and decoding instruction in supplementary reading programs.* Austin, TX: Texas Education Agency.

Cheour, M., Ceponiene, R., Lehtokoski, A., Luuk, A., Allik, J., Alho, K., et al. (1998, September). Development of language-specific phoneme representations in the infant brain. *Nature Neuroscience, 1,* 351–353.

Choudhury, N., & Benasich, A. A. (2003, April). A family aggregation study: The influence of family history and other risk factors on language development. *Journal of Speech, Language, and Hearing Research, 46,* 261–272.

Christakis, D. A., Ebel, B. E., Rivara, F. P., & Zimmerman, F. J. (2004, November). Television, video, and computer game usage in children under 11 years of age. *Journal of Pediatrics, 145,* 652–656.

Clements, D. H. (2000, Summer). Translating lessons from research into mathematics classrooms: Mathematics and special needs students. *International Dyslexia Association: Perspectives, 26,* 31–33.

Cole, P. G., & Mengler, E. D. (1994). Phonemic processing of children with language deficits: Which tasks best discriminate children with learning disabilities from average readers? *Reading Psychology, 15,* 223–243.

College Board. (2005). *SAT scores for 2005 highest on record.* New York: Author. Available online at www.collegeboard.com/press.

Cone-Wesson, B. (2005, July-August). Prenatal, alcohol and cocaine exposure: Influences on cognition, speech, language, and hearing. *Journal of Communication Disorders, 38,* 279–302.

Courchesne, E., Carper, R., & Akshoomoff, N. (2003). Evidence of brain overgrowth in the first year of life in autism. *Journal of the American Medical Association, 290,* 337–344.

Craig, H. K., Thompson, C. A., Washington, J. A., & Potter, S. L. (2003, June). Phonological features of child African American English. *Journal of Speech, Language, and Hearing Research, 46,* 623–635.

D'Agostino, J. V., & Murphy, J. A. (2004). A meta-analysis of Reading Recovery in United States schools. *Educational Evaluation and Policy Analysis, 26,* 23–38.

Dale, P. S., Simonoff, E., Bishop, D.V. M., Eley, T. C., Oliver, B., Price, T. S., et al. (1998, August). Genetic influence on language delay in two-year-old children. *Nature Neuroscience, 1,* 324–328.

Dalton, K. M., Nacewicz, B. M., Johnstone, T., Schaefer, H. S., Gernsbacher, M. A., Goldsmith, H. H., et al. (2005, April). Gaze fixation and the neural circuitry of face processing in autism. *Nature Neuroscience, 8,* 519–526.

Damasio, A. (2003). *Looking for Spinoza: Joy, sorrow, and the feeling brain.* New York: Harcourt.

D'Amico, A., & Guarnera, M. (2005). Exploring working memory in children with low arithmetical achievement. *Learning and Individual Differences, 15,* 189–202.

Dapretto, M., Davies, M. S., Pfeifer, J. H., Scott, A.A., Sigman, M., Bookheimer, S. Y., et al. (2006, January). Understanding emotions in others: Mirror neuron dysfunction in children with autism spectrum disorders. *Nature Neuroscience, 9,* 28–30.

Davidson, R. J. (2000). The neuroscience of affective style. In R. D. Lane & L. Nadel (Eds.), *Cognitive neuroscience of emotion* (pp. 129–155). New York: Oxford University Press.

DeGrandpre, R. J., & Hinshaw, S. P. (2000, Summer). ADHD: Serious psychiatric problem or all-American copout? *Cerebrum: The Dana Forum on Brain Science,* 12–38.

Dehaene, S., Piazza, M., Pinel, P., & Cohen, L. (2003). Three parietal circuits for number processing. *Cognitive Neuropsychology, 20,* 487–506.

Demb, J. B., Boynton, G. M., & Heeger, D. J. (1998). Functional magnetic resonance imaging of early visual pathways in dyslexia. *Journal of Neuroscience, 18,* 6939–6951.

Diamond, M., & Hopson, J. (1998). *Magic trees of the mind: How to nurture your child's intelligence, creativity, and healthy emotions from birth through adolescence.* New York: Dutton.

Dinklage, K. T. (1971). Inability to learn a foreign language. In G. Blaine, and C. MacArthur (Eds.), *Emotional problems of the student* (pp. 185–206). New York: Appleton-Century-Crofts.

Dyslexia International—Tools and Technology (DITT). (2001). *Language shock—Dyslexia across cultures.* Brussels: Author.

Eckert, M. M., Leonard, C. M., Richards, T. L., Aylward, E. H., Thomson, J., & Berninger, V. W. (2003). Anatomical correlates of dyslexia: Frontal and cerebellar findings. *Brain, 126,* 482–494.

Edelen-Smith, P. J. (1998). How now brown cow: Phoneme awareness activities for collaborative classrooms. *Intervention in School and Clinic, 33,* 103–111.

Elbaum, B., & Vaughn, S. (2001). School-based interventions to enhance the self-concept of students with learning disabilities: A meta-analysis. *The Elementary School Journal, 101,* 303–329.

Evans, A. C. (2006, March). The NIH MRI study of normal brain development. *NeuroImage, 30,* 184–202.

Fadiga, L., Craighero, L., & Olivier, E. (2005, March). Human motor cortex excitability during the perception of others' action. *Current Opinion in Neurobiology, 15,* 213–218.

Farber, N. B., & Olney, J. W. (2003, December). Drugs of abuse that cause developing neurons to commit suicide. *Developmental Brain Research, 147,* 37–45.

Farkas, R. D. (2003, September-October). Effects of traditional versus learning-styles instructional methods on middle school students. *Journal of Educational Research, 97,* 42–52.

Fassbender, C., & Schweitzer, J. B. (2006). Is there evidence for neural compensation in attention-deficit hyperactivity disorder? A review of the functional neuroimaging literature. *Clinical Psychology Review, 26,* 445–465.

Feifer, S. G., & De Fina, P. A. (2000). *Neuropsychology of written language disorders: Diagnosis and intervention.* Middletown, MD: School Neuropsych Press.

Ferguson, P. M. (2002). A place in the family: An historical interpretation of research on parental reactions to having a child with a disability. *Journal of Special Education, 36,* 124–130, 147.

Fisher, S. E., & DeFries, J. C. (2002). Developmental dyslexia: Genetic dissection of a complex cognitive trait. *Nature Reviews Neuroscience, 30,* 767–780.

Fisk, C. & Hurst, B. (2003, October). Paraphrasing for comprehension. *The Reading Teacher, 57,* 182–185.

Fletcher, J. M. (2005, July-August). Predicting math outcomes: Reading predictors and comorbidity. *Journal of Learning Disabilities, 38,* 308–312.

Flett, A., & Conderman, G. (2002, March). Twenty ways to promote phonemic awareness. *Intervention in School and Clinic, 37,* 242–245.

Foorman, B. R., & Ciancio, D. J. (2005, November-December). Screening for secondary intervention: Concept and context. *Journal of Learning Disabilities, 38,* 494–499.

Forness, S. R. (2003, November). Parting reflections on education of children with emotional and behavioral disorders. *Education and Treatment of Children, 26,* 320–324.

Foss, J. M. (2001). *Nonverbal learning disability: How to recognize it and minimize its effects* (ERIC Digest E-619). Arlington, VA: ERIC Clearinghouse on Disabilities and Gifted Eudcation.

Fowler, M. (2002, April). Attention-deficit/hyperactivity disorder. *National Information Center for Children and Youth with Disabilities Briefing Paper,* 1–16.

Frazier, T. W., Demaree, H. A., & Youngstrom, E. A. (2004, July). Meta-analysis of intellectual and neuropsychological test performance in attention-deficit hyperactivity disorder. *Neuropsychology, 18,* 543–555.

Fuchs, L. S., Compton, D. L., Fuchs, D., Paulsen, K., Bryant, J. D., & Hamlett, C. L. (2005, August). The prevention, identification, and cognitive determinants of math difficulty. *Journal of Educational Psychology, 97,* 493–513.

Fuchs, L. S., & Fuchs, D. (2002). Mathematical problem-solving profiles of students with mathematical disabilities with and without comorbid reading disabilities. *Journal of Learning Disabilities, 35,* 563–573.

Fuchs, L. S., Fuchs, D., & Speece, D. L. (2002). Treatment validity as a unifying construct for identifying learning disabilities. *Learning Disability Quarterly, 25,* 33–45.

Fulk, B. (2000, January). Twenty ways to make instruction more memorable. *Intervention in School and Clinic, 35,* 183–184.

Gaillard, R., Naccache, L., Pinel, P., Clémenceau, S., Volle, E., Hasboun, D., et al. (2006, April). Direct intracranial, fMRI, and lesion evidence for the causal role of left inferotemporal cortex in reading. *Neuron, 50,* 191–204.

Gans, A. M., Kenny, M. C., & Ghany, D. L. (2003, May-June). Comparing the self-concept of students with and without learning disabilities. *Journal of Learning Disabilities, 36,* 287–295.

Ganschow, L., & Sparks, R. (1995). Effects of direct instruction in Spanish phonology on native language skills and foreign language aptitude of at-risk foreign language learners. *Journal of Learning Disabilities, 28,* 107–120.

Ganschow, L., & Sparks, R. (2001). Learning difficulties and foreign language learning: A review of research and instruction. *Language Teaching, 34,* 79–98.

Gathercole, S. E., Alloway, T. P., Willis, C., & Adams, A. (2006, March). Working memory in children with reading disabilities. *Journal of Experimental Child Psychology, 93,* 265–281.

Gazzaniga, M. S., Ivry, R. B., & Mangun, G. R. (2002). *Cognitive neuroscience: The biology of the mind.* New York: Norton.

Geary, D. C. (2000, Summer). Mathematical disorders: An overview for educators. *International Dyslexia Association: Perspectives, 26,* 6–9.

Giedd, J. N., Blumenthal, J., Jeffries, N. O., Castellanos, F. X., Liu, H., Zijdenbos, A., Paus, T., Evans, A. C., & Rapoport, J. L. (1999). Brain development during childhood and adolescence: A longitudinal MRI study. *Nature Neuroscience, 2,* 861–863.

Gillies, R. M. (2002, September-October). The residual effects of cooperative-learning experiences: A two-year follow-up. *Journal of Educational Research, 96,* 15–20.

Goldberg, E. (2001). *The executive brain: Frontal lobes and the civilized mind.* New York: Oxford.

Graham, S., & Harris, K. R. (2005). Improving the writing performance of young struggling writers. *Journal of Special Education, 39,* 19–33.

Graham, S., Harris, K. R., & Larsen, L. (2001). Prevention and intervention of writing difficulties for students with learning disabilities. *Learning Disabilities Research and Practice, 16,* 74–84.

Gray, K. A., Day, N. L., Leech, S., & Richardson, G. A. (2005, May-June). Prenatal marijuana exposure: Effect on child depressive symptoms at ten years of age. *Neurotoxicology and Teratology, 27,* 439–448.

Grigg, J. (2004, March). Environmental toxins: Their impact on children's health. *Archives of Disease in Childhood, 89,* 244–250.

Günther, T., Holtkamp, K., Jolles, J., Herpertz-Dahlmann, B., & Konrad, K. (2004, October). Verbal memory and aspects of attentional control in children and adolescents with anxiety disorders or depressive disorders. *Journal of Affective Disorders, 82,* 265–269.

Guterl, F. (2003, Sept. 8) Overloaded? *Newsweek,* E4–E8.

Haberstick, B. C., Smolen, A., & Hewitt, J. K. (2006, May). Family-based association of 5HTTLPR and aggressive behavior in a general population sample of children. *Biological Psychiatry, 59,* 836–843.

Hadjikhani, N., Joseph, R. M., Snyder, J., Chabris, C. F., Clark, J., Steele, S., et al. (2004, July). Activation of the fusiform gyrus when individuals with autism spectrum disorder view faces. *NeuroImage, 22,* 1141–1150.

Hafström, O., Milerad, J., Sandberg, K. L., & Sundell, H. W. (2005, November). Cardiorespiratory effects of nicotine exposure during development. *Respiratory Physiology & Neurobiology, 149,* 325–341.

Happé, F. G. E. (1997). Central coherence and the theory of mind in autism: Reading homographs in context. *British Journal of Developmental Psychology, 15,* 1–12.

Harm, M. W., & Seidenberg, M. S. (1999). Phonology, reading acquisition, and dyslexia: Insights from connectionist models. *Psychological Review, 106,* 491–528.

Hawi, Z., Segurado, R., Conroy, J., Sheehan, K., Lowe, N., Kirley, A., et al. (2005, December). Preferential transmission of paternal alleles at risk genes in attention-deficit hyperactivity disorder. *American Journal of Human Genetics, 77,* 958–965.

Heilman, K. M. (2002). *Matter of mind: A neurologist's view of brain-behavior relationships.* New York: Oxford University Press.

Helenius, P., Salmelin, R., Richardson, U., Leinonen, S., & Lyytinen, H. (2002). Abnormal auditory cortical activation in dyslexia 100 msec after speech onset. *Journal of Cognitive Neuroscience, 14,* 603–617.

Herbert, M. R. (2005, October). Large brains in autism: The challenge of pervasive abnormality. *Neuroscientist, 11,* 417–440.

Ho, C. S.-H., Chan, D. W.-O., Lee, S.-H., Tsang, S.-M., & Luan, V. H. (2004, February). Cognitive profiling and preliminary subtyping in Chinese developmental dyslexia. *Cognition, 91,* 43–75.

Hollander, E., Anagnostou, E., Chaplin, W., Esposito, K., Haznedar, M. M., Licalzi, E., et al. (2005, August). Striatal volume on magnetic resonance imaging and repetitive behaviors in autism. *Biological Psychiatry, 58,* 226–232.

Hollander, E., King, A., Delaney, K., Smith, C. J., & Silverman, J. M. (2003, January). Obsessive-compulsive behaviors in parents of multiplex autism families. *Psychiatry Research, 117,* 11–16.

Howes, N., Bigler, E. D., Burlingame, G. M., & Lawson, J. S. (2003). Memory performance of children with dyslexia: A comparative analysis of theoretical perspectives. *Journal of Learning Disabilities, 36,* 230–246.

Howlin, P. (2003). Outcome on high-functioning adults with autism with and without language delays: Implications for the differentiation between autism and Asperger syndrome. *Journal of Autism and Developmental Disorders, 33,* 3–13.

Iacoboni, M., Molnar-Szakacs, I., Gallese, V., Buccino, G., Mazziotta, J. C., & Rizzolatti, G. (2005). Grasping the intentions of others with one's own mirror neuron system. *PloS Biology, 3,* e79.

Individuals with Disabilities Education Improvement Act (IDEA) of 2004, PL 108–446, 20 U.S.C. §§ 1400 *et seq.*

International Dyslexia Association (IDA). (2000). *Dysgraphia.* Baltimore, MD: Author.

International Dyslexia Association (IDA). (2003). *Common signs of dyslexia.* Baltimore, MD: Author.

Idol, L. (1987). Group story mapping: A comprehension strategy for both skilled and unskilled readers. *Journal of Learning Disabilities, 20,* 196–205.

James, L. A., Abbott, M., & Greenwood, C. R. (2001). How Adam became a writer: Winning writing strategies for low-achieving students. *Teaching Exceptional Children, 33,* 30–37.

Johnson, D.W., & Johnson, R. T. (1989). Cooperative learning: What special educators need to know. *The Pointer, 33,* 5–10.

Johnson, E., Mellard, D. F., & Byrd, S. E. (2005, November-December). Alternative models of learning disabilities identification: Considerations and initial conclusions. *Journal of Learning Disabilities, 38,* 569–572.

Jones, S. (2000). Accommodations and modifications for students with handwriting problems and/or dysgraphia. *LDOnline* [Online]. Available at http://www.ldonline.org/ld_indepth/writing/dysgraphia

Kalinowski, J., & Saltuklaroglu, T. (2003, June). Choral speech: The amelioration of stuttering via imitation and the mirror neuronal system. *Neuroscience & Biobehavioral Reviews, 27,* 339–347.

Kaminen, N., Hannula-Jouppi, K., Kestila, M., Lahermo, P., Muller, K., Kaaranen, M., et al. (2003, May). A genome scan for developmental dyslexia confirms linkage to chromosome 2p11 and suggests a new locus on 7q32. *Journal of Medical Genetics, 40,* 340–345.

Kaplan, B. J., Crawford, S. G., Dewey, D. M., & Fisher, G. C. (2000, October). The IQs of children with ADHD are normally distributed. *Journal of Learning Disabilities, 33,* 425–432.

Kaufman, N. K., Rohde, P., Seeley, J. R., Clarke, G. N., & Stice, E. (2005, February). Potential mediators of cognitive-behavioral therapy for adolescents with comorbid major depression and conduct disorder. *Journal of Consulting and Clinical Psychology, 73,* 38–46.

Kavale, K. A. (2005, November-December). Identifying specific learning disability: Is responsiveness to intervention the answer? *Journal of Learning Disabilities, 38,* 554–562.

Kavale, K. A., & Forness, S. R. (2000). What definitions of learning disability say and don't say: A critical analysis. *Journal of Learning Disabilities, 33,* 239–256.

Kim, Y., Park, J., Ko, M., Jang, S. H., & Lee, P. K. W. (2004, September). Facilitative effect of high frequency subthreshold repetitive transcranial magnetic stimulation on complex sequential motor learning in humans. *Neuroscience Letters, 367,* 181–185.

King, C. A., Knox, M. S., Henninger, N., Nguyen, T. A., Ghaziuddin, N., Maker, A., et al. (2006, February). Major depressive disorder in adolescents: Family psychiatric history predicts severe behavioral disinhibition. *Journal of Affective Disorders, 90,* 111–121.

Klingner, J. K., Vaughn, S., Arguelles, M. E., Hughes, M. T., & Leftwich, S. A. (2004, September-October). Collaborative strategic reading: "Real-world" lessons from classroom teachers. *Remedial and Special Education, 25,* 291–302.

Klingner, J. K., Vaughn, S., Dimino, J., Schumm, J. S., & Bryant, D. (2001). *From clunk to click: Collaborative reading strategies.* Longmont, CO: Sopris West.

Klingner, J. K., Vaughn, S., & Schumm, J. S. (1998). Collaborative strategic reading during social studies in heterogeneous fourth grade classrooms. *Elementary School Journal, 99,* 3–22.

Kolodziej, N. J., & Columba, L. (2005, Winter). Invented spelling: Guidelines for parents. *Reading Improvement, 42,* 212–223.

Korvatska, E., Van de Water, J., Anders, T. F., & Gershwin, M. E. (2002). Genetic and immunologic considerations in autism. *Neurobiology of Disease, 9,* 107–125.

Kouri, T. A. (2005, February). Lexical training through modeling and elicitation procedures with late talkers who have specific language impairment and developmental delays. *Journal of Speech, Language, and Hearing Research, 48,* 157–171.

Labov, W. (2003). When ordinary children fail to read. *Reading Research Quarterly, 38,* 128–131.

Lacourse, M. G., Orr, E. L. R., Cramer, S. C., & Cohen, M. J. (2005, September). Brain activation during execution and motor imagery of novel and skilled sequential hand movements. *NeuroImage, 27,* 505–519.

Lane, K. L., Menzies, H. M., Barton-Arwood, S. M., Doukas, G. L., & Munton, S. M. (2005, Winter). Designing, implementing, and evaluating social skills interventions for elementary students: Step-by-step procedures based on actual school-based investigations. *Preventing School Failure, 49,* 18–26.

Latterell, C. M. (2005, Fall). Social stigma and mathematical ignorance. *Academic Exchange Quarterly, 9,* 167–171.

Lavezzi, A. M., Ottaviani, G., & Matturri, L. (2005, November). Adverse effects of prenatal tobacco smoke exposure on biological parameters of the developing brainstem. *Neurobiology of Disease, 20,* 601–607.

Learning Disabilities Association of America (LDA). (2006a). Speech and language milestones chart. *LDOnline* [Online]. Available at http://www.ldonline.org/ld_indepth/speech-language/lda_milestones. html

Learning Disabilities Association of America (LDA). (2006b). Preventing antisocial behavior in disabled and at-risk students. *LDOnline* [Online]. Available at http://www.ldonline.org/ld_indepth/add_adha/ ael_behavior.html

LeDoux, J. (2002). *Synaptic self: How our brains become who we are.* New York: Viking.

Lemer, C., Dehaene, S., Spelke, E., & Cohen, L. (2003). Approximate quantities and exact number words: Dissociable systems. *Neuropsychologia, 41,* 1942–1958.

Leonard, C. M. (2001). Imaging brain structure in children: Differentiating language disability and reading disability. *Learning Disability Quarterly, 24,* 158–176.

Levy, S., Kim, A.-H., & Olive, M. L. (2006, Spring). Interventions for young children with autism: A synthesis of the literature. *Focus on Autism and Other Developmental Disabilities, 21,* 55–62.

Lewis, B. A., Singer, L. T., Short, E. J., Minnes, S., Arendt, R., Weishampel, P., et al. (2004, September-October). Four-year language outcomes of children exposed to cocaine in utero. *Neurotoxicology and Teratology, 26,* 617–627.

Lieberman, B. (2005, June). Study narrows search for brain's memory site. *Brain in the News, 12,* 4.

Luciana, M., Conklin, H. M., Hooper, C. J., & Yarger, R. S. (2005). The development of nonverbal working memory and executive control processes in adolescents. *Child Development, 76,* 697–712.

Masi, G., Milone, A., Canepa, G., Millepiedi, S., Mucci, M., & Muratori, F. (2006, January). Olanzapine treatment in adolescents with severe conduct disorder. *European Psychiatry, 21,* 51–57.

Mather, D. S. (2003, July-August). Dyslexia and dysgraphia: More than written language difficulties in common. *Journal of Learning Disabilities, 36,* 307–317.

McAfee, J. (2002). *Navigating the social world: A curriculum for individuals with Asperger's syndrome, high functioning autism, and related disorders.* Arlington, TX: Future Horizons.

McCandliss, B. D., Cohen, L., & Dehaene, S. (2003, July). The visual word form area: Expertise for reading in the fusiform gyrus. *Trends in Cognitive Sciences, 7,* 293–299.

McInnes, A., Humphries, T., Hogg-Johnson, S., & Tannock, R. (2003, August). Listening comprehension and working memory are impaired in attention-deficit hyperactivity disorder irrespective of language impairment. *Journal of Abnormal Child Psychology, 31,* 427–443.

Menon, V., & Desmond, J. E. (2001, October). Left superior parietal cortex involvement in writing: Integrating fMRI with lesion evidence. *Brain Research: Cognitive Brain Research, 12,* 337–340.

Meyer-Lindenberg, A., Buckholtz, J. W., Kolachana, B., Hariri, A. R., Pezawas, L., Blasi, G., et al. (2006, April). Neural mechanisms of genetic risk for impulsivity and violence in humans. *Proceedings of the National Academy of Sciences USA, 103,* 6269–6274.

Miller-Loncar, C., Lester, B. M., Seifer, R., Lagasse, L. L., Bauer, C. R., Shankaran, S., et al. (2005, March-April). Predictors of motor development in children prenatally exposed to cocaine. *Neurotoxicology and Teratology, 27,* 231–220.

Millichap, J. G., & Yee, M. M. (2003). The diet factor in pediatric and adolescent migraine. *Pediatric Neurology, 28,* 9–15.

Molko, N., Cachia, A., Rivière, D., Mangin, J-F., Bruandet, M., LeBihan, D., et al. (2003 November). Functional and structural alterations of the intraparietal sulcus in a developmental dyscalculia of genetic origin. *Neuron, 40,* 847–858.

Montgomery, J. W. (2000, April). Verbal working memory and sentence comprehension in children with specific language impairment. *Journal of Speech, Language, and Hearing Research, 43,* 293–308.

Monuteaux, M. C., Faraone, S. V., Herzig, K., Navsaria, N., & Biederman, J. (2005, January-February). ADHD and dyscalculia: Evidence for independent familial transmission. *Journal of Learning Disabilities, 38,* 86–93.

Morge, S. (2005, Fall). High school students' math beliefs and society. *Academic Exchange Quarterly, 9,* 182–187.

Munk, D. D. (2003). *Solving the grading puzzle for students with disabilities.* Whitefish Bay, WI: Knowledge by Design.

Murphy, M. M., Mazzocco, M., Gerner, G., & Henry, A. E. (2006). Mathematics learning disability in girls with Turner syndrome or fragile X syndrome. *Brain and Cognition, 61,* 195–210.

Myles, B. S. (2005). *Children and youth with Asperger syndrome: Strategies for success in inclusive settings.* Thousand Oaks, CA: Corwin Press.

National Association for the Education of Young Children (NAEYC). (1998). *Learning to read and write: Developmentally appropriate practices for young children.* Available online at http://www.naeyc.org/about/positions/pdf/psread98.pdf

National Center for Educational Statistics (NCES). (2004). *NAEP Mathematics 2004.* Washington, DC: Author.

National Institute of Mental Health (NIMH). (2001). *Eating disorders.* Bethesda, MD: Author.

National Institute of Mental Health (NIMH). (2002a). *Anxiety disorders.* Bethesda, MD: Author.

National Institute of Mental Health (NIMH). (2002b). *Depression.* Bethesda, MD: Author.

National Institute of Mental Health (NIMH). (2004). *Autism spectrum disorders.* Bethesda, MD: Author.

National Institute on Alcohol Abuse and Alcoholism (NIAAA). (2000). *Alcohol alert.* Bethesda, MD: Author.

National Institute on Deafness and Other Communication Disorders (NIDCD). (2000, April). *Speech and language: Developmental milestones.* Bethesda, MD: Author.

National Joint Committee on Learning Disabilities (NJCLD). (2005). *Responsiveness to intervention and learning disabilities.* Available at http://www.nasponline.org

National Reading Panel (NRP). (2000). *Teaching children to read: An evidence-based assessment of the scientific research literature and it implications for reading instruction.* Washington, DC: National Institute of Child Health and Human Development.

National Science Foundation (NSF). (2004). *Science and engineering indicators: Elementary and secondary education.* Arlington, VA: Author.

Nicolson, R. I., Fawcett, A. J., & Dean, P. (2001, September). Developmental dyslexia: The cerebellar deficit hypothesis. *Trends in Neuroscience, 24,* 508–511.

Niogi, S. N., & McCandliss, B. D. (2006). Left lateralized white matter microstructure accounts for individual differences in reading ability and disability. *Neuropsychologia, 44,* 2178–2188.

Noland, J. S., Singer, L. T., Short, E. J., Minnes, S., Arendt, R. E., Kirschner, H. L., et al. (2005, May-June). Prenatal drug exposure and selective attention in preschoolers. *Neurotoxicology and Teratology, 27,* 429–438.

Nomura, Y., Wickramaratne, P. J., Warner, V., Mufson, L., & Weissman, M. M. (2002, April). Family discord, parental depression, and psychopathology in offspring: Ten-year follow-up. *Journal of the American Academy of Child and Adolescent Psychiatry, 41,* 402–409.

Northwest Regional Educational Laboratory (NWREL). (2006). *6+1 Trait Writing.* Available online at http://www.nwrel.org/assessment

Oberer, J. J. (2003, Spring). Effects of learning-style teaching on elementary students' behaviors, achievement, and attitudes. *Academic Exchange Quarterly, 7,* 193–199.

Oberman, L. M., Hubbard, E. M., McCleery, J. P., Altschuler, E. L., Ramachandran, V. S., & Pineda, J. A. (2005, July). EEG evidence for mirror neuron dysfunction in autism spectrum disorders. *Cognitive Brain Research, 24,* 190–198.

O'Brien, E. K., Zhang, X., Nishimura, C., Tomblin, J. B., & Murray, J. C. (2003, June). Association of specific language impairment (SLI) to the region of 7q31. *American Journal of Human Genetics, 72,* 1536–1543.

Oudeans, M. K. (2003, Fall). Integration of letter-sound correspondence and phonological awareness skills of blending and segmenting: A pilot study examining the effects of instructional sequence on word reading for kindergarten children with low phonological awareness. *Learning Disability Quarterly, 26,* 258–280.

Palincsar, A. S., & Brown, A. L. (1984). The reciprocal teaching of comprehension-fostering and comprehension-monitoring activities. *Cognition and Instruction, 1,* 117–175.

Palladino, P., & Cornoldi, C. (2004). Working memory performance of Italian students with foreign language learning difficulties. *Learning and Individual Differences, 14,* 137–151.

Paulesu, E., Démonet, J.-F., Fazio, F., McCrory, E., Chanoine, V., Brunswick, N., et al. (2001, March). Dyslexia: Cultural diversity and biological unity. *Science, 291,* 2165–2167.

Paus, T. (2005). Mapping brain maturation and cognitive development during adolescence. *Trends in Cognitive Sciences, 9,* 60–68.

Pelham, W. E., Gnagy, E. M., Greiner, A. R., Hoza, B., Hinshaw, S. P., Swanson, J. M., et al. (2000). Behavioral vs. behavioral and pharmacological treatment in ADHD children attending a summer treatment program. *Journal of Abnormal Child Psychology, 28,* 507–526.

Penhune, V. B., & Doyon, J. (2005, July). Cerebellum and M1 interaction during early learning of timed motor sequences. *NeuroImage, 26,* 801–812.

Perchemlides, N., & Coutant, C. (2004, October). Growing beyond grades. *Educational Leadership, 62,* 53–56.

Pinker, S. (1994). *The language instinct: How the mind creates language.* New York: William Morrow.

Plomin, R., & Kovas, Y. (2005, July). Generalist genes and learning disabilities. *Psychological Bulletin, 131,* 592–617.

Powers, M. D. (2000). What is autism? In M. D. Powers (Ed.), *children with autism: A parent's guide* (2nd ed.). Bethesda, MD: Woodbine House.

Press, D. Z., Casement, M. D., Pascual-Leone, A., & Robertson, E. M. (2005). The time course of off-line motor sequence learning. *Cognitive Brain Research, 25,* 375–378.

Purves, D., Augustine, G. J., Fitzpatrick, D., Katz, L. C., LaMantia, A.-S., McNamara, J. O., et al. (2001). *Neuroscience* (2nd ed.). Sunderland, MA: Sinauer Associates.

Qin, Y., Carter, C. S., Silk, E. M., Stenger, A., Fissell, K., Goode, A., et al. (2004, April). The change of the brain activation patterns as children learn algebra equation solving. *Proceedings of the National Academy of Sciences USA, 101,* 5686–5691.

Rapcsak, S. Z., & Beeson, P. M. (2004, June). The role of left posterior inferior temporal cortex in spelling. *Neurology, 62,* 2221–2229.

Rayner, K., Foorman, B. R., Perfetti, C. A., Pesetsky, D., & Seidenberg, M. S. (2001, November). How psychological science informs the teaching of reading. *Psychological Science in the Public Interest, 2,* 31–74.

Raz, A. (2004, August). Brain imaging data of ADHD. *Psychiatric Times, 21.* Available online at www.psychiatrictimes.com/p040842.html.

Rees, S., & Inder, T. (2005, September). Fetal and neonatal origins of altered brain development. *Early Human Development, 81,* 753–761.

Reid, R., Trout, A. L., & Schartz, M. (2005, Summer). Self-regulation interventions for children with attention-deficit hyperactivity disorder. *Exceptional Children, 71,* 361–377.

Reilly, P. R. (2004). *Is it in your genes? The influence of genes on common disorders and diseases that affect you and your family.* Cold Spring Harbor, NY: Cold Spring Harbor Laboratory Press.

Reis, S. M., & Ruban, L. (2005, Spring). Services and programs for academically talented students with learning disabilities. *Theory into Practice, 44,* 148–159.

Reiss, A. L., Kesler, S. R., Vohr, B., Duncan, C. C., Katz, K. H., Pajot, S., et al. (2004, August). Sex differences in cerebral volumes of 8-year-olds born preterm. *Journal of Pediatrics, 145,* 242–249.

Renvall, H., & Hari, R. (2002). Auditory cortical responses to speech-like stimuli in dyslexic adults. *Journal of Cognitive Neuroscience, 14,* 757–768.

Rescorla, L. (2002, April). Language and reading outcomes to age 9 in late-talking toddlers. *Journal of Speech, Language, and Hearing Research, 45,* 360–371.

Rescorla, L. (2005, April). Age 13 language and reading outcomes in late-talking toddlers. *Journal of Speech, Language, and Hearing Research, 48,* 459–472.

Restak, R. (2000). *Mysteries of the mind.* Washington, DC: National Geographic Society.

Richards, R. G. (1998). *The writing dilemma: Understanding dysgraphia.* Riverside, CA: RET Center Press.

Richards, T. (2001, Summer). Functional magnetic resonance imaging and spectroscopic imaging of the brain: Application of fMRI and fMRS to reading disabilities and education. *Learning Disability Quarterly, 24,* 189–204.

Rimland, B. (2000). The autism epidemic, vaccinations and mercury. *Journal of Nutritional and Environmental Medicine, 10,* 261–266.

Rockstroh, S., & Scuweizer, K. (2001, January). The contributions of memory and attention processes to cognitive abilities. *Journal of General Psychology, 128,* 30–42.

Rosenberg, D. R., Davanzo, P. A, & Gershon, S. (2002). *Pharmacotherapy for child and adolescent psychiatric disorders* (2nd ed.). New York: Marcel Dekker.

Rowe, K., Pollard, J., & Rowe, K. (2005). *Literacy, behavior, and auditory processing.* Paper presented at the Royal Australasian College of Physicians Scientific Meeting, May 8–11, 2005, Wellington, New Zealand.

Rumsey, J., Horwitz, B., Donohue, B. C., Nace, K. L., Maisog, J. M., & Andreason, P. (1999). A functional lesion in developmental dyslexia: Left angular gyral flow predicts severity. *Brain and Language, 70,* 187–204.

Samaco, R. C., Hogart, A., & LaSalle, J. M. (2005). Epigenetic overlap in autism-spectrum neurodevelopmental disorders: MECP2 deficiency causes reduced expression of UBE3A and GABRB3. *Human Molecular Genetics, 14,* 483–492.

Santi, K. L., Menchetti, B. M., & Edwards, B. J. (2004, May-June). A comparison of eight kindergarten phonemic awareness programs based on empirically validated instructional principles. *Remedial and Special Education, 25,* 189–196.

Schack, T., & Mechsner, F. (2006, January). Representation of motor skills in human long-term memory. *Neuroscience Letters, 391,* 77–81.

Schultz, R. T. (2005, April-May). Developmental deficits in social perception in autism: The role of the amygdala and fusiform face area. *International Journal of Developmental Neuroscience, 23,* 125–141.

Schumacher, J., Anthoni, H., Dahdouh, F., Konig, I. R., Hillmer, A. M., Kluck, N., et al. (2006, January). Strong genetic evidence of DCDC2 as a susceptibility gene for dyslexia. *American Journal of Human Genetics, 78,* 52–62.

Scott, M. M., & Deneris, E. S. (2005, April-May). Making and breaking serotonin neurons and autism. *International Journal of Developmental Neuroscience, 23,* 277–285.

Scott, S., & Manglitz, E. (2000). Foreign language learning: A process for broadening access for students with learning disabilities. *Journal of Postsecondary Education and Disability, 17,* 23–37.

Seminowicz, D. A., Mayberg, H. S., McIntosh, A. R., Goldapple, K., Kennedy, S., Segal, Z., et al. (2004, May). Limbic-frontal circuitry in major depression: A path modeling metanalysis. *NeuroImage, 22,* 409–418.

Semrud-Clikeman, M. (2005, November-December). Neuropsychological aspects for evaluating learning disabilities. *Journal of Learning Disabilities, 38,* 563–568.

Serlier-van den Bergh, A. (2006). *NLD primary materials: Basic theory, approach, and hands-on strategies.* Paper presented at the Symposium of the Nonverbal Learning Disorders Association, March 10–11, 2006, San Francisco, CA.

Serna, L., Nielsen, E., Mattern, N., & Forness, S. R. (2003). Primary mental health prevention in Head Start classrooms: Partial replication with teachers as intervenors. *Behavioral Disorders, 23,* 124–129.

Shalev, R., Auerbach, J., Manor, O., & Gross-Tsur, V. (2000). Developmental dyscalculia: Prevalence and prognosis. *European Child and Adolescent Psychiatry, 9,* 58–64.

Sharma, M. (2006). *How children learn mathematics.* Framingham, MA: Center for Teaching/Learning Mathematics.

Shaywitz, S.E. (2003). *Overcoming dyslexia: A new and complete science-based program for reading problems at any level.* New York: Knopf.

Shaywitz, S. E., & Shaywitz, B. A. (2005, June). Dyslexia (Specific reading disability). *Biological Psychiatry, 57,* 1301–1309.

Simos, P. G., Breier, J. I., Fletcher, J. M., Bergman, E., & Papanicolaou, A. C. (2000). Cerebral mechanisms involved in word reading in dyslexic children: A magnetic source imaging approach. *Cerebral Cortex, 10,* 809–816.

Simpson, R. L. (2001). ABA and students with autism spectrum disorders: Issues and considerations for effective practice. *Focus on Autism and Other Developmental Disabilities, 16,* 68–71.

Simpson, R. L. (2005). *Autism spectrum disorders: Interventions and treatments for children and youth.* Thousand Oaks, CA: Corwin Press.

Singer, T., Seymour, B., O'Doherty, J., Kaube, H., Dolan, R. J., & Frith, C. D. (2004) Empathy for pain involves the affective but not sensory components of pain. *Science, 303,* 1157–1162.

Singh, K., Granville, M, & Dika, S. (2002). Mathematics and science achievement effects of motivation, interest, and academic engagement. *Journal of Educational Research, 95,* 323–332.

Siok, W. T., Perfetti, C. A., Jin, Z., & Tan, L. H. (2004, September). Biological abnormality of impaired reading is constrained by culture. *Nature, 431,* 71–76.

Sipe, L. R. (2001). Invention, convention, and intervention: Invented spelling and the teacher's role. *The Reading Teacher, 55,* 264–273.

Smith, K. S., & Geller, C. (2004, Summer). Essential principles of effective mathematics instruction: Methods to reach all students. *Preventing School Failure, 48,* 22–29.

Snow, C. E., Burns, M. S., & Griffin, P. (Eds.). (1998). *Preventing reading difficulties in young children.* Washington, DC: National Academy Press.

Sousa, D. A. (2003). *How the gifted brain learns.* Thousand Oaks, CA: Corwin Press.

Sousa, D. A. (2005). *How the brain learns to read.* Thousand Oaks, CA: Corwin Press.

Sousa, D. A. (2006). *How the brain learns* (3rd ed.). Thousand Oaks, CA: Corwin Press.

Sowell, E. R., Thompson, P. M., Welcome, S. E., Henkenius, A. L., Toga, A. W., & Peterson, B. S. (2003, November). Cortical abnormalities in children and adolescents with attention-deficit hyperactivity disorder. *Lancet, 362,* 1699–1707.

Sparks, R., & Ganschow, L. (1993). Searching for the cognitive locus of foreign language learning difficulties: Linking first and second language learning. *Modern Language Journal, 77,* 289–302.

Sparks, R. L., Philips, L., & Javorsky, J. (2003, July-August). Students classified as LD who petitioned to or fulfilled their college language requirement—are they different? A replication study. *Journal of Learning Disabilities, 36,* 348–362.

Speece, D. L., & Mills, C. (2003). Initial evidence that letter fluency tasks are valid indicators of early reading skill. *Journal of Special Education, 36,* 223–233.

Spence, S. J. (2004, September). The genetics of autism. *Seminars in Pediatric Neurology, 11,* 196–204.

Stanberry, L. I., Richards, T. L., Berninger, V. W., Nandy, R. R., Aylward, E. H., Maravilla, K. R., et al. (2006, April). Low-frequency signal changes reflect differences in functional connectivity between good readers and dyslexics during continuous phoneme mapping. *Magnetic Resonance Imaging, 24,* 217–229.

Sterzer, P., Stadler, C., Krebs, A., Kleinschmidt, A., & Poustka, F. (2005, January). Abnormal neural responses to emotional visual stimuli in adolescents with conduct disorder. *Biological Psychiatry, 57,* 7–15.

Stoodley, C. J., Harrison, E. P. D., & Stein, J. F. (2006). Implicit motor learning deficits in dyslexic adults. *Neuropsychologia, 44,* 795–798.

Stormshak, E. A., Dishion, T. J., Light, J., & Yasui, M. (2005, December). Implementing family-centered interventions within the public middle school: Linking service delivery to change in student problem behavior. *Journal of Abnormal Child Psychology, 33,* 723–733.

Sturomski, N. (1997, July). Teaching students with learning disabilities to use learning strategies. *NICHCY News Digest, 25,* 2–12.

Sunohara, G. A., Roberts, W., Malone, M., Schachar, R. J., Tannock, R., Basile, V. S., et al. (2000, December). Linkage of the dopamine D4 receptor gene and attention-deficit hyperactivity disorder. *Journal of the American Academy of Child and Adolescent Psychiatry, 39,* 1537–1542.

Suresh, P. A., & Sebastian, S. (2000). Developmental Gerstmann's syndrome: A distinct clinical entity of learning disabilities. *Pediatric Neurology, 22,* 267–278.

Swanson, J., Castellanos, F. X., Murias, M., LaHoste, G., & Kennedy, J. (1998). Cognitive neuroscience of attention deficit hyperactivity disorder and hyperkinetic disorder. *Current Opinion in Neurobiology, 8,* 263–271.

Teicher, M. H. (2002, March). Scars that won't heal: The neurobiology of child abuse. *Scientific American, 286,* 68–75.

Teicher, M. H., Anderson, C. M., Polcari, A., Glod, C. A., Maas, L. C., & Renshaw, P. F. (2000, April). Functional deficits in basal ganglia of children with attention-deficit hyperactivity disorder shown with functional magnetic resonance imaging relaxonmetry. *Nature Medicine, 6,* 470–473.

Teicher, M. H., Ito, Y., Glod, C. A., & Barber, N. I. (1996, March). Objective measurement of hyperactivity and attentional problems in ADHD. *Journal of the American Academy of Child and Adolescent Psychiatry, 35,* 334–342.

Temple, E., Deutsch, G. K., Poldrack, R. A., Miller, S. L., Tallal, P., Merzenich, M. M., & Gabrieli, J. D. E. (2003, March). Neural deficits in children with dyslexia ameliorated by behavioral remediation: Evidence from functional MRI. *Proceedings of the National Academy of Sciences, 100,* 2860–2865.

Toll, M. F. (1993). Gifted learning disabled: A kaleidoscope of needs. *Gifted Child Today, 16,* 34–35.

Torgesen, J. K. (2001). Individual differences in response to early intervention in reading: The lingering problem of treatment resisters. *Learning Disabilities Research and Practice, 15,* 55–64.

Treffert, D. A., & Wallace, G. L. (2002, June). Islands of genius. *Scientific American, 286,* 76–85.

Tryon, P. A., Mayes, S. D., Rhodes, R. L., & Waldo, M. (2006, Spring). Can Asperger's disorder be differentiated from autism using DSM-IV criteria? *Focus on Autism and Other Developmental Disabilities, 21,* 2–6.

Uhry, J. (1999). Invented spelling in kindergarten: The relationship with finger-point reading. *Reading and Writing, 11,* 441–464.

United States Department of Education (USDE). (2003, July). *Annual report to Congress on the implementation of the Individuals with Disabilities Education Act.* Washington, DC: U.S. Government Printing Office.

Van Petten, C., & Bloom, P. (1999, February). Speech boundaries, syntax, and the brain. *Nature Neuroscience, 2,* 103–104.

Varley, R. A., Klessinger, N. J. C., Romanowski, C. A. J., & Siegal, M. (2005). Agrammatic but numerate. *Proceedings of the National Academy of Sciences USA, 102,* 3519–3524.

Vaughn, S., & Fuchs, L. S. (2003). Redefining learning disabilities as inadequate response to instruction: The promise and potential problems. *Learning Disabilities Research to Practice, 18,* 137–146.

Vaughn, S., Linan-Thompson, S., & Hickman, P. (2003). Response to instruction as a means for identifying students with reading/learning disabilities. *Exceptional Children, 69,* 391–409.

Vlachos, F., & Karapetsas, A. (2003, December). Visual memory deficit in children with dysgraphia. *Perceptual Motor Skills, 97,* 1281–1288.

Wachelka, D., & Katz, R. C. (1999, September). Reducing test anxiety and improving academic self-esteem in high school and college students with learning disabilities. *Journal of Behavior Therapy and Experimental Psychiatry, 30,* 191–198.

Wagner, A. D., Schacter, D. L., Rotte, M., Koutstaal, W., Maril, A., Dale, A. M., et al. (1998, August). Building memories: Remembering and forgetting of verbal experiences as predicted by brain activity. *Science, 281,* 1188–1191.

Walker, M. P., Stickgold, R., Alsop, D., Gaab, N., & Schlaug, G. (2005). Sleep-dependent motor memory plasticity in the human brain. *Neuroscience, 133,* 911–917.

Waugh, C. K. (2002, Summer). Raising self-expectations: The key to motivating students with disabilities. *Academic Exchange Quarterly, 6,* 68–72.

Weismer, S. E., Evans, J., & Hesketh, L. J. (1999, October). An examination of verbal working memory capacity in children with specific language impairment. *Journal of Speech, Language, and Hearing Research, 42,* 1249–1260.

Willard-Holt, C. (1999). *Dual exceptionalities* (ERIC Digest E574). Reston, VA: ERIC Clearinghouse on Disabilities and Gifted Education.

Williams, D., Stott, C. M., Goodyer, I. M., & Sahakian, B. J. (2000, June). Specific language impairment with or without hyperactivity: Neuropsychological evidence for frontostriatal dysfunction. *Developmental Medical Child Neurology, 42,* 368–375.

Williams, D. L., Goldstein, G., & Minshew, N. J. (2006, January). The profile of memory function in children with autism. *Neuropsychology, 20,* 21–29.

Williams, J. H. G., Waiter, G. D., Gilchrist, A., Perrett, D. I., Murray, A. D., & Whiten, A. (2006). Neural mechanisms of imitation and mirror neuron functioning in autistic spectrum disorder. *Neuropsychologia, 44,* 610–621.

Wing, A. M. (2000). Mechanisms of motor equivalence in handwriting. *Current Biology, 10,* R245-R248.

Wright, B. A., Bowen, R. W., & Zecker, S. G. (2000). Nonlinguistic perceptual deficits associated with reading and language disorders. *Current Opinion in Neurobiology, 10,* 482–486.

Zachry, T., Wulf, G., Mercer, J., & Bezodis, N. (2005, October). Increased movement accuracy and reduced EMG activity as a result of adopting an external focus of attention. *Brain Research Bulletin, 67,* 304–309.

Zimmer, C. (2003, May). How the mind reads other minds: Understanding what others are thinking is a human exclusive. *Science, 300,* 1079–1081.

Resources

Texts & Documents

Barkley, R. A. (2000). *Taking charge of ADHD: The complete, authoritative guide for parents.* New York: Guilford Press.

Bender, W. N., & Larkin, M. J. (2003). *Reading strategies for elementary students with learning difficulties.* Thousand Oaks, CA: Corwin Press.

Butterworth, B. (2004). *Dyscalculia guidance: Helping pupils with specific learning difficulties in maths.* London: David Fulton.

Cavey, D.W. (2000). *Dysgraphia: Why Johnny can't write.* Austin, TX: Pro-Ed.

Diamond, M., & Hopson, J. (1998). *Magic trees of the mind: How to nurture your child's intelligence, creativity, and healthy emotions from birth through adolescence.* New York: Dutton.

Grandin, T. (1996). *Thinking in pictures: And other reports from my life with autism.* New York: Vintage Books.

Harwell, J. M. (2001). *Complete learning disabilities handbook: Ready-to-use strategies & activities for teaching students with learning disabilities* (2nd ed.). San Francisco: Jossey-Bass.

Myles, B. S. (2005). *Children and youth with Asperger syndrome: Strategies for success in inclusive settings.* Thousand Oaks, CA: Corwin Press.

Sicile-Kira, C. (2004). *Autism spectrum disorders: The complete guide to understanding autism, Asperger's syndrome, pervasive developmental disorder, and other ASDs.* New York: Perigee Books.

Simpson, R. L., et al. (2005). *Autism spectrum disorders: Interventions and treatments for children and youth.* Thousand Oaks, CA: Corwin Press.

Sousa, D. A. (2006). *How the brain learns* (3rd ed.). Thousand Oaks, CA: Corwin Press.

U.S. Department of Education (2004). *Teaching children with attention-deficit hyperactivity disorder: Instructional strategies and practices.* Washington, DC: Author.

Publishers

Earobics Literacy Launch
Cognitive Concepts, Inc.
Web: www.earobic.com

Fast ForWord Reading Language Program
Scientific Learning Corporation
Web: www.scientificlearning.com

Lindamood Phonemic Sequencing Program (LiPS)
Lindamood Bell Learning Processes
Web: www.lindamoodbell.com

READ 180
Scholastic, Inc.
Web: http://teacher.scholastic.com/read180

Organizations   (Note: All Internet sites were active at time of publication)

American Speech-Language Hearing Association
  (ASHA)
10801 Rockville Pike
Rockville, MD 20852
(800) 638-8255
Web: www.asha.org

Anxiety Disorders Association of America
8730 Georgia Ave, Suite 600
Silver Spring, MD 20910
(240) 485-1001
Web: www.adaa.org

Asperger Syndrome Education Network (ASPEN)
9 Aspen Circle
Edison, NJ 08820
(732) 321-0880
Web: www.aspennj.org

Attention Deficit Disorder Association
P.O. Box 543
Pottstown, PA 19464
(484) 945-2101
Web: www.add.org

Autism Society of America, Inc.
7910 Woodmont Avenue
Suite 300
Bethesda, MD 20814
(800) 3-AUTISM or (800) 328-8476
Web: www.autism-society.org

Autism Treatment Network
16868 S.W. 65th Avenue, #240
Lake Oswego, OR 97035
(503) 783-2710
Web: www.autisntreatmentnetwork.org

Children and Adults with Attention Deficit
  Hyperactivity Disorder (CH.A.D.D.)
8181 Professional Place, Suite 150
Landover, MD 20785
(800) 233-4050
Web: www.chadd.org

Council for Exceptional Children
1110 North Glebe Road
Suite 300
Arlington, VA 22201-5704
(888) 232-7733
Web: www.cec.sped.org

Council for Learning
  Disabilities (CLD)
P.O. Box 4014
Leesburg, VA 20177
Web: www.cldinternational.org

Cure Autism Now
5455 Wilshire Boulevard, Suite 2250
Los Angeles, CA 90036
(888)8-AUTISM or (888) 828-8476
Web: cureautismnow.org

International Dyslexia Association
8600 LaSalle Road, Suite 382
Baltimore, MD 21286-2044
(800) 222-3123
Web: www.interdys.org

International Reading Association (IRA)
800 Barksdale Road
P.O. Box 8139
Newark, DE 19714-8139
(800) 336-READ or (800) 336-7323
Web: www.reading.org

Learning Disabilities Association of America
4156 Liberty Road
Pittsburgh, PA 15234-1349
(888) 300-6710
Web: www.ldanatl.org

National Alliance for Autism Research
99 Wall Street, Research Park
Princeton, NJ 08540
(888) 777-NAAR or (888) 777-6227
Web: www.naar.org

National Center for Learning Disabilities
381 Park Avenue, Suite 1401
New York, NY 10016
(888) 575-7373
Web: www.ncld.org

National Mental Health Association
2001 N. Beauregard Street 12th floor
Alexandria, VA 22311
(800) 969-NMHA (-6642) / (703) 684-7722
Web: www.nmha.org

National Information Center for Children and Youth
  with Disabilities (NICHCY)
P.O. Box 1492
Washington, DC 20013-1492
(800) 695-0285
Web: www.nichcy.org

National Institute on Deafness and Other
  Communication Disorders
31 Center Drive, MSC 2320
Bethesda, MD 20892-2320
(800) 241-1044
Web: www.nidcd.nih.gov

National Institute of Mental Health
6001 Executive Boulevard, Room 8184, MSC 9663
Bethesda, MD 20892-9663
(866) 615-6464
Web: www.nimh.nih.gov

Nonverbal Learning Disorders Association
2446 Albany Avenue
West Hartford, CT 06117
(860) 570-0217
Web: www.nlda.org

Obsessive Compulsive (OC) Foundation
337 Notch Hill Road
North Branford, CT 06471
(203) 315-2190
Web: www.ocfoundation.org

Reading Recovery Council of North America
1926 Kenny Road, Suite 100
Columbus, OH 43210-1069
(614) 292-7111
Web: www.readingrecovery.org

U.S. Department of Education
600 Maryland Avenue SW
Washington, DC 20202
(800) USA-LEARN (872-5327)
Web: www.ed.gov

Index

Page numbers in **boldface** are **Strategies to Consider**.

CORWIN PRESS

The Corwin Press logo—a raven striding across an open book—represents the union of courage and learning. Corwin Press is committed to improving education for all learners by publishing books and other professional development resources for those serving the field of PreK–12 education. By providing practical, hands-on materials, Corwin Press continues to carry out the promise of its motto: **"Helping Educators Do Their Work Better."**